Sex and Gender Crimes in the
New International Law

Nijhoff Law Specials

VOLUME 75

The titles published in the series are listed at brill.nl/nlsp

Sex and Gender Crimes in the New International Law

Past, Present, Future

By

Alona Hagay-Frey

MARTINUS
NIJHOFF
PUBLISHERS

LEIDEN • BOSTON
2011

Cover illustration: Peter Paul Rubens, *The Rape of the Daughters of Leucippus* (1617/18). With kind permission of The Art Gallery Collection / Alamy/ asap creative

Translated from Hebrew by Stefanie Raker

This book is printed on acid-free paper.

Library of Congress Cataloging-in-Publication Data

Hagay-Frey, Alona.
 Sex and gender crimes in the new international law : past, present,
future / by Alona Hagay-Frey ; Translated from Hebrew by Stefanie Raker.
    p. cm. -- (Nijhoff law specials ; v. 75)
 Adapted from the author's thesis (LLM)---Universitat Tel-Aviv, 2009.
 Includes bibliographical references and index.
 ISBN 978-90-04-18912-6 (pbk. : alk. paper)
 1. Rape as a weapon of war. I. Raker, Stefanie. II. Title.
 KZ7162.H34 2011
 345'.02532--dc22

                                            2011017043

ISSN 0924-4549
ISBN 978 9004 18912 6

Copyright 2011 by Koninklijke Brill NV, Leiden, The Netherlands.
Koninklijke Brill NV incorporates the imprints Brill, Global Oriental, Hotei Publishing,
IDC Publishers, Martinus Nijhoff Publishers and VSP.

PRINTED BY DRUKKERIJ WILCO B.V. - AMERSFOORT, THE NETHERLANDS

To my grandmother Rachel who inspires me every step of my way.

I do not fear the shells and bombs that may fall on my house. They do not ask for my name. I fear the foot soldiers who break into my house and kill and wound in a very personal way and commit atrocities in front of my children.

A Muslim Woman from Bosnia-Herzegovina[1]

---

1 Testimony of a Moslem woman from Bosnia-Herzegovina, quoted in Catharine A. MacKinnon, "Genocide's Sexuality", in Melissa S. Williams and Stephen Macedo, eds., *Political Exclusion and Domination: NOMOS XLVI* (New York University Press, 2004) 313 (hereinafter *Catharine MacKinnon, Genocide's Sexuality*), quoting Prosecutor v. Kupreskic, Transcript, Case No. IT-95-16-T (ICTY, 14 January 2000).

PART THREE: SEX AND GENDER CRIMES UNDER THE NEW
INTERNATIONAL LAW AND A PROPOSED SOLUTION

PROLOGUE[2]

My inquiries into the roots and the coverage of gender[3] crimes in international law began coincidentally. The vast number of rapes being committed in Sudan, Rwanda, and Yugoslavia were reported frequently in the newspapers. Blurred photos obscured the rape victims' faces, and the interviewees were confused, scarred, and shaken. However, the injured, the family members of people killed in the war, and other random speakers were filmed in color, interviewed and documented not only as refugees and victims, but also as heroes. The images and reports about this distorted reality correlated with my experiences working at the Tel Aviv Rape Crisis Center. Over many months, I learned first-hand about how those who have been sexually assaulted feel guilty, stigmatized, and rejected. Yet at the same time, I saw instances in Israeli society of men holding senior positions who were accused of sexual assault, adorned with high status and a supportive wife, casting a look that seemed to convey a belief that the bodies of all subordinate women are permitted to them.

In my research, I plunged into the depths of international law and I identified various legal eras, until I finally reached the most current law,

---

2 Most of this prologue and the preliminary findings of my research have been published as an article in an edited collection. See Alona Hagay-Frey, "Sex and Gender Crimes in International Law: Silence, Honor or New International Crime?" in Klaus Hoffman-Holland, ed., *Ethics and Human Rights in a Globalized World* (Mohr Siebeck, 2009) 179.

3 The term "gender" as opposed to the term "sex" points to those perceived differences between women and men that are socially constructed, i.e., those differences between women and men that do not stem from physiological-biological differences, but rather from culture and society. Similarly, in my approach the term "gender-based crimes" or "gender crimes" is preferable to the term "sex crimes" because it includes crimes against a man or a woman due to gender status. This status will sometimes include a sexual component. See Barbara Bedont & Katherine Hall Martinez, "Ending Impunity for Gender Crimes under the International Criminal Court", VI(1) *Brown J. World Aff.* 65, 69 (1999) (hereinafter *Barbara Bedont & Katherine Hall Martinez*); Janet Halley, "Rape at Rome: Feminist Interventions in the Criminalization of Sex-Related Violence in Positive International Criminal Law", 30(1) *Michigan J. Int'l Law* 75 (2008) (hereinafter *Janet Halley, Rape at Rome*). Nevertheless, in this book, I also refer to "sex crimes" in light of the common usage of this term.

the modern criminal code – the Rome Statute.[4] I conducted my journey armed with several tools, including insights about the development of the crime of rape in domestic law and feminist critical theories, which enable exposure of the gaps and silences and allow us to paint a transparent reality with prominent colors.

I discovered that the gender subordination that exists in day-to-day reality has dictated the slow and differential development of the crime of rape within domestic law, and, in parallel, within international criminal law. This gender subordination led to the exclusion of the crime of rape from the general norms of international law for an entire era, which I call the *Era of Silence*. When the silence was breached, the crime of rape was categorized in international law as an attack on "honor". This categorization as an attack on "honor" gave sex crimes an inferior status under international law. I call this stage of development the *Era of Honor*.

Subsequently, and gradually, a *Third Era* began and a *New Status Quo* has emerged. International criminal law began taking shape in a process that led to the Rome Statute, the most up-to-date criminal code, which rests on the broad agreement of 113 states. However, sex crimes are explicitly included in only *some* of the traditional crime categories anchored in the Rome Statute – despite the fact that in the judgments of the international criminal tribunals for Rwanda and the former Yugoslavia, sex crimes were ultimately anchored in *all* of the categories of crime in international criminal law.

My argument is that in each and every one of the categories of crime existing in international law, it is appropriate to include certain aspects of sex crimes; there is no legal or other justification for the fact that sex crimes are not included in *all* the categories of crime that exist in international criminal law. However, my argument does not end there. Even if the Rome Statute were to recognize sex crimes under all of the traditional crime categories, it would be insufficient. The deeper problem lies in the fact that sex crimes

---

4   Rome Statute of the International Criminal Court, 17 July 1998, UN Doc. A/CONF. 183/9, 2187 U.N.T.S. 3 (hereinafter *Rome Statute*). The Rome Statute unified the entire history of criminal law in an organized manner and thus today it arguably constitutes the modern code of international criminal law. This document summarizes the normative doctrine of international criminal law. Furthermore, as discussed in Part Two below, since it is the most recent treaty establishing the first permanent international criminal court, and since it rests on a broad consensus comprising most of the countries of the world, at least a significant part of it should therefore be treated as international customary criminal law. However, although the vast majority of the Rome Statute reflects international customary criminal law, a few countries, such as the United States and Israel, have reservations about a few controversial provisions and thus chose not to sign and/or ratify the treaty.

in international law contain two distinct crimes: (i) sexual crimes perpetrated in the context of inter-group conflicts based on group identities such as nationality, religion, race, or ethnicity, which I refer to as "ethnic sex crimes" or "inter-ethnic sex crimes", and (ii) sexual crimes perpetrated on the basis of gender. These crimes have different characteristics and, therefore, at times they require different legal treatment. The silence has been breached with respect to the ethnic sex crime, and its recognition under international law is nearly complete, but the gender sex crime remains without an adequate solution, and is only partially recognized.

In the darkness of war, women were excluded from protection of the law and abandoned. Their bodies were permitted to all, without impunity. Gender oppression is exacerbated during times of conflict, when rape becomes a tool of war. I aim to show that any attempt to understand and contend with rape during war as ordinary violence, without addressing it as both an ethnic sex crime and a gender sex crime, will inevitably overlook certain aspects of this crime and, therefore, will be ineffective. This attempt to include women in the general norms according to their masculine characteristics will inevitably leave gaps in those places where there are differences. Furthermore, I claim that the inclusion of violent sexual offenses under the existing crime categories of international law equates these crimes with other international crimes, leading to problems such as the inappropriate application of certain elements of those crime categories to sex crimes. Therefore, despite the significance of this development, it is insufficient.

My view is that the underlying stratum of sex crimes – the gender stratum – must be exposed, which requires recognizing a new international crime. This new crime category will enable full protection against and enforcement of sex crimes under international law. Those aspects of sex and gender crimes that have been marginalized and excluded from the legal norms would be brought into the mainstream of international law, with full protection. Moreover, this new crime category will enable international coordination as to the elements of the crime of rape. It also would create incentives for domestic enforcement of these serious offenses and help establish appropriate content for the offense of rape in the domestic law of every country.

I wish to emphasize that I am not arguing that crimes against women are more serious than other crimes – only that each offense possesses its own unique traits. My argument is that sex and gender crimes need to be addressed by a crime category suited to their unique features, and this crime category must stand alongside the other existing serious offenses.

Sex crimes are egregious offenses which still lack effective legal treatment. The international legal community must unite to condemn them, as has occurred with other intolerable crimes. In the same way that international law pursued the pirate and deemed him *hostis humani generis*,[5] so too must international criminal law, after hundreds of years of silence, mercilessly pursue sex criminals.

---

5   Yoram Dinstein, *The Internal Powers of the State* (Schocken, Tel Aviv University Press, 1972) 76 [Hebrew].

ACKNOWLEDGMENTS

This book is adapted from the thesis I submitted to Tel Aviv University as part of my masters' degree in law (LL.M.). My research was awarded The Raoul Wallenberg Prize on Human Rights from the Israel-Sweden Friendship League and Tel Aviv University.

I owe special thanks to my supervisors, Professor Daphne Barak-Erez and Professor Aeyal Gross, for their guidance, support and insight at every stage of this enterprise. I also wish to thank Professor Natan Lerner, my first international law professor, who taught me, inspired me, and opened doors for me. I also thank Professor Leora Bilsky and Dr. Hilly Moodrick-Even Khen for their important comments on previous drafts of this book. I am grateful to my friends who held patient, professional and serious discussions with me about every issue, idea, new source, and potential legal argument, especially Dr. Daphné Richemond-Barak, who supported and advised me every step of the way, and Ofra Henman, Yaniv Roznai, Barak Atiram and Ron Avital.

I thank the law faculty of Tel Aviv University for support and financial assistance, and the International Raoul Wallenberg Foundation for its generous prize, which enabled me to devote the time and effort to my research. I wish to thank Brill Publications for publishing my research, and especially Lindy Melman, Alan Stephens and Bea Timmer for their professionalism and patience.

I am also grateful to Stefanie Raker, my translator, for her patience, hard work and precision, our substantive discussions about even the smallest details, and her assistance in translating this book. I also thank Jonathan Braverman and Adi Copel, my research assistants, for their invaluable help.

Finally, I would like to thank my family for their love, warmth and belief in me – my mother Miri Aminadav Hagay and my father Efi Hagay, for their constant support, even when the end was not apparent and my confidence faltered; my dear husband and best friend Asaf Hagay-Frey, who is always there for me, for his infinite assistance and continuous encouragement; and, last but not least, my son Arbel and my daughter Ella, for their love, curiosity, and wisdom, which always give me positive energy and strength.

Alona Hagay-Frey
Neve Yahud Monoson, Israel

INTRODUCTION
THE HISTORICAL VACUUM

The exception is a kind of exclusion. What is excluded from the general rule is an individual case. But the most proper characteristic of the exception is that what is excluded in it is not, on account of being excluded, absolutely without relation to the rule. On the contrary, what is excluded in the exception maintains itself in relation to the rule in the form of the rule's suspension. *The rule applies to the exception in no longer applying, in withdrawing from it.* The state of exception is thus not the chaos that precedes order but rather the situation that results from its suspension. In this sense, the exception is truly, according to its etymological root, *taken outside (ex-capere),* and not simply excluded.[6]

Giorgio Agamben

Throughout history, the rape[7] of women[8] during war has been deemed an unavoidable consequence of wartime, essential to preserving the troops' morale,

---

6   Giorgio Agamben, *Homo Sacer, Sovereign Power and Bare Life* (Daniel Heller-Roazen, trans., Stanford University Press, 1998) 17–18 (emphases added by the author) (hereinafter *Giorgio Agamben*).

7   Note that the term "rape" in this context refers to all violent sex crimes and not only rape in its classic meaning. This broad meaning encompasses various other crimes, including sexual enslavement, forced impregnation, sexual torture, forced sterilization, and forced prostitution. These crimes are termed "gender-based crimes" because they are perpetrated nearly exclusively against women because of their gender. See Brook Sari Moshan, "Women, War, and Words: The Gender Component in the Permanent International Criminal Court's Definition of Crimes against Humanity", 22 *Fordham Int'l L.J.* 154, 156–159 (1998) (hereinafter *Brook Sari Moshan*).

8   In her article, ibid., Brook Sari Moshan discusses a broad array of crimes that have been termed "gender-based crimes" and which share a common foundation: women are exclusively the victims, or they are the victims to a greatly disproportionate degree. Therefore, I will refer to rape victims in the feminine language, as it is indisputable that the majority of rape victims are women. By using this language, *it is not my intent to exclude male victims.* See, e.g., Sandesh Sivakumaran, "Sexual Violence against Men in Armed Conflict", 18 *Eur. J. Int'l L.* 253 (2007). To emphasize this point: in the vast majority of sex crimes the victims are women. In addition, rape of men by men is committed mostly against a one-dimensional background, the inter-ethnic background of the war – the first stratum. In contrast, rape of women is committed mostly against a bi-dimensional background – inter-ethnic and inter-gender/sexual – two distinct strata. Therefore, my argument is that this crime is more complex. See also infra notes 167, 480.

along with pillaging and property crimes.[9] The phrase "to the victor go the spoils" has referred to women since Helen of Troy[10] – except that the value of women solely as property has been replaced over time by a more sophisticated values system. For centuries, the conquering of women by rape served as a mark of victory, proof of the soldier's masculinity and success, and compensation for his service. Since the days when women constituted property, unrestricted access to a woman's body was considered a reward for participating in war. The widespread belief was that incidents of rape would take place, against all logic or morality, and that they were unpreventable.[11]

Subsequently, rape during armed conflict came to be perceived as a crime against the honor of the family and the nation. Rape by the invading army's soldiers destroyed any illusions still held by the defeated party's men as to their power and ownership of property. The body of the raped woman became a symbolic battlefield, ground that was trampled upon by the march of victorious troops. The spectacle played out on the stage of the woman's body was a message transmitted between men – persuasive proof of one side's victory and the other side's defeat.[12]

Rape was recognized as a crime against women under international law only during the second half of the twentieth century – as a crime against their honor.[13] As discussed at length below, linking rape to an attack on

---

9   Kelly Dawn Askin, *War Crimes against Women: Prosecution in International War Crimes Tribunals* (M. Nijhoff, 1997) 18–23 (hereinafter *Kelly Dawn Askin, War Crimes against Women*).

10   Jonathan Gottschall, *The Rape of Troy: Evolution, Violence, and the World of Homer* (Cambridge University Press, 2008) 55.

11   Susan Brownmiller, *Against Our Will: Men, Women and Rape* (Simon & Schuster, 1975) 31 (hereinafter *Susan Brownmiller*). In the introduction to the third chapter, Susan Brownmiller quotes General George S. Patton from his book, *War as I Knew It*:

> I told him that, in spite of my most diligent efforts, there would unquestionably be some raping, and that I should like to have the details as early as possible so that the offenders could be properly hanged.

12   Ibid., p. 38. This concept was already part of the Roman legal system, in which the rapist was responsible towards the father or the brother of the raped woman, and rape was perceived as their failure to protect their females. For more about the roots of the crime of rape, see Mustafa K. Kasubhai, "Destabilizing Power in Rape: Why Consent Theory in Rape Law is Turned on its Head", 11 *Wis. Women's L.J.* 37, 52 (Summer 1996).

13   Rana Lehr-Lehnardt, "One Small Step for Women: Female-Friendly Provisions in the Rome Statute of the International Criminal Court", 16 *BYU J. P. L.* 317, 320–322 (2002) (hereinafter *Rana Lehr-Lehnardt*). For more about the critical importance of the differences between honor and dignity, see Orit Kamir, *Israeli Honor and Dignity: Social Norms, Gender Politics and the Law* (Carmel, 2004) [Hebrew] (hereinafter *Orit Kamir, Israeli Honor and Dignity*). See also infra notes 233, 234.

honor obscures the cruelty of the physical injury and adopts society's viewpoint, rather than the injured woman's, as the focal point of the discussion. This perspective often views the woman as damaged and worthless. Moreover, treating rape as solely an injury to honor reduces the motivation to prosecute an attacker for this crime, as compared to a "more serious" physical injury.

In recent years, the International Criminal Tribunal for the Former Yugoslavia (ICTY), the International Criminal Tribunal for Rwanda (ICTR) and the International Criminal Court (ICC) defined the crime of rape in the international arena as a crime of violence. They distinguished fairly effectively between the honor aspect and the violence aspect.

Due to the intensive involvement of non-governmental organizations (NGOs), the ad hoc international criminal tribunals began to deal with sex crimes. For example, the ICTY invested significant resources in prosecuting rape cases and recognized rape as torture, while the ICTR recognized rape as an act of genocide. However, in the initial Preparatory Committee on the Establishment of an International Criminal Court at The Hague, there were only a few references to sex crimes, and these were concentrated in the category of "honor".[14] Moreover, because women are not considered a people, there is no international norm that prohibits destroying a group of women as such, and "sex" is not a category on the list for defining the prohibition of genocide.[15] Therefore, international law tried – and still tries – to deal with sex crimes by categorizing them under the traditional crime categories that already exist in international law.[16]

The Rome Statute, which established the ICC in 1998, constitutes an additional stepping stone by subjecting gender and sex crimes to the ICC's jurisdiction and instituting clear procedures to deal appropriately with these crimes and their victims. Many international women's organizations see the establishment of the ICC as an essential step for protecting women and promoting equality.[17]

This book's premise is that satisfactory achievements have yet to be attained, despite the growing recognition of the need to act to protect women's rights as victims during battle. The social discrimination against women makes them

---

14   Barbara Bedont & Katherine Hall Martinez, supra note 3, pp. 65–85.

15   Catharine MacKinnon, Genocide's Sexuality, supra note 1, p. 337.

16   The traditional crime categories, which I discuss later in the book, are "genocide", "war crime" (which today includes the crime of "grave breach of the Geneva Conventions") and "crime against humanity".

17   Kelly Dawn Askin, War Crimes against Women, supra note 9, pp. xiii-xviii.

especially vulnerable during armed conflict.[18] Hence, their inferior social status impacts the distorted way their experiences are reflected in the principles
of international criminal law, which is intended to deal with the consequences
of armed conflict.[19] My book both analyzes the way international law has con-
tended with sex crimes in recent decades and examines the need for separate
and special recognition of sex crimes under international law.

The significance of my research is not solely that it reflects the widely-held
perception that something must be done about the way international law has
practically ignored sex crimes. My book attempts more than the presentation
of justifications supporting a change in the traditional approach. Specifically,
I suggest that we view sex crimes as two-dimensional crimes: ethnic crimes
and gender crimes. I analyze the argument that rape during war is not only a
crime linked to the national or international conflict, but that it also includes
an additional stratum: it is a tool for the subordination of women, for male
sexual satisfaction and empowerment, and for the confirmation of male control over the female gender. Hence, it is not sufficient to treat rape as solely
another offense under the existing traditional crime categories in international
law. It must be anchored as a discrete crime that will formally and clearly establish the boundaries of the legal norm, harmonize different nations' laws, and
eradicate the remnants of patriarchy linked to this offense.

In Part One, I present the tools which will be used to enrich this study's
critique of the development of international criminal law, beginning with the
initial stage of excluding sex crimes and concluding with the current normative situation. Toward this end, I begin with the feminist discourse. I discuss
various feminist theories' critiques of international criminal law in general,
and the relationship of international law to sex crimes, in particular. I conclude Part One with a look at the domestic criminal law of nation-states.
I survey certain connections between international law and domestic law
and demonstrate their interdependence. I present the unique nature of sex
crimes from the perspectives of the perpetrator, the victim and society, and
I discuss the elements of the crime of rape. In that context, I focus on consent,
particularly in those situations in which a relationship of subordination is
incontestable.

---

18   Significantly, the degree and extent of violence against women rise dramatically during
periods of national as well as international tensions. For example, Fionnuala Ni Aolain cites the
violence during the period when President Suharto was deposed in Indonesia. Fionnuala Ni
Aolain, "Rethinking the Concept of Harm and Legal Categorizations of Sexual Violence During
War", 1(2) *Theoretical Inquiries in Law* 307, 309 (2000).
19   Judith G. Gardam & Michelle J. Jarvis, *Women, Armed Conflict and International Law*
(Kluwer International Law, 2001).

In Part Two, I embark on an historical journey, progressing through the different eras of international criminal law, based on my identification of certain unique characteristics of each era. This survey commences with the period that I refer to as the *Era of Silence*, beginning with the creation of international law and concluding in 1949 with the drafting of the Geneva Conventions. The Geneva Conventions mark the start of the period that I refer to as the *Era of Honor* – when, for the first time, the offense of rape was anchored as a crime under international law, enumerated in the list of crimes against honor. I discuss the problems inherent in this link between rape and honor and its roots, as well as the importance of separating the crime of rape from issues of honor and anchoring rape as a "war crime" and "crime against humanity" in all respects. The period that I refer to as the *Third Era* commences in the 1990s, with the establishment of the ICTY and the ICTR. These ad hoc tribunals created a temporary revolution in their treatment of sex crimes in international law. This era also includes the establishment of the first permanent international criminal court, the ICC. My historical journey ends with the *New Status Quo* that the establishment of the ICC has created.[20]

In Part Three, I seek to deepen the discussion and tie all the loose ends together. First, I summarize international law's achievements concerning treatment of sexual offenses in recent years, primarily the addition of sex crimes to the existing categories of crime under international law. Simultaneously, I expose the problems inherent in these developments. I analyze the current treatment of sex crimes as "war crimes" and "crimes against humanity" and examine the continued exclusion of sex crimes from the serious crime of "genocide" and the Rome Statute's abstention from explicitly defining them as a "grave breach of the Geneva Conventions". I also demonstrate how the group "gender" could have been included among the protected groups in the definition of the crime of "genocide" and how sex crimes could have been included in the list of prohibited acts for this international crime. I then offer a new perspective for analyzing sex crimes as a discrete international crime. In the end of this final part of the book, I contribute a normative proposal to this important discussion, which is built on three parallel routes: (i) retain sex crimes under the existing crime categories; (ii) add them to the

---

20   As discussed, supra note 4, my treatment of the Rome Statute as a modern criminal code representing current international criminal law is based on its provision of organized modern definitions for the existing international criminal offenses, with broad international agreement. This statute looks to the future and is not restricted by time or place, as were its predecessors. Hence, the Rome Statute creates a stable legal foundation for future prosecutions in the international arena. See Darryl Robinson, "Defining 'Crimes Against Humanity' at the Rome Conference", 93(1) *Am. J. Int'l L.* 57 (1999).

crime categories of "genocide" and a "grave breach of the Geneva Conventions"; and (iii) under certain circumstances, recognize sex and gender crimes as a discrete international crime. In conclusion, in chapter ten, I present a preliminary draft of a new proposed international crime category – "sex and gender crimes". This new crime category will compel the international community to take action in order to harness collective efforts, apprehend, prosecute and convict those sex criminals who, until now, have committed their crimes with impunity.

Part One

BEGINNING THE JOURNEY, COLLECTING THE TOOLS

CONTENTS

INTRODUCTION TO PART ONE

This Part gathers the tools that both enrich and lay a foundation for the rest of this study's critique of the inadequate treatment of sex crimes under international law, from its inception through today. Using insights gained from different feminist theories, I claim that a connection exists between the two legal spheres – the national and the international. This connection requires us to address the developments in the crime of rape in domestic law. I claim that changes in the law in this field are likely to have a significant impact on both the international legal realm and the domestic legal realm – in addition to the symbolic importance of such changes. Furthermore, in order to analyze sex crimes in international law, we must first understand the roots of the crime of rape in domestic law and its development: its unique characteristics, the problematic nature of its definition, and its different impacts on the victim, the perpetrator and society.

Chapter 1

INTERNATIONAL LAW FROM A FEMINIST PERSPECTIVE

The aspirations of the feminist analysis of international law go beyond the objective of advancing women's issues. It has the ability to contribute to the development and advancement of international law as a legal branch with relevance to modern reality. For example, the feminist "search for silences" inquires into those subjects that international law chooses to leave unaddressed or treated only partially or secondarily,[21] such as the subject of this book.[22]

Several steps must be taken in order to analyze the way sexual offenses are and should be covered under international law. First, international criminal law's silence about sexual offenses, and the underlying gender bias that this silence reflects, must be exposed. Second, the archaic dichotomy between the private sphere and the public sphere, which international law maintained for centuries, must be shattered, because, as I demonstrate in this chapter, the line drawn by this dichotomy overlaps to a great extent with the gender line. Finally, we must draw upon the important lessons of how the offense of rape has developed in the domestic law of nation-states. I discuss the first two issues in this chapter one, and the third point in chapter three.

The feminist argument is, primarily, that international law was invented and formulated by men in order to protect men, and therefore, historically, it ignored violence against women.[23] This argument is similar to feminist claims concerning other subjects, but in this area of law the argument is even stronger in light of the incontestable historical maleness of the battlefield. The lack of women's involvement in decisions to instigate armed conflicts, the minimal

---

21   Gilad Noam, "A Feminist Perspective of Public International Law", in Daphne Barak-Erez, *et al.*, eds., *Studies in Feminism, Gender and Law* (Nevo, 2007) 195 [Hebrew] (hereinafter *Gilad Noam*).

22   As I discuss below in Part Two, chapter 4: "The Era of Silence", over many decades during the *Era of Silence*, international law treated the rape of women during war as an inseparable, integral element of the battlefield. As a result, sex crimes during battle were not deemed worthy of condemnation. The dramatic change and new status quo resulting from establishment of the ICC has led to a new criminal boundary that may not be breached, internationally or nationally.

23   Kelly Dawn Askin, War Crimes against Women, supra note 9, pp. 47–48.

number of women in the international legal field, and the nearly exclusive involvement of men as legislators and judges in international law, contributed to the failure of international law to deal appropriately with violence against women. These factors have perpetuated female inferiority and prevented advancements in the issues related to women.

The continued silencing of the female voice in international law seems to stem from two central reasons:

(1) The organizational structure of international law, which focuses on states and organizations. In both, women are absent from positions of influence and the public sphere.

(2) The normative structure of international law.[24] Because the principal players in international law are states, the widespread assumption over hundreds of years was that international laws directly impact states and not individuals. The premise of international law is that its norms apply to individuals within states in a universal and neutral manner. Thus, international law traditionally has not recognized the fact that these norms are likely to have a differential impact on men and women.[25]

In my opinion, the varied tools arising from different feminist theories enable a sharper and more accurate exposure of the gender bias in international law. They also create an opening for an intensive and challenging discussion about various aspects of international law from different feminist perspectives.[26] Therefore, as have many others before me, I adopt a research approach which draws on a number of feminist streams of thought.[27]

Despite the developments in humanitarian law with respect to women's rights, the role of women in international law remains peripheral. For example, in all the years that the International Court of Justice has existed, one woman was appointed to serve as a judge in 1995, former President Rosalyn Higgins, who served until 2009, and two women were appointed only in 2010.[28] Women have never served as members of the United Nations International

---

24 Hilary Charlesworth, Christine Chinkin & Shelley Wright, "Feminist Approaches to International Law", 85 *Am. J. Int'l L.* 613, 621–634 (1991) (hereinafter *Hilary Charlesworth, Christine Chinkin & Shelley Wright*).

25 For example, Hilary Charlesworth, Christine Chinkin & Shelley Wright claim that the private/state and public/international dichotomy, which I discuss below in subchapter 1.1, serves a masculine world view and supports male dominance of international law's agenda. Ibid., p. 627.

26 For a discussion of the eclectic feminist approach to international law, see Gilad Noam, supra note 21, p. 191.

27 Ibid., p. 192.

Law Commission, nor has a woman ever served as the general secretary of the United Nations (UN).[29, 30] Moreover, in recent years there has not been any significant increase in the miniscule number of women serving in professional and senior positions within the UN system.[31]

Accordingly, an analysis of international law's view of women demonstrates that in each of those rare instances in which international law does relate to women, they are viewed primarily as victims (particularly as mothers or potential mothers) and, on that basis, they are considered worthy of defense. Hence, the absence of women in the international arena highlights the lack of political equality and the inferior power of women, as expressed by radical feminism, which I discuss below in this chapter.[32] Resolution Number 1820, adopted unanimously by the UN Security Council in 2008, is significant to this issue because, although it lacks strong operative measures, it emphasizes

---

28   Note that at the ICTY, there is one woman among the 16 permanent judges and four women who are *ad litem* judges out of 11, and at the ICTR there are three women among the 13 permanent judges and three *ad litem* judges out of 12. However, at the ICC, there is a dramatic increase in the proportion of women serving as judges: two out of five in the appeals division, five out of eight in the trial division, and four out of six in the pre-trial division. I discuss this development below in Part Two, subchapter 6.3: "The ICC – A New Status Quo".

29   See Hilary Charlesworth, Christine Chinkin & Shelley Wright, supra note 24, pp. 624–626.

30   Note that the lack of representation of women in the international sphere is but a mirror of the lack of parliamentary representation of women in the domestic legal system. Every few months, the Inter-Parliamentary Union conducts a survey of women in national parliaments, which demonstrates that the percentage of women in national parliaments is far from satisfactory. Surprisingly, the Rwandan parliament consistently ranked first place. Some will breathe a sigh of relief that, finally, the percentage of women in a parliament approaches their percentage of the population, but I have disappointing news. The primary reason why Rwanda has so many women in parliament is the slaughter of so many men in that state's genocide. "Inter-Parliamentary Union, Women in National Parliaments" in http://www.ipu.org/wmn-e/classif-arc.htm (last accessed 14 April 2011).

31   On 22 December 2003, the UN General Assembly adopted a resolution (G.A. Res. 58/144) expressing concern that for two consecutive years there had been a slowdown in the narrowing of the representation gap between women and men in UN professional and senior positions. The resolution states that from 1998 to 2003, the representation of women in professional and/or senior positions showed almost no increase. The resolution instructs the UN Secretary General to prepare a detailed report, including statistical data, regarding underrepresentation of women in the UN. The report was submitted to the UN General Assembly on 20 September 2004 (Report of Secretary General, "Improvement of the Status of Women in the United Nations System", Doc. A/59/357 (20 September 2004). For discussion about this resolution, see Gilad Noam, supra note 21, p. 198.

32   See Catharine A. MacKinnon, *Feminism Unmodified: Discourses on Life and Law* (Harvard University Press, 1987) (hereinafter *Catharine MacKinnon, Feminism Unmodified*).

the importance of women's participation in peace conferences and dispute resolution:

> Reaffirming the important role of women in prevention and resolution of conflicts and in peace-building, and stressing the importance of their equal participation and full involvement in all efforts for the maintenance and promotion of peace and security, and the need to increase their role in decision-making with regard to conflict prevention and resolution.[33]

In other words, the call for appropriate representation of women in the current international legal system is not just an expression of the doctrine of liberal feminism that accepts the existing "masculine" system as the environment within which women must seek influence and equal opportunities. The demand for equal representation exposes the silencing and the subjects that international law avoids treating, and points to the boundary line dividing those subjects covered under the wing of international law from those that are not. *This boundary line overlaps to a great degree with the gender line.*

The liberal argument that it is sufficient to provide formal equal opportunities to women and men to serve in these roles turns out to be problematic for two fundamental reasons. The first is the different starting point that men enjoy due to their roles as the major-generals and generals in war, especially in the political and military arenas. The second reason is that, although subjects such as maintaining peace and human rights are not inherently gendered, nonetheless, women's voice, in its distinctiveness, uniqueness, and decision-making style, can add variety and stimulate creativity in the international arena with respect to these subjects. The liberal claim about equal opportunities ignores this potential positive contribution of women in law, and therein lies its weakness. Moreover, the impact of these subject areas on men and women is not uniform.[34]

In their books, both Carol Gilligan[35] and Catharine MacKinnon[36] use the terminology of the "voice" and expose the silence and silencing of the

---

33   S.C. Res. 1820, 19 June 2008, U.N. Doc. S/RES/1820 (hereinafter *Resolution 1820*) (addressing widespread sexual violence in conflict).

34   On this point, I disagree with the view expressed by Gilad Noam in his article. See Gilad Noam, supra note 21, p. 198.

35   See Carol Gilligan, *In a Different Voice: Psychological Theory and Women's Development* (Harvard University Press, 1982) (hereinafter *Carol Gilligan*).

36   Catharine A. MacKinnon, *Only Words* (Harvard University Press, 1993) 3 (hereinafter *Catharine MacKinnon, Only Words*).

feminine voice in modern society,[37] although they use different techniques.[38] Giving a "voice" in law in general, and in a legal proceeding in particular, is a political act constituting part of the struggle for change in the hierarchical power structure of society.[39]

Gilligan and "cultural feminism" emphasize the differences between women and men in various contexts and women's "different voice".[40] Hence, for example, in the international context, on the basis of empirical research it has been claimed that women tend to support peace initiatives, environmental protection, and social services to a greater extent than men.[41] Another claim is that the decision-making style in entities with greater female representation fosters discussions rooted in more open and inclusive language, as distinct from "male" discussions characterized by polarized claims and conflict.[42]

MacKinnon's view is that it is the long-term silencing of women which is the source of the difference. Male freedom of speech has silenced female freedom of speech. Trampling of women and their subordination has weakened their voice and created an internalized consciousness of subordination. Therefore, maintains MacKinnon, we should not sanctify the difference. According to MacKinnon's view, Gilligan's celebration of difference is unwarranted:

> The work of Carol Gilligan on gender differences in moral reasoning gives it a lot of dignity, more than it has ever had, more frankly, than I thought it ever could have. But she achieves for moral reasoning what the special protection rule achieves in law: the affirmative rather than the negative valuation of that which has accurately distinguished women from men, by making it seem as though those attributes, with their consequences, really are somehow ours, rather than what male supremacy has attributed to us for its own use. For women to affirm difference, when difference

---

37   Liora Bilsky [sic], "The Violence of Silence: Legal Proceeding between Distribution and Voice", 23 *Tel Aviv Univ. L. Rev.* 421, 425–431 (2000) [Hebrew] (hereinafter *Leora Bilsky*).

38   Carol Gilligan calls for listening to the different and silenced female voice, supra note 35. In contrast, Catharine MacKinnon believes that this listening is essential, but that it is impossible without fundamental changes in male-female relationships. I discuss this point below in this chapter.

39   Leora Bilsky, supra note 37, p. 421; Katherine T. Bartlett, "Feminist Legal Methods", 103 *Harv. L. Rev.* 829 (1990) (hereinafter *Katherine Bartlett*).

40   See Carol Gilligan, supra note 35, pp. 25–51, for a discussion of Gilligan's theory, which is based on the assumption that the way in which women think is different from men's thinking, within an ethic of care and connection.

41   See Gilad Noam, supra note 21, p. 198; Hilary Charlesworth, Christine Chinkin & Shelley Wright, supra note 24, p. 616.

42   Gilad Noam, supra note 21, pp. 191–192, 198.

means dominance, as it does with gender, means to affirm the qualities and characteristics of powerlessness.

.... Further, when you are powerless, you don't just speak differently. A lot, you don't speak. Your speech is not just differently articulated, it is silenced. Eliminated, gone. You aren't just deprived of a language with which to articulate your distinctiveness, although you are; you are deprived of a life out of which articulation might come. *Not being heard is not just a function of lack of recognition, not just that no one knows how to listen to you, although it is that; it is also silence of the deep kind, the silence of being prevented from having anything to say.* Sometimes it is permanent. *All I am saying is that the damage of sexism is real, and reifying that into differences is an insult to our possibilities.*[43, 44]

[Emphasis added by the author]

In my opinion, the roots of the difference should indeed be condemned and altered, yet if the results of this oppression lend variation and a positive nuance to the discussion and to the international discourse, then those results should be embraced. In addition, shattering the existing frameworks and thinking beyond traditional categories is likely to lead to substantive change.

Moreover, in my opinion, the discussion about human rights has a different impact on women than on men. Women have the most to lose and the most to gain from any change, even the slightest, in the human rights arena, particularly concerning sex crimes during armed conflicts. In other words, any changes regarding human rights are likely to have a greater impact on women than on men, even marginally – not due to differences between the two genders, but rather due to the relationships of subordination and control, which to some extent still remain. As expressed by MacKinnon:

---

43   Catharine MacKinnon, Feminism Unmodified, supra note 32, pp. 38–39.

44   There are, of course, other critiques of the cultural feminist viewpoint. For example, one critique discussed by Gilad Noam is that women who seek integration into influential positions need to pave their way in an environment which is constructed as masculine. As a result, women are in perpetual conflict over whether to accept the "masculinity" of the system, thereby renouncing their feminine characteristics, or whether to emphasize their multi-faceted feminine characteristics, thereby risking being pushed to the margins of the "accepted" public discourse. See Gilad Noam, supra note 21; see also Hilary Charlesworth & Christine Chinkin, *The Boundaries of International Law: A Feminist Analysis* (Manchester University Press, 2000) 192, 193 (hereinafter *Hilary Charlesworth & Christine Chinkin, The Boundaries of International Law*). Another radical feminist critique of cultural feminism is that the adherence to difference perpetuates myths about women's nature and obscures the understanding of society's power relations of male dominance and female weakness. Moreover, this adherence to difference is a product of the false consciousness of those who are subordinate and submissive because of their forced silence and the continuation of their inferior status. Catharine MacKinnon, Feminism Unmodified, supra note 32, p. 29.

The question of equality, from the standpoint of what it is going to take to get it, is at root a question of hierarchy, which – as power succeeds in construction social perception and social reality – derivatively becomes a categorical distinction, a difference. Here, on the first day that matters, dominance was achieved, probably by force. By the second day, division along the same lines had to be relatively firmly in place. On the third day, if not sooner, differences were demarcated, together with social systems to exaggerate them in perception and in fact, *because* the systematically differential delivery of benefits and deprivations required making no mistake about who was who. Comparatively speaking, man has been resting ever since.[45]

This process also applies to the subject of this book: for years, international law kept silent about sex crimes, which primarily affect women, and, for that reason, presumably, it both turned a blind eye and chose to exclude sex crimes from the law.[46]

Janet Halley disagrees with the radical feminist approach represented by MacKinnon, particularly in the international arena, and she crowns it with unflattering names: Governance Feminism (due to its attempt to garner power),[47] Carceral Feminism (due to its preoccupation with positive law),[48] and Feminist Universalism (due to its creation of a separate women's universe that ignores male victims). Halley contends that feminist NGOs are creating norms that aim to become part of the rules, and claims:

> The feminists doing this work discovered ways of implementing their structuralist view that rape was not merely a tool of belligerent forces (Croat v. Serb; Serb v. Muslim; Hutu v. Tutsi; etc.) but part of a global *war against women*.[49]

Halley contends that the radical feminists view women not as a group within humanity but rather a separate universe unto themselves. Rape during war,

---

45   Catharine MacKinnon, Feminism Unmodified, supra note 32, p. 40.

46   Regarding the fact that on occasion human rights have a different impact on women and men, see Hilary Charlesworth & Christine Chinkin, "The Gender of Jus Cogens", 15 *Hum. Rts. Q.* 63, 75 (1993) (hereinafter *Hilary Charlesworth & Christine Chinkin, The Gender of Jus Cogens*).

47   Janet Halley, Prabha Kotiswaran, Hila Shamir & Chantal Thomas, "From the International to the Local in Feminist Responses to Rape, Prostitution/Sex Work, and Sex Trafficking: Four Studies in Contemporary Governance Feminism", 29 *Harv. J. L. & Gender* 335, 340–347 (2006).

48   Janet Halley, Rape at Rome, supra note 3, p. 5.

49   Ibid., p. 6.

like rape during peace, is viewed as part of a comprehensive war between women and men. For this reason, Halley argues, men who are killed in the same battle are ignored.[50]

Despite the significance of Halley's critique, it must not provide grounds for halting the efforts to contend with this historical injury to women. Sex crimes, as described below,[51] are an historical weapon for subordinating women and the struggle against them need not be carried out at the expense of contending with other harms.

Thus the conclusion is clear: the silence of international law must be broken, the feminine voice must be heard. To do so, the walls between the public and the private, which have been built and maintained over centuries, must be breached, as I discuss in the next subchapter.

1.1 PRIVATE V. PUBLIC IN INTERNATIONAL HUMANITARIAN LAW

In the spirit of the liberal tradition, international law distinguished between those areas deemed to be of "public" interest, in which intervention of the international community is justified, and those areas deemed to be solely of "private" interest and under the sovereign state's authority.[52] This dichotomy, covered with a cloak of objectivity and neutrality, has clear and decisive impli-cations. International law traditionally acted in the most quintessentially "pub-lic" framework: the inter-state arena. It distinguished between issues relevant to the international community, which could be organized under international law, and issues under the private sovereignty of the state as to which, as a gen-eral rule, the international community could not interfere.[53, 54]

This method of decoding and analyzing the silence of international law exposes the dichotomies at the foundation of international law, such as law/politics, logic/emotion, order/anarchy, international/national, and public/private. Many feminist scholars have drawn attention to the distinct gender

---

50   Ibid.

51   See chapter 3: "Rape as a Unique Crime under Domestic Law".

52   Hilary Charlesworth, Christine Chinkin & Shelley Wright, supra note 24, pp. 625–630.

53   Arguably, this distinction has become obscured in recent decades by developments in international criminal law. However, it seems that the international community still elects to intervene only in matters related to a public international interest that is precious to the inter-national community, such as systematic crime. Thanks to my colleague Ron Avital for this comment.

54   See Hilary Charlesworth, Christine Chinkin & Shelley Wright, supra note 24, p. 625.

code underlying this division, with one value relating to "male" and the other relating to "female", respectively.[55]

The feminist critique seeks to expose these "silences" of international law – i.e., areas international law does not deal with, because they are deemed "private" or "political" – and to show the gendered basis underlying the preference not to deal with these areas. Moreover, this silence is what enables male dominance and sustains it.[56]

Torture, an international crime codified in the Convention against Torture from 1984,[57] could be an example of this phenomenon.[58] A human rights violation that can be inflicted on both men and women, torture was given a central place in international law at the end of World War II (WWII). Yet, in contrast with the central place given to torture, the silence surrounding sex crimes – which are perpetrated primarily against women – was thundering.

Torture as a discrete crime, rather than a "crime against humanity" or a "war crime", can be committed during either times of conflict or peace.[59] However, it is important to note that under Article 1(1) of the Convention against Torture, sexual violence or other violence against women can be considered the international crime of torture *only if the act can be linked to the public realm* – perpetrated as part of an "official" policy.[60] Under those circumstances, the provision can be interpreted so that rape meets the legal definition of torture. But note the private/public dichotomy embedded in the requirement that torture be perpetrated *by a public official*. The testimony of women about systematic and mass rape during wars, even in modern times, indicates that rape is not always committed by a "public official" or soldiers. In many instances, acts

---

55   See Aeyal M. Gross & Amalia Ziv, "Between Theory and Politics: Gay and Lesbian Studies and Queer Theory" in Yair Kedar, Amalia Ziv & Oren Kenner, eds., *Beyond Sexuality: Selected Articles in Gay and Lesbian Studies and Queer Theory* (Hakibbutz Hemeuchad, 2001) 10, 14 [Hebrew]; Hilary Charlesworth & Christine Chinkin, The Gender of Jus Cogens, supra note 46, pp. 69–74.

56   See Gilad Noam, supra note 21, p. 200.

57   Convention against Torture and Other Cruel, Inhuman or Degrading Treatment or Punishment, 10 December 1984, UN Doc. A/39/46 (hereinafter *Convention against Torture*).

58   Shelley Hoffman, "Violence against Women in Armed Conflicts", available at http://lib .civics.cet.ac.il/pages/item.asp?item=16937 (last accessed 14 April 2011) [Hebrew] (hereinafter *Shelley Hoffman*).

59   Antonio Cassese, *International Criminal Law* (Oxford, 2008) 149–151 (hereinafter *Antonio Cassese*).

60   Hilary Charlesworth, "Feminist Methods in International Law", 93 *AJ.I.L. (Symposium on Method in International Law)* 379, 387 (1999) (hereinafter *Hilary Charlesworth, Feminist Methods in International Law*); Andrew Byrnes, "The Convention Against Torture", in Kelly Dawn Askin & Dorean M. Koening, eds., *Women and International Human Rights Law*, Vol. II (1999–2001) 183, 189–194.

of rape were committed by other forces accompanying an army[61] and in some cases even by neighbors.[62] Those acts of rape committed by "private persons" cannot meet the definition of torture under the Convention against Torture.[63]

While torture by "public officials" is given special treatment under the Convention against Torture, general human rights treaties contain no specific provisions prohibiting violence within the family, or any of the other widespread forms of violence against women. Although there are declarations in the international arena which denounce and prohibit violence against women, and explicitly state that they cover both public officials as well as private individuals, these declarations are not legally binding.[64, 65]

As we have seen, the feminist discourse exposes the silence of international law, which has developed from a male perspective, regarding all matters related to sex crimes. This silence has been reinforced by the walls that create a dichotomy between public and private. However, this discussion about the feministic

---

61   See, for example, the article about trials following the exposure of trafficking in women as sex slaves in Bosnia. Soldiers employed by a private army participated in the trafficking. Powerhouse: Robert Capps, "Sex-slave Whistle-blowers Vindicated", salon.com, 6 August 2002, http://archive.salon.com/news/feature/2002/08/06/dyncorp/index.html (last accessed 25 September 2010).

62   For example, during the Bosnian genocide, Serbian men who for years had lived as neighbors of Muslim women raped these neighbors in the name of "Greater Serbia". Catharine MacKinnon, Genocide's Sexuality, supra note 1, p. 314.

63   Shelley Hoffman, supra note 58, p. 3.

64   See Declaration on Elimination of Violence against Women, 20 December 1993, G.A. Res. 48/104, UN Doc A/Res/48/104; Vienna Declaration and Programme of Action, World Conference on Human Rights, 25 June 1993, UN. Doc. A/Conf.157/23, part II, paras. 36–44. The Vienna Declaration provides, *inter alia*, in Article 42:

> 42. … Steps should also be taken by the Division for the Advancement of Women in cooperation with other United Nations bodies, specifically the Centre for Human Rights, to ensure that the human rights activities of the United Nations regularly address violations of women's human rights, including gender-specific abuses. Training for United Nations human rights and humanitarian relief personnel to assist them to recognize and deal with human rights abuses particular to women and to carry out their work without gender bias should be encouraged.

For an interesting discussion about whether battered women can be recognized as victims of torture, see Liora Rofman, "Battered Women as Torture Victims? A Feminist Critique of Women's Human Rights Discourse", 2006 (unpublished master's thesis, Bar Ilan University) [Hebrew].

65   Note that in 1998, rape was recognized for the first time by the ICTY as a type of torture. Prosecutor v. Delalic, Case No. IT-96–21-T, T. Ch. II (ICTY, 16 November 1998) paras. 943, 965 (hereinafter *Delalic Judgment*).

critique of international law would be incomplete without addressing its self-critique, which I briefly present and discuss in the following subchapter.

1.2 FEMINIST SELF-CRITIQUE DISCOURSE: VICTIM/AGENT, VIOLENCE/ SEX

Conflicts among various feminist viewpoints about the silencing of the female voice and how to enable it to be heard, generally, as well as how to make the female voice heard in the international law arena, specifically, was discussed above in the previous subchapter. Now it is appropriate to expand this discussion, with a focus on the subject of this study: how to handle sex crimes in the framework of international law.

The critique of the feminist discourse that focuses on sex crimes, particularly the radical feminist discourse, is primarily that it ignores the possibility that women can be independent agents. For example, the discourse's focus on German women raped by Russian soldiers toward the end of WWII views them solely as victims and absolves them of all responsibility for the Holocaust.[66]

More specifically, one of the critiques of MacKinnon, as the prominent spokesperson of the radical perspective, is that her view of "sex" solely as a site of danger means that women are always potential victims of sex crimes.[67] Halley comments that MacKinnon's model is based on the perception of a hierarchy between men and women, and that, consequently, her analysis of all sexual issues takes place through this prism of the domination of women. Halley claims that this absolutist viewpoint is likely to overlook other interests of justice, and also to cause harm from this type of analysis of every sexual act.[68]

In addition, a fundamental paradox exposed by the critique of the feminist discourse is that the feminist appeal to courts of law (whether state or international) accepts the rules of the game of the international institutions.

---

66   On this issue, see the article by Pascala R. Bos, "Feminists Interpreting the Politics of War Time Rape: Berlin, 1945; Yugoslavia, 1992–1993", 31(4) *Signs J. Women Culture & Soc'y* 995 (2006) (hereinafter *Pascala Bos*).

67   Moreover, because radical feminism views sexuality as the site of male dominance, even sexual intercourse that is not acknowledged by law or society as rape could be considered a form of male dominance. Aeyal M. Gross, "Impersonation as Another Person: Imitation and Gender Insubordination in the Trial of Hen Alkobi" in Orna Ben-Naftali & Hannah Naveh, eds., *Trials of Love*, (Ramot, Tel-Aviv University, 2005) 365, 392 [Hebrew] (hereinafter *Aeyal Gross*).

68   Janet Halley, "Take a Break from Feminism?" in Karen Knop, ed., *Gender and Human Rights* (Oxford, 2004) 57, 65–66 (hereinafter *Janet Halley, Take a Break from Feminism?*); Janet Halley, Rape at Rome, supra note 3, pp. 6–8.

And because those institutions were created by male eyes and hands, this appeal also accepts the gender arrangement that the court imposes – the same patriarchal social structure that harms the status of women.[69] Another critique is that the definition of rape as a war crime could embed the offense into this crime category in such a way that other incidents of rape will be left without an appropriate solution.

In general, the feminist streams of thought can be divided into radical feminism, identified with MacKinnon, which fought for the recognition of rape as a war crime and as "genocide" under certain circumstances, and other approaches which express concern that recognition of these crimes will perpetuate the status of women as victims and create distinctions between one rape and another. According to this latter view, rape is a serious offense which must be denounced as such, irrespective of which party perpetrates it or how.

An issue that proponents of both feminist streams of thought agree upon is that women who have been raped during conflict must be treated as war victims.[70] However, they are likely to disagree about the definition of some of the situations I call "survival sex". These are acts of sexual intercourse between women who are prisoners and the soldiers in charge of them, or between a population that has been conquered and the conquering army, on the basis of "consent" given in a general context of coercion and lack of freedom.[71]

The discussion about sex and gender crimes in international law must continue, but with an awareness of the potential risks that exist. Examples of these risks are that (i) women may become stigmatized as victims; (ii) the inclusion of the offense of rape in the existing crime categories in international law could result in the exclusion of other sex and gender crimes that do not fit into the criteria of the existing crime categories; and (iii) the way the male legal system deals with issues perceived as "female" can create certain problems.

---

69   Daphne Barak-Erez, "Introduction: The Legal Feminism of Catharine A. MacKinnon and the Move from the Margin to the Center" in Daphne Barak-Erez, ed., *Legal Feminism in Theory and Practice* (Resling, 2005) 18–19 [Hebrew]; Janet Halley, Take a Break from Feminism?, supra note 68, pp. 65–66; Aeyal Gross, supra note 67, p. 395.

70   Karen Engle, "Feminism and Its (Dis)Contents: Criminalizing Wartime Rape in Bosnia and Herzegovina", 99 *Am. J. Int'l L.* 778, 786 (2005) (hereinafter *Karen Engle*).

71   I expand upon this topic below in Part Three, subchapter 9.5.2: "The Presumption of Nonconsent".

Chapter 2

LAW REFORM AND REALITY?

Before undertaking the journey through history in Part Two below, another question remains to be addressed: do changes in international law have merely symbolic significance, or do they lead to meaningful operative changes at the level of both national norms *and* the reality on the battlefield? International law has traditionally been characterized by the absence of a central authority holding exclusive power to create law, implement it and oversee it. Accordingly, one may ask: what is its significance? Why is it important to fill in its gaps and address its weaknesses?

Christine Chinkin and Hilary Charlesworth address this question. They claim that international law's importance lies not only in its immediate enforceability, but also in its ability to provide a theoretical and conceptual foundation for the distribution of power and the allocation of resources in the international community – a community whose influence (on domestic matters as well as international) has greatly increased as a result of globalization.[72] This ability exists alongside the processes discussed below in Part Two that have led to the establishment of international courts and tribunals with authority to criminally prosecute individuals.

The academic, political, and legal discourse is another component in the struggle to change the governing systems. This discourse, which Nancy Fraser calls "the 'experts' discourse", links the unorganized social discourse to the state. This professional discourse coins new terms and adds them to the lexicon.[73]

The radical feminist discourse focuses on the patterns and modes that will lead to a fundamental change in society by abolishing the situation of inequality between women and men. The change sought by radical feminism is not just in how the law is implemented, but also a substantive and fundamental change in the content of the law. This goal arises from a belief in the power of law as a tool of social formation:

> The project of constructing feminist jurisprudence is thus an ambitious as well as radical one: it seeks not only to challenge values and the goals of the

---

72   See Hilary Charlesworth, Christine Chinkin & Shelley Wright, supra note 24, pp. 619–622; Gilad Noam, supra note 21, pp. 190–191.

73   Nancy Fraser, *Unruly Practices: Power, Discourse and Gender in Contemporary Social Theory* (University of Minnesota Press/Polity Press, 1989) 166–181.

existing legal order, but also (like the Marxist theory) to undermine its epistemological foundations, by exposing the ways in which law constitutes "reality" – objective, true and gender neutral.[74]

Radical feminism is based on the assumption that law is a primary tool for legitimizing the existing social order. Moreover, because the liberal perspective views law as a tool for shaping social life (and not as a product that reflects the power relations in society), then from the moment the masculine view becomes embedded in the law, it attains an objective status. As a result, in order to change women's status in society and in law, the change in consciousness must be integrated with a fresh analysis of the institutions, conventions, norms and existing legal criteria.[75]

As discussed above in chapter one, the metaphor of the "voice" has attained a central place in current feminist literature. Listening to the victims enables them to bring their stories to the world. Giving a voice in law, in general, and in the judicial process, in particular, is a political act which is part of the struggle to change society's hierarchical power structures by means of the courts.[76] In effect, the court is one of the focal points in which the human voice still enjoys an advantage in western culture. By changing the law, the historical silence will disappear and new colors will paint the crimes that in the past were transparent.

Consequently, the existence of this discourse in the international arena has an impact and defines new terms. These changes have stimulated discussion and given a voice to the silent. Simultaneously, this international discourse has had an impact on what is taking place in the private realm of domestic law. Halley calls this the "politics of recognition".[77]

Now the question arises: are the rationales for conducting this discourse indeed relevant to situations of armed conflict? In other words, is the aspiration to establish normative arrangements for the behavior of fighting forces at the height of battle realistic?

---

74   Nicola Lacey, "Feminist Legal Theory", 9 *Oxford J. Legal Stud.* 383, 385 (1989).

75   See Ayelet Shachar, "The Sexuality of Law: The Legal Discourse About Rape", 18(1) *Tel Aviv Univ. L. Rev.* 160, 173 (1994) [Hebrew] (hereinafter *Ayelet Shachar*), quoting Catharine A. MacKinnon, *Toward a Feminist Theory of the State* (Harvard University Press, 1989) 113–114 (hereinafter *Catharine MacKinnon, Toward a Feminist Theory of the State*):

   Feminism has a theory of power: sexuality is gendered as gender is sexualized. Male and female are created through the eroticization of dominance and submission.… This is the social meaning of sex and the distinctively feminist account of gender inequality.

76   See Leora Bilsky, supra note 37; Katharine Bartlett, supra note 39.

77   Janet Halley, Rape at Rome, supra note 3, p. 51.

Arguably, these kinds of normative arrangements could be viewed as, ultimately, undesirable, on the grounds that they heighten the long-term risk of harm to innocent people. For example, Chris Jochnick and Roger Normand have argued that the laws of war grant legal legitimization to war and its continued existence and undermine the most important goal of preventing war in the first place. In their view, the expression "laws of war" is an oxymoron and any attempt to impose a behavioral code on soldiers at the height of anarchy is doomed to failure.[78]

These arguments, in addition to being highly controversial, ignore the position of those sitting on the other side of the fence of this dispute, the humanists or the regulators. I believe that humanity is morally obligated to do everything in its capacity to diminish the horrendousness of war. Even in wartime, basic humanitarian laws must be observed. In most instances, the humanitarian interests and the military needs of the fighting forces can be harmonized through the potential for mutual application and mutual welfare, which is integral to international humanitarian law.[79] Law contains the potential to organize the full range of human activity, and the destructive character of the actions carried out during war mandate rigorous legal intervention to protect the human interests likely to be harmed by it.

Moreover, empirical studies indicate that many of the world's armies generally honor the core principles of humanitarian law.[80] Also, the claim that organizing war constitutes recognition of its legitimacy is a naïve view, given the reality that wars continue to take place without the international community being capable of preventing them.[81]

As I demonstrate in the next chapter, the two legal universes of the national and international are interdependent and interconnected. One impacts the other. The latter was born from the former, and then created norms affecting the former, such that the historic gender subordination exists in both. Consequently, in order to see the whole picture when analyzing how international law relates to sex crimes, it is critical to first analyze sex crimes from the perspective of national laws.

---

78 Chris Jochnick & Roger Normand, "The Legitimization of Violence: A Critical History of the Law of War", 35 *Harv. Int'l L.J.* 49, 55–56 (1994).

79 Michael Howard, "Temperamenta Belli: Can War Be Controlled?" in Michael Howard, ed., *Restraints on War: Studies in the Limitation of Armed Conflict* (Oxford, 1979) 1.

80 Of course, the motives are not always humanitarian, but rather more often are concerned with image, acts of revenge, etc. Perhaps today the long arm of the ICC can also be included as a motive.

81 For more on this issue, see Orna Ben-Naftali & Yuval Shany, *International Law Between War and Peace* (Ramot, Tel Aviv University, 2006) 117–120 [Hebrew] (hereinafter *Orna Ben-Naftali & Yuval Shany*).

Chapter 3

RAPE AS A UNIQUE CRIME UNDER DOMESTIC LAW

The importance of analyzing the offense of rape under domestic law is based not only on the fact that women's historic inferiority was not born on the battlefield. As explained above in chapter one, and as I explain further in this chapter, international law was shaped in light of national legal values, and vice versa. This chapter presents the complexities of the domestic offense of rape with respect to its development and the remnants of patriarchy still embedded in it, which have been preserved in many countries.

I first discuss the symbiotic relationship between international law and domestic law. This connection explains the significance of the study that I undertake in the remainder of the chapter about the way in which domestic law, first, chose to exclude rape, and subsequently, decided how to include sex and gender crimes. Domestic law will be examined from the social perspective and then from the legal perspective. Particular focus will be given to those crimes for which the domestic law has adopted a presumption that I have termed "the presumption of nonconsent".

3.1 THE NEXUS BETWEEN INTERNATIONAL LAW AND NATIONAL LAW

National law is both the background to and a source of international law in cases of lacunae in international law. For example, Article 21(1)(c) of the Rome Statute, the treaty that established the ICC, refers the ICC to national laws when the ICC's own governing documents and international law do not provide a solution:

21. The Court shall apply:
    (a) In the first place, this Statute, Elements of Crimes and its Rules of Procedure and Evidence;
    (b) In the second place, where appropriate, applicable treaties and the principles and rules of international law, including the established principles of the international law of armed conflict;
    (c) Failing that, *general principles of law derived by the Court from national laws* of legal systems of the world including, as appropriate, *the national laws of States that would normally exercise jurisdiction over the crime*, provided that those principles are not inconsistent with this Statute

and with international law and internationally recognized norms and standards.

[Emphasis added by the author]

In this context, note that Article 38 of the Statute of the International Court of Justice (ICJ) also provides the sources of international law. It enumerates the following sources – international conventions, international custom, and "the general principles of law recognized by civilized nations."[82] Because parties can set conditions to the applicability of customary law (unlike the principles of *jus cogens*),[83] in order to identify the law applicable to a given event, one must first determine whether the specific issue is subject to an agreement among the relevant states. In the absence of an agreement, one must look to the customary law and the principles of general law.[84] Article 38(1)(d) specifies that certain subsidiary sources are also applicable, specifically "judicial decisions" and the "teachings of the most highly qualified publicists". The expression "judicial decisions" includes the decisions of other international courts, but it also includes decisions of national courts related to international law. Significantly, as opposed to the first three sources of law, these subsidiary sources do not create international law, although the line distinguishing between the sources is not always clear.[85]

Another nexus between national and international law is found in Article 8(2)(e)(vi) of the Rome Statute, which subjects certain crimes of sexual violence to the ICC's jurisdiction if they are deemed "war crimes", even if the crimes are perpetrated in local or non-international armed conflicts:

> 2. For the purpose of this Statute, "war crimes" means: ....
>
>   (e) Other serious violations of the laws and customs applicable in *armed conflicts not of an international character*, within the established framework of international law, namely, any of the following acts: ....

---

82   Statute of the International Court of Justice, 26 June 1945, 59 Stat. 1055.

83   In general, international law is dispositive (*jus dispositivum*). In other words, it is permissible to alter it by consent of the states affected by a matter. Exceptions are certain cognate laws (*jus cogens*), from which it is not permissible to derogate. Although no complete agreement exists regarding which rules constitute "peremptory norms", there is no controversy that the list includes genocide, piracy torture, slave trade, war crimes, crimes against humanity and aggression. These crimes have always been prohibited because they are grave crimes threatening all of humanity. In this book, I argue that sex and gender crimes should also be considered part of this list. See also infra note 206.

84   However, note that it is not always possible to distinguish because the different sources overlap to a great extent. For example, in many cases, treaties adopted the rules of customary law. Malcolm Shaw, *International Law* (Cambridge University Press, 5th ed., 2005) 67, 88, 91–92 (hereinafter *Malcolm Shaw*); Robbie Sabel, "Sources of International Law", in Robbie Sabel, ed., *International Law* (Hebrew University, 2d ed., 2010) 60 [Hebrew] (hereinafter *Robbie Sabel*).

85   Malcolm Shaw, supra note 84, p. 107; Robbie Sabel, supra note 84, p. 61.

(vi) Committing rape, sexual slavery, enforced prostitution, forced pregnancy, as defined in article 7, paragraph 2 (f), enforced sterilization, and any other form of sexual violence also constituting a serious violation of article 3 common to the four Geneva Conventions.

[Emphasis added by the author]

Hence, there is a threefold basis to examine sexual offenses under the domestic laws of nation-states in the context of this study: *first*, to better understand the implications of the unique characteristics of sex crimes as compared to other criminal offenses in the international arena; *second*, because these laws, so long as they do not conflict with the Rome Statute or the principles of international law, may be integrated into the international law in the event of a legal lacuna which cannot be resolved under existing international law; and *third*, if the offenses are committed in the context of domestic conflicts within a state and defined under the Rome Statute as "war crimes", then the perpetrators of the crimes could be prosecuted at the ICC.

3.2 RAPE AS A GENDER CRIME – ATTACKER, VICTIM AND SOCIETY

As I discuss above, it is not sufficient to expose the silence of international law and the line dividing the public realm (covered by international law) from the neglected private realm, and the gender bias underlying both. After the discussion in the previous subsection about the nexus between international law and domestic law, and in order to finish laying the background for the discussion below in Part Two about how sex and gender offenses are anchored in the international criminal law, it is also important to examine the complexity and distinct nature of the offense of rape compared to other crimes.

The criminal laws of each nation-state reflect the needs of organized society to protect the values essential for its orderly conduct and desired development, as suited to its worldview in any given time period.[86] Historically, as Simone de Beauvoir wrote, "society has always been male; political power has always been in the hands of men."[87] Woman was perceived as an absolute other, subject to the good will of her patron.[88] Against this background, a woman's inferiority was expressed by her being denied legal and social status, and she was considered to be part of her patron's property. Consequently, rape was first defined as a property crime – harm to the property of the father or husband of the woman who was raped. In this context, of course, a husband's use of force against his

---

86   S.Z. Feller, *Foundations of Criminal Law*, Vol. A (1984) 1 [Hebrew].
87   Simone de Beauvoir, *The Second Sex* (H.M. Parshley, trans., Vintage Classics, 1997) 102.
88   Ibid.

wife – whether to cause her to submit to sexual relations or otherwise – was not considered a criminal offense, since he was entitled to use his property as he saw fit.[89]

Anne Coughlin believes that the historical source of the elements of the offense of rape as a crime lies in the defense a woman could raise when charged with a crime of unlawful sexual relations, i.e., outside of the marital relationship.[90] The complaint of rape constituted a woman's defense in that it transferred guilt for the criminal act onto the man with whom she was accused of having unlawful sexual relations. In effect, she could claim that she was not criminally responsible for the forbidden contact because she was like an object, lacking control or desire, absent voluntary will[91] – or, alternatively, that the man whom she was accusing of rape had overcome her opposition after threatening her with death or grave bodily harm (the defense of necessity).[92]

The law has indeed changed since those dark days, and the crime of rape now stands on its own two feet. However, it still retains certain remnants of patriarchy, and, as I discuss in this chapter below, in many cases the complainant is still "rewarded" by being treated as if she is the guilty party.

To this day, the female gender inferiority attributed to sex victims which turns them into a target, as contrasted with the gender superiority linked to male sexual capabilities, correlates with the social perceptions about femininity and masculinity. One cannot ignore the prominent consistency in which men are more frequently the attackers and women are more frequently the victims.[93] As Orit Kamir remarks:

> In the modern world, as in the traditional world, the gendered construction of masculinity is still based to a great extent on assertiveness, activeness, aggressiveness, combativeness, hunting, overcoming obstacles, achievement, triumph and conquest. "Masculinity" is still identified with traditional, patriarchal, masculine honor, and all of its implications. A man is

---

89   Susan Brownmiller, supra note 11, p. 18. For example, the English law enacted in 1861 prohibited the following sexual acts:

> Unlawful sexual intercourse, act of sodomy, carnal knowledge of a person against the order of nature, carnal knowledge of an animal, consummation of marriage, indecent act, and indecent suggestion.

90   According to Coughlin, the common law defined the crime of unlawful relations as sexual relations outside the framework of marriage, whether adultery or premarital sex. See Anne M. Coughlin, "Sex and Guilt", 84 *Virginia L. Rev.* 7, 8 (1998).

91   Orit Kamir, Israel's Dignity-based Feminism, infra note 94, pp. 142–143.

92   Ibid., pp. 143–144.

93   Catharine A. MacKinnon, "A Sex Equality Approach to Sexual Assault", 989 *Annals of the New York Academy of Sciences* 265 (2003) (hereinafter *Catharine MacKinnon, A Sex Equality Approach*). See also supra note 8 and infra notes 167, 480.

expected to display masculine characteristics in the social sphere, which includes his family, his professional world, economics, military service, as well as his sexual contacts with women. His social status and masculine honor are derived directly from the degree of assertiveness, aggressiveness and conquest he displays. ...

Accordingly, "normal" sexual contact is perceived as including a man's conquest of a woman and a woman's surrender to her conqueror.[94]

In a certain sense, rape can be viewed as a tool in the subordination of women, as a "gender crime" – a crime committed by one gender against the other. Recognition of this view has been expressed in a range of legal documents issued by various international institutions, including the UN General Assembly, the Committee on the Elimination of Discrimination against Women, the Organization of American States, the Beijing Committee, and the European Union. Each of these institutions defined and denounced sexual violence as stemming from unequal social power between the sexes, meaning gender.[95] UN Security Council Resolution 1820, which I discuss in chapter one above, also explicitly recognizes sex crimes as a weapon in times of conflict, and states:

Noting ... that women and girls are particularly targeted by the use of sexual violence, including as a tactic of war to humiliate, dominate, instill fear in, disperse ...[96]

To recapitulate, the offense of rape carries complicated historical baggage. The remnants of this historical baggage are rooted in our time as well, and this has led to increasing international recognition of the gender elements of subordination and control that are embedded in sex crimes. These elements are discussed in the subchapter below, which analyzes the offense of rape from society's perspective.

3.2.1 SOCIETY'S ATTITUDE TOWARD RAPE

Brownmiller describes the power of rape as a political tool to preserve male control as follows:

Man's discovery that his genitalia could serve as a weapon to generate fear must rank as one of the most important discoveries of prehistoric times,

---

94   Orit Kamir, *Israel's Dignity-based Feminism in Law and Society* (Carmel, 2007) 142 [Hebrew] (hereinafter *Orit Kamir, Israel's Dignity-based Feminism*), p. 153.

95   For more on this point, see Catharine MacKinnon, A Sex Equality Approach, supra note 93, pp. 265–266.

96   Resolution 1820, supra note 33.

along with the use of fire and invention of the first crude stone axe. From prehistoric times to the present, I believe, rape has played a critical function. It is nothing more or less than a conscious process of intimidation by which *all men* keep *all women* in a state of fear.[97]

This perpetual fear is also expressed in the victim's sense of guilt. In many cases, the knowledge that she became a victim of rape – despite being aware of the threat in advance – is transformed into a sense of guilt for having assisted the attacker. In contrast with victims of other crimes, rape victims generally feel blame and encounter the problem of social judgment. Sometimes they are considered to have been defiled, even by their family members. Their partner and family members hold prejudices about what rape is and what a rape victims' appropriate response should be. Judith Lewis Herman compares the trauma of rape to the trauma of war veterans returning home from battle. However, she notes the contrast between the public recognition awarded to seasoned war veterans and the conspicuous lack of recognition which is the fate of the rape victim.[98] Public opinion generally not only fails to recognize many incidents of rape as rape, but it also tends to interpret them as consensual sexual relations for which the victim bears responsibility. The women, therefore, discover this alarming contradiction between their actual experience and society's interpretation of this reality.[99]

Women who are raped learn that not only were they raped, but also their dignity has been stolen from them. They are treated with greater contempt than soldiers defeated in war. They are not recognized as having lost in an unfair battle and they are blamed for betraying their own moral norms and bringing defeat upon themselves.[100]

The psychological harm caused by rape has been extensively described in the literature. This harm can be expressed as, among other things, fear, insecurity, anger, feelings of revenge, depression, sleep disturbances and nightmares, eating disorders, guilt feelings, shame and low self-image, anxiety, exhaustion, and sexual frigidity. In many cases, the reaction is severe, similar

---

97   Susan Brownmiller, supra note 11, p. 15.

98   Judith Lewis Herman, *Trauma and Recovery: The Aftermath of Violence – From Domestic Abuse to Political Terror* (BasicBooks, Harper Collins, 1992) 67 (hereinafter *Judith Lewis Herman*).

99   Regarding the gap between the rape victim's perception of the experience and society's perception, which can cause the victim to wonder if she really was raped, if what she experienced as rape was really rape, see Susan Estrich, *Real Rape* (Harvard University Press, 1987); Catharine A. MacKinnon, "Feminism, Marxism, Method and the State: Toward Feminist Jurisprudence", 8 *Signs J. Women Culture & Soc'y* 515 (1983).

100   Judith Lewis Herman, supra note 98, p. 51.

to other crises that are unexpected and life-threatening.[101] Despite the fact that each rape experience is different, three common factors characterize the harm caused to the victim: dehumanization, objectification, and domination.[102]

The foregoing indicates that the psychological harm to the victim is not a secondary response to the trauma. Rather, it is a primary response affecting both the person's psychological construct of self as well as her relationship with the community.[103]

Legal efforts to seek justice or compensation for the victim are likely to involve additional trauma because the legal system often treats rape victims with open hostility. This is a genuine additional trauma, "a second rape" by the lawyers for the accused.[104] The legal system by its nature constitutes a hostile environment: it is organized like a battlefield in which strategies of aggressive claims and psychological attack replace the strategies and attack that used physical force. Once again, power has been wrested away from the woman – the decision about what happens to her body and her heart-rending personal story is expropriated and converted to public property, sometimes without her consent. Taking the decision, for example, to open the doors of the courtroom, to expose her name, her identity and her story as the victim, has a deep impact on the continuation of her psychological therapy and her future desire to be helped by the professional to whom she would reveal her innermost secrets.[105] Even without this violation of her trust, the ability of a sexual abuse victim to expose her distress is already diminished and is accompanied by feelings of shame and guilt.[106]

> The process of the police investigation, the medical examinations and testifying in court involve the exposure of intimate details about the event itself and the complainant's personal life. This exposure takes place in settings that are not necessarily careful about respect for privacy, and is sometimes accompanied by degrading treatment by the investigators. In this context, it is often said that a woman who was raped is victimized

---

101   Leslie Sebba, "The Crime of Rape: Legal Trends and Criminality", 3 *Plilim* 46, 58–59 (1993) [Hebrew].

102   See Michelle J. Anderson, "All-American Rape", 2 *St. John's L. Rev.* 625 (2005) (hereinafter *Michelle Anderson*).

103   Judith Lewis Herman, supra note 98, p. 51.

104   Regarding the phenomenon of women who sought justice in the legal system and experienced it as a second rape, see Judith Lewis Herman, supra note 98, p. 72.

105   Ibid.

106   Ibid.

twice: first by the rapist's aggression and afterwards by society's treatment of her.[107, 108]

Unfortunately, it is not difficult to find instances of this kind of "second rape".

For example, Binaifer Nowrogee reports about an egregious incident in 2001 in the Butare trial, when the ICTR judges laughed during the testimony of a woman who was the victim of multiple rapes during the Rwandan genocide (referred to by Nowrogee as TA). TA was also asked highly offensive questions by the defense attorneys, including one which referred to the fact she had not taken a bath and implied that she could not have been raped because she smelled. Other questions asked by defense counsel included: "Did you touch the accused's penis?" and "How was it introduced into your vagina?" Moreover, TA underwent a day and a half of questioning by the prosecutor, before undergoing a week of cross-examination by defense counsel.[109]

The results of publicizing a rape can be especially severe in patriarchal and traditional societies, where the woman who has been raped is often ostracized by her family and society. Frequently, husbands react by scornfully banishing their wives if they have been raped. During wartime, just as during times of peace, they impose on their wives a considerable share of the blame for the atrocious event of being raped. The husband's ownership rights were violated and the property itself is held to blame.[110]

---

107   Nitza Shapiro-Libai, "The Requirement for a 'Dvar Mah' in Sexual Offenses– An Unjustified Exception", 33 *Hapraklit* 422, 427 (1979–1980) [Hebrew]; Ayelet Shachar, supra note 75, p. 159.

108   Moreover, the myth that "women complain about rape in order to get revenge on men" is incorrect. Reported sexual assaults are true, with very few exceptions. FBI crime statistics indicate that only 2% of reported rapes are false. This is the same rate of false reporting as other major crime reports. See Website of the Connecticut Sexual Assault Crisis Services, Inc., http://www.connsacs.org/learn/index.htm. (last accessed 14 April 2011). For example, the Portland, Oregon police reported in 1990 that 1.6% of rape complaints were determined to be false, compared to 2.6% of false stolen vehicle reports. See Tamara Larsen, "Comment, Sexual Violence is Unique: Why Evidence of Other Crimes Should be Admissible in Sexual Assault and Child Molestation Cases", 29 *Hamline L. Rev.* 177, 200 (2006), citing Sharon Hunter, Gail Burns-Smith & Carol Walsh, "Equal Justice? Not Yet for Victims of Sexual Assault" (Newsletter, Connecticut Sexual Assault Crisis Services, 1996); see also Morrison Torrey, "When Will We Be Believed? Rape Myths and the Idea of a Fair Trial in Rape Prosecutions", 24 *U.C. Davis L. Rev.* 1013, 1028 (1991).

109   Binaifer Nowrogee, "'Your Justice Is Too Slow': Will the ICTR Fail Rwanda's Rape Victims?" *UNRISD Occasional Paper Gender Policy* 10 (UNRISD, 2005) 23–24 (hereinafter *Binaifer Nowrogee*).

110   Susan Brownmiller, supra note 11, pp. 39–40. An interesting exception is the following response of a rabbi in the Kovno ghetto in Lithuania, who was asked by the husband of a

For example, the victim TA, who lost all of her family during the genocide in Rwanda, told the following story during an interview:

> My parents, my brother and my sister were killed. I'm all alone. My relatives were killed in a horrible fashion. But I survived – to answer the strange questions that were asked by the ICTR. If you say you were raped, that is something understandable. How many times do you need to say it? When the judges laughed, they laughed like they could not stop laughing. I was angry and nervous.
>
> When I returned, everyone knew I had testified. My fiancé refused to marry me once he knew I had been raped. He said, you went to Arusha and told everyone that you were raped. Today I would not accept to testify, to be traumatized for a second time. No one apologized to me. Only Gregory Townsend [the ICTR prosecuting lawyer] congratulated me after the testimony for my courage. When you return you get threatened. My house was attacked. My fiancé has left me. In any case, I'm already dead.[111]

Social ostracism as described by this witness in the ICTR can also be found in Jewish tradition in which a woman who had been raped was condemned and considered impure. According to early Jewish law, a woman who was raped became forbidden both to her husband and the man who had raped her, due to the concern that what began as rape would end as consensual intercourse.[112] This law was revised, and ultimately the position was adopted that only the wife of a member of the priestly caste would be prohibited to her husband, whereas other Jewish women were prohibited to their husbands only in cases of betrayal.[113, 114]

Jewish woman whether he was permitted to have relations with her after she had been raped by Nazis during the Holocaust and her arm had been tattooed with the words "Prostitute of Hitler's Military Corps":

> Far be it from any man to cast aspersion on pious Jewish women in such a plight as this. Rather … [w]e must avoid causing them any unnecessary anguish. Certainly husbands who have divorced their wives under similar circumstances have acted reprehensibly.

Ibid. p. 54.

111   Binaifer Nowrogee, supra note 109, p. 24, quoting an interview, rape victim, Butare, 2003.

112   Yaacov Shapira, "Preserving the Relationship between a Cohen and his Wife who has been Raped – Law and Cinema", 1 *Family Law* 303, 309–319 (2007) [Hebrew].

113   Ibid.

114   The second century compilation of Jewish law, the Mishnah, records that this law was changed due to the rabbis' concerns that women would exploit this law in order to obtain a divorce even when their husbands had not agreed to end the relationship. Note that this change

Even a woman with the capacity to cope with the legal process is likely to find herself a priori in an inferior position due to prejudices that have been incorporated into the justice system. Herman sarcastically notes that one could not devise a better system for causing severe post-traumatic symptoms than a courtroom trial.[115]

The conclusion is incontrovertible: in order to enable victims' voices to be heard and to expose their historic silences, rules of procedures that are more flexible, and some would even say more feminine, must be adopted. These procedures would protect and support the victim, and enable her to tell her story.

When we examine the evolution of the crime of rape in international law, we must understand that its roots lie in both the gender inferiority of the victim and the gender superiority of the attacker under the domestic law. These are relationships characterized by subordination and dominance, as they are termed by radical feminism, which have yet to become equal. This inequality is intensified during wartime conditions. Under cover of war, the national struggle legitimizes the day-to-day subordination.[116] Moreover, the impact of rape on the victim, in most instances, will be of major significance – the victim's ability to pursue the perpetrator will be impaired by personal and societal constraints, the support she will receive from her environment will be minimal, and she may be designated as the guilty party.

3.3 THE ELEMENTS OF THE CRIME OF RAPE UNDER DOMESTIC LAW[117]

Under common law, the criminal law divided the elements of a crime into two key elements: the guilty act (the *actus reus*) and the mental state (the *mens rea*) of the accused at the time of committing the offense.[118] In order to provide a

---

was not based on concern for women who were divorced by their husbands after becoming victims of rape. Ibid, p. 311.

115   Judith Lewis Herman, supra note 98, p. 72.

116   "In times of war, the laws are silent" *(inter arma enim silent leges)*, in the famous saying attributed to the Roman legislator Cicero. For further discussion of this issue, see Orna Ben-Naftali & Yuval Shany, supra note 81, pp. 117–120. See also supra note 18 and infra note 182.

117   Since this subchapter is intended to illuminate the discussion about international law in Part Two and to help map out this subject, I have chosen to focus primarily on the crime of rape under the common law, while bringing examples from other legal systems to clarify some of the legal issues.

118   Samuel H. Pillsbury, *How Criminal Law Works* (Carolina Academic Press, 2009) 57–58 (hereinafter *Samuel Pillsbury*); M. Cherif Bassiouni, *Introduction to International Criminal Law* (Transnational Publishers, 2003) 281.

complete picture of the issues discussed in this book, this subchapter briefly discusses these two aspects of the crime of rape.

3.3.1 The Guilty Act – *Actus Reus*

As discussed above in the previous subchapter, the elements of the crime of rape were originally formulated to protect a man's property rights in the women he possessed and, later, to protect a woman's honor against a foreign man's trespass upon her sexuality.[119] Moreover, the issue of consent originated as a defense that a woman could raise against a charge of unlawful sexual relations. This historical development of the offense of rape sheds light on the connections between the elements of the offense of rape in many legal systems: the complainant's lack of consent, her active resistance, and the accused's use of force. For example, the canonic definition of the crime of rape under the common law, as expressed by William Blackstone in the 18th century, provided that rape was "the carnal knowledge of a woman forcibly and against her will." The elements of the criminal behavior were (i) "carnal knowledge", defined as the penetration of the penis into the vagina; (ii) "forcibly", meaning with the use of more force than necessary to effect penetration, and (iii) "against her will", which was interpreted to require that the woman resisted to the extent of her ability.

In feudal England, rape was primarily considered as an attack upon a family's honor by the violation of a female's chastity. The wrong was suffered not only by the victim, but also by her male patron (father, husband or other male relative), who was the keeper of the family honor. In many states in the United States (U.S.), during the nineteenth and early twentieth centuries, the wrong became personal to the victim, but it still centered on her chastity. As a result, attacks on the complainant's prior sexual virtue – or rather its lack – were permitted in defense of rape charges.[120]

The offense of rape rests on the perception that rape is exceptional and pathological behavior – and that it can be distinguished from "normal sex". However, the "neutral" standard courts use to determine whether the sexual relations were "normal" is a male standard.[121] Therefore, it is not surprising that of all the different kinds of force, the doctrine of force in the criminal law

---

119   Orit Kamir, Israel's Dignity-based Feminism, supra note 94, p. 145.

120   Samuel Pillsbury, supra note 118, p. 254.

121   Catherine MacKinnon, Toward a Feminist Theory of the State, supra note 75, pp. 126–154, 171–183. Ayelet Shachar, supra note 75, p. 164; Catharine MacKinnon, Feminism Unmodified, supra note 32.

of rape recognized only physical force.[122] As MacKinnon comments, only extreme physical force, preferably using a weapon in addition to the penis, was generally considered sufficient force for sex to be considered rape.[123] Ayelet Shachar describes this phenomenon as follows:

> [T]he group holding the power to define reality as unequal on the basis of sexual identity will be capable of institutionalizing these hierarchical relations in the form of laws and statutes that are presented as neutral. The establishment of such laws will ensure the continuation of male domination, and even convert it into an entrenched situation that appears to be impartial.[124]

The foregoing discussion demonstrates that (i) the offense of rape was traditionally perceived as a crime of dramatic and brutal violence by a man, usually a stranger, against a woman, and (ii) proof of the defendant's use of overwhelming force and the victim's physical resistance was required for conviction.[125]

This requirement regarding the element of force that must accompany the sexual act for a conviction of rape has been the subject of extensive critique.[126] *First*, from that which is prohibited, we can derive that which is permitted – in other words, this requirement concerning the use of force makes those sexual acts that are accompanied by some lesser degree of force permissible. This requirement regarding the element of force also applied in the case of incidents not accompanied by any force whatsoever because the rape victim became paralyzed with fear, and hence did not actively resist. Non-resistance was deemed consent, based on the requirement for the factual elements of "forcibly and against her will". If we consider what these elements would mean in the battlefield, in which the victim's fear and subordination to the rapist's domination are already day-to-day facts, then the lack of a reaction – her paralysis – are entirely understandable. From this perspective, it is apparent why women in these circumstances would rarely actively resist an attacker.

Second, no other assault offense requires that the victim actively express the lack of consent, yet with rape, it is a central element. In contrast, explicit

---

122   Stephen J. Schulhofer, *Unwanted Sex: The Culture of Intimidation and the Failure of Law* (Harvard University Press, 1998).

123   Catharine MacKinnon, Feminism Unmodified, supra note 32, p. 67.

124   Ayelet Shachar, supra note 75, p. 173.

125   Samuel Pillsbury, supra note 118, p. 254.

126   Catharine MacKinnon, Feminism Unmodified, supra note 32.

consent is required for every other kind of physical invasion, such as, for example, dental care.[127]

Third, a woman's resistance to rape can lead to very grave injuries, even death, if she chooses to struggle rather than submit to her bitter fate. Consequently, as opposed to the commonly-accepted view, the better choice would usually be *not* to resist.

Fourth, many women have been socialized to be passive, both accepting and satisfying other people's wishes. Hence, actively resisting someone's demands, as heinous as they may be, feels foreign to them. Moreover, the fact that the type of resistance and its strength will be analyzed from a male point of view leads to a distortion of the factual reality when it is translated into a legal reality.

Orit Kamir links the two requirements of "lack of consent" and "active resistance" to the historic roots of the offense of rape – the social construction of the conquering male and the conquered female.[128] However, beyond these historic roots, it is significant even today to recall that:

> an interpretative point of view which maintains that it is theoretically possible to separate the isolated sexual act before the court from the social-aggressive context of sexual relationships can infringe upon the woman's capacity to provide a "reasonable" explanation for her behavior, thereby diminishing her chances of convincing the court of the reliability of her version.[129]

Rape law reforms have addressed various problems in the domestic law of rape. For example, one area addressed by these reforms concerns the definition of the prohibited sexual act. At common law, rape required an act of sexual intercourse, defined as vaginal penetration by a penis. This pedantic and narrow factual element led to the victim always being a woman, meaning that a man could not be raped.[130] Furthermore, any other forced sexual assault was considered a lesser offense. Recent reforms of rape law have broadened the definition of the sexual act. Under modern legislation, rape often includes the penetration of the mouth or anus and the use of any body part or physical objects to penetrate the vagina or anus.[131]

---

127   For additional examples, see Orit Kamir, Israel's Dignity-based Feminism, supra note 94, pp. 164–165.

128   Ibid., p. 145.

129   Ayelet Shachar, supra note 75, p. 150.

130   A man could be the victim of the common law offense of sodomy, a crime defined without the element of nonconsent. Samuel Pillsbury, supra note 118, p. 256.

131   Ibid.

Another area addressed by rape law reform concerns the two active require-ments for the accused's use of force and physical resistance by the complainant. These requirements were eliminated in some common law states and miti-gated in other legal systems. However, the reforms split into two similar but different directions: on the one hand, in England (in 1976), in some states in the U.S., and in some other places, the use of force was eliminated from the definition of the crime of rape, and new statutes provided that rape is defined as the sexual penetration of a woman's body without her consent. On the other hand, in certain states in the U.S.,[132] Canada, and other jurisdictions, the ele-ment of force was emphasized for the offense of rape, rather than the victim's lack of consent. Also, the term "rape" was replaced by terms that emphasize the violence of the sexual assault. Hence, the element of the "lack of consent" was eliminated and the offense of rape joined the ranks of other violent offenses. Rape, according to this approach, is an assault – the violent penetration of a person's body.[133] This issue is highly relevant to our discussion of *how sex crimes should be recognized under international law.*[134]

However, even the modern liberal attempt to eliminate the two active ele-ments of "forcibly" and "against her will", and to analyze the victim's consent from a clean and autonomous point of view, has become a double-edged sword. As Kamir explains:

> Feminist research into the common law demonstrates that, to the extent the legal system focuses on the element of free consent, it increases judi-cial inquiry of the complainant rather than the accused. To the extent that

---

132   Note, however, that in most states in the U.S., the "classic" definition of rape has remained unchanged:

> The vast majority of state laws in the United States derive from the classic rape narrative: they basically require a defendant to exert force against his victim before the state may convict him of what is commonly thought of as rape. ... In order to be convicted of a state's highest, non-aggravated sexual offense, statutes in forty-three states and the District of Columbia require that the defendant use force against his victim. Although eight of these forty-four statutes appear to require only non-consent, they include the use of force in the definition of "non-consent". Sixteen states and the District of Columbia *do criminalize sex-ual penetration that is non-consensual and without force.* These states, however, impose less punishment upon nonconsensual penetration, with greater than half of them categorizing these offenses as mere misdemeanors. Overall, then, in under just six state statutes does the All-American rape constitute the highest, non-aggravated sexual offense.... Culturally, as well as legally, the classic rape narrative remains the public face of rape in this country.
> [Emphasis added by the author]

Michelle Anderson, supra note 102.
133   Orit Kamir, Israel's Dignity-based Feminism, supra note 94, p. 132.
134   See Janet Halley, Rape at Rome, supra note 3, p. 58.

her consent takes on a more central role in the distinction between rape and legitimate sexual contact, the judicial motivation to thoroughly analyze every bit of her behavior and personality is thus enhanced. As the weight of influence given to the violence used by the accused diminishes, so, too, the legal concern with him is diminished, and it turns instead to analyzing the complainant and her role in the event. Her every word, every movement, every article of clothing, every intuition, become relevant and significant facts, and the legal system analyzes them over and over again....

In other words, the complainant stands in the dock in place of the accused. And because she doesn't benefit from the defendant's rights, the presumption of innocence does not apply, but rather its opposite: as the prosecution's witness, she must convince the court beyond a reasonable doubt of the truth of every detail of her complaint.[135]

In other words, while in the past the prosecution labored to overcome evidence brought by the defense about the victim's prior sexual history in order to prove her resistance, now the prosecution itself must bring evidence about the victim to prove that she did not consent.

As the foregoing indicates, the physical elements of the offense differ in certain respects from one legal system to another. Nevertheless, it is apparent that the modern liberal solution, which focuses on eliminating the two active elements of "forcibly" and "against her will" from the traditional offense and replacing them with an analysis of the element of consent, is not without its problems.

3.3.2 The Guilty Mind – *Mens Rea*

At the heart of criminal law is *mens rea*, a Latin term meaning guilty mind, which refers to the requirement that a person must have had the intention to commit a wrongful act in order to be convicted of a crime.[136] Like the *actus reus*, the mental state required for the crime of rape has also been revised over the years, as I discuss in this subchapter.

The traditional legal requirement for a criminal's *mens rea* is "knowledge" or "awareness", meaning that conviction requires not only proof of the factual elements of the offense, but also subjective proof that the accused was aware of each of the factual elements. As exceptions to this general rule, a different *mens rea* is required for strict liability offenses, for which the factual element alone is sufficient, and crimes of negligence, which justify an objective

---

135   Orit Kamir, Israel's Dignity-based Feminism, supra note 94, pp. 134–135.
136   Samuel Pillsbury, supra note 118, p. 101.

standard of conduct for the accused. At the other end of the spectrum, there is another exception: there are offenses in which a higher threshold of *mens rea* is required, such as intent, which is necessary for the offense of murder, for example.[137]

Clearly, where an offense is located on the *mens rea* scale has an impact on the prosecution's burden of proof and burden of persuasion. Crimes of strict liability and negligence ease the prosecution's burden of proving the guilt of the accused. Crimes requiring a *mens rea* of intent and knowledge place a higher burden on the prosecution and a lower burden on the accused. As another exception, the range also includes offenses requiring a slightly lower threshold for *mens rea* than knowledge, called "recklessness" or "gross negligence", which typically requires proof that the accused willfully disregarded or was indifferent to the factual elements of the offense and their consequences.[138]

Historically, the offense of rape was one of the exceptions to the standard requirements for proof of *mens rea*. The court had to focus on the *actus reus* and practically ignore the *mens rea* of the accused regarding the physical acts other than, of course, penetration. This approach was accepted in all common law systems, including most of the states in the U.S. The reason was logical and simple: it is nearly impossible to prove beyond a reasonable doubt that the accused heard, saw, listened, internalized and understood the woman's position regarding the sexual contact – meaning, that he was aware. Even if it could be objectively proven that under the circumstances, it would have been reasonable for him to be aware, it would almost always be impossible to prove that he had actually formed this awareness. Hence, at common law, rape was a general intent crime; the defendant only needed to intend penetration.[139] Since penetration does not occur by accident, there was no *mens rea* requirement with respect to the lack of consent of the victim.[140]

During the mid-1970s, the question first arose: *is proof of the actus reus alone sufficient to convict a person for the offense of rape?* This question was answered differently in different jurisdictions. In most of the states in the U.S., the offense was revised and the *mens rea* requirement became one of "negligence" – an

---

137   Moreover, with respect to murder, "premeditation" is also required.

138   Samuel Pillsbury, supra note 118, p. 106.

139   David P. Bryden, "Forum on the Law of Rape: Redefining Rape", 3 *Buff. Crim. L. Rev.* 317, 325 (2000).

140   Donald Dripps, "After Rape Law: Will the Turn to Consent Normalize the Prosecution of Sexual Assault?" 41 *Akron L. Rev.* 957, 961 (2008).

objective test.[141, 142] "The majority of states require some form of notice of non-consent. A defendant will not be convicted if he honestly and reasonably believed that his partner consented to the sexual act."[143] In England the House of Lords, in a controversial judgment, held that the crime of rape should require the mental state of "recklessness" – a subjective test.[144] In other words, the *mens rea* requirement would not be met if a defendant honestly and genuinely believed that the woman was consenting, however unreasonable that belief was. "This was known formally as the 'mistaken belief' clause and informally as the 'rapist charter' because it meant that the woman could be actively non consenting, even shouting 'no' and struggling to free herself, and the man could still be acquitted of rape."[145] This controversial decision led in 2003 to new legislation for the crime of rape, which provided that the required *mens rea* would be "negligence" (if "A does not reasonably believe that B consents"),[146] meaning that a person cannot be convicted for the offense of rape if his mistake was reasonable. In other words, the transition was made from a "subjective mistake" to an "objective mistake" – it would be sufficient for the prosecution to prove that a reasonable person under the circumstances would have suspected that the victim did not consent.

141　"Negligent behavior", in contrast with "purpose", "knowledge" and "recklessness", which focus on what the accused *actually* intended or realized, is manifested by a lack of awareness of the existence of the factual elements of the circumstances, and its unacceptable nature is derived from the assessment that a reasonable person in the actor's position would have been aware of the risk, and, therefore, would have acted differently. Yuval Levy & Eliezer Lederman, *Principles of Criminal Responsibility* (1981) 504 [Hebrew]; Samuel Pillsbury, supra note 118, p. 109.

142　See Stephen J. Schulhofer, *Unwanted Sex: The Culture of Intimidation and the Failure of Law* (Harvard University Press, 1998) 258; Andrew E. Taslitz, "Willfully Blinded: On Date Rape and Self-Deception", 28 *Harv. J.L. & Gender* 381, (2005). Taslitz explains, on page 384, that today most jurisdictions in the U.S. require the *mens rea* of negligence, and Hodak summarizes the required *mens rea* for the crime of rape when there is reasonable doubt as to whether the victim consented to the sexual act. Kerry M. Hodak, Note, "Court Sanctioned Mediation in Cases of Acquaintance Rape: A Beneficial Alternative to Traditional Prosecution", 19 *Ohio St. J. Disp. Resol.* 1089, 1095–1096 (2004).

143　Samuel Pillsbury, supra note 118, p. 270.

144　Kim Stevenson, "Observations on the Law Relating to Sexual Offences: The Historic Scandal of Women's Silence", *Web J. Current Legal Issues* in association with Blackstone Press Ltd. (1999).

145　Nicole Westmarland, "Rape Law Reform in England and Wales", *University of Bristol, School for Policy Studies, Working Paper Series* 13 (2004).

146　The *mens rea* element for rape in the Sexual Offenses Act, 2003, sets a standard of "negligence" whereby the defendant's honest but unreasonable belief in his victim's consent will not negate liability.

The *mens rea* for the offense of rape under Canadian law is especially interesting, as it integrates elements of recklessness with the logic of negligence. In order for an accused to claim that he did not have the requisite *mens rea*, he must prove that he undertook a reasonable effort, under the circumstances, to know and understand whether the woman actually consented to penetration.[147] But notice again the problem with respect to gender. This may be yet another instance where the reasonable man and reasonable woman would disagree. If so, the gender perspective of reasonableness may decide the case.[148]

The foregoing discussion indicates that the definition of the mental element for the offense of rape is significant both with respect to the burden of proof for this offense and the way that society perceives this offense. As we shall see, to the extent that the circumstances in which the offense is committed involve subordination and coercion, then the law will tend towards an objective standard for *mens rea*, as I demonstrate in the following subsection.

3.4 THE PRESUMPTION OF NONCONSENT IN DOMESTIC LAW

In contrast with the focus of the domestic law on proving the lack of consent to convict for the crime of rape, there are other situations in which domestic law is willing to accept a presumption of nonconsent, which are worth examining in our context because they involve an inherent inequality between the parties. This presumption of nonconsent is relevant to other situations in which there is an inherent inequality between the parties – such as the battlefield. The problem of inequality is intensified during conflicts and is a focus of this book. In this context, the heroic soldier, who represents the victorious party, the more powerful ethnic group in the inter-ethnic war, sometimes believes that rape is for the good of the woman who is raped. The confusion and moral ambiguity during armed conflict highlights the gender gaps that have survived

---

147   The Canadian Criminal Code, sec. 273(2), provides that a belief the complainant consented is not a defense if (i) the belief arose from the accused's "self-induced intoxication" or "recklessness or willful blindness", or (ii) "the accused did not take reasonable steps, in the circumstances known to the accused at the time, to ascertain that the complainant was consenting." See also Kwong-leung Tang, "Rape Law Reform in Canada: The Success and Limits of Legislation", 42(3) *Intl. J. Offender Therapy & Comp. Criminology* 258, 263–265 (1998).

148   Samuel Pillsbury, supra note 118, pp. 270–271.

from patriarchal rule. These power gaps can cause a victim's will to survive to be misinterpreted as consent.[149]

In order to illustrate my argument about the presumption of nonconsent during conflict arising from the inherent inequality that prevails during conflict, I discuss the offenses of sexual harassment and statutory rape in this subchapter. In both of these legal situations, which lead to criminal liability in many countries, there is a power gap between the parties that gives rise to the legal presumption of a lack of consent, and thus to the lower bar for *mens rea* (strict liability or negligence, i.e., objective awareness). Moreover, as I demonstrate in the next subchapter, the confusion and moral ambiguity present in the battlefield are also present in sexual harassment.

3.4.1 Sexual Harassment

Sexual harassment is a new offense which was only given a name in some countries about thirty years ago.[150] As described by MacKinnon:

> Sexually diddling the staff or the students used to be an open secret or joke, regarded as a perhaps deplorable but trivial peccadillo of some men, a tic of the person or perk of the position or both. Whatever else the man did or was outweighed the importance of whatever she said he did to her sexually.[151]

Sexual harassment laws have turned what used to be seen as a moral failure, deplorable and censurable behavior, or perhaps what some considered to be

---

149   For example, the anonymous woman who wrote *A Woman in Berlin* describes how she planned the next rape that would be committed against her by a high-ranking officer who would keep other potential rapists away, because of the coercive and surreal circumstances in which she found herself: bombed-out Berlin after it fell to the Soviets. The men of the city had been taken to the front, the enemy's soldiers were raping and pillaging, and Berlin's women – left without running water, food or electricity – were hiding out. *Is this consent?* In my opinion, it most certainly is not. Sex in the absence of any choice is rape. See Anonyma, *Eine Frau in Berlin: Tagebuch-aufzeichnungen vom 20, April bis 22. Juni 1945* (2005) [German]. I discuss the issue of consent at greater length below in Part Three, subchapter 9.5.2: "The Presumption of Nonconsent".

150   The term sexual harassment was used in 1973 by Dr. Mary Rowe in a report to the then President and Chancellor of MIT about various forms of gender issues. Note that "sexual harassment" is a crime in some countries in the world, and in others it is solely a civil wrong. In the U.S., for example, as discussed below in this subchapter, it is grounds for a civil claim under federal equality laws.

151   Catharine A. MacKinnon, "Afterword", in Catharine A. MacKinnon & Reva B. Siegel, eds., *Directions in Sexual Harassment Law* (Yale University Press, 2003) 672–673 (hereinafter *Catharine MacKinnon, Afterword*).

one of life's small pleasures, into a legal wrong. Sexual harassment laws have led to the recognition that sexual exploitation is behavior that reflects sexual inequality. The laws of countries around the world and various international forums are increasingly adopting and expanding upon this recognition, even accepting it as a given fact.[152]

The broad forces of patriarchy that discriminate against and subordinate all women are reinforced by each act of sexual harassment, according to MacKinnon's view. The sexual harassment of a single woman not only harms her and her right to dignity and equality. It reinforces the systemic discrimination of all women, because the sexual harassment compels her to see herself as "female" in the patriarchal sense of a second class citizen and as a sexual object for men.[153]

The concept that sexual harassment in the workplace was unlawful emerged in the U.S. in the 1970s.[154] However, even today, there is no express prohibition against sexual harassment under U.S. federal law. The growing body of federal case law rests on the narrow prohibition against employment discrimination on the basis of sex in Title VII of the Civil Rights Act of 1964,[155] which states that in businesses with 15 or more employees an employer may not:

> fail or refuse to hire or discharge any individual or otherwise discriminate against any individual with respect to his compensation, terms, conditions, or privileges of employment, because of such individual's race, color, religion, sex, or national origin.[156]

---

152   For articles discussing sexual harassment around the world, see Catherine A. MacKinnon & Reva B. Siegel, eds., *Directions in Sexual Harassment Law* (Yale University Press, 2003); Catharine MacKinnon, Afterword, supra note 151, p. 677.

153   Orit Kamir, Israel's Dignity-based Feminism, supra note 94, p. 295.

154   Sexual harassment in the workplace has been a well-known phenomenon ever since women began working outside of the home. Firing or not promoting women who refused to submit to an employer's or supervisor's sexual demands was not invented in the 1970s. Prior to that time, such harassment was considered a natural part of male-female relationships. Sexual harassment was seen as the female employee's personal problem, not one justifying intervention of the legal system. See Sharon Rabin-Margaliot, "Who is Concerned about Sexual Harassment at Work?" in Aharon Barak & Haim Berenzon, eds., *Berenzon Yearbook* (Nevo, 1997) 697, 701 [Hebrew].

155   Ibid.

156   Abigail C. Saguy, "Employment Discrimination or Sexual Violence? Defining Sexual Harassment in American and French Law", 34 *Law & Soc'y Rev.* 1091, 1096 (2000) (hereinafter *Abigail Saguy*); Heather L. Kleinschmidt, "Comment, Reconsidering Severe or Pervasive: Aligning the Standards in Sexual Harassment and Racial Harassment Causes of Action", 80 *Ind. L.J.* 1119, 1134 (2005).

The theory was, and still is, that sexual harassment discriminates against women (or men) on the basis of their sexuality. The plaintiff's claim must rest on the argument that "if I wasn't a man/woman, I wouldn't have been harassed". In other words a woman must prove that she was harassed because she is a woman.

It is significant to note that, unlike in the U.S., in many countries sexual harassment is both a civil wrong and a criminal offense.[157] One of my main arguments in this book is that *categorization is essential and has many implications, legal and otherwise.* Therefore, if one situates sexual harassment among other forms of sexual violence, one is, in effect, defining it as a form of sexual violence itself.[158] Abigail Saguy expresses this point:

> A basic insight of the sociology of culture is that human beings need categories, definitions, frames, or accounts (I am using these terms loosely, almost interchangeably) to make sense of the world.... Any given account, however, presents experience from a particular angle, making certain aspects of the phenomenon extremely clear, but obscuring others. In the case of sexual harassment, definitions that rely on a sex-discrimination frame focus on how sexual harassment can be motivated by and can contribute to gender inequality in employment, but they are less useful for making sense of a generally sadistic boss who thrives on making life miserable for his subordinates, men and women alike.... A discrimination frame, which stresses employment repercussions, is also of little help in conceptualizing the denigration or fear many women feel in the streets when ogled or threatened by men. Nor is an employment discrimination frame very useful in understanding the sense of violation and betrayal a woman may feel when her psychiatrist abuses her trust and sense of vulnerability by initiating sexual relations.[159]

Unlike in the U.S., in France, for example, three laws are applicable to sexual harassment: the Criminal Code, the Labor Code and the Civil Code. Article 222–33 of the French Criminal Code defines sexual harassment as: "The fact of harassing anyone using orders, threats or constraint, in order to obtain favors

---

157 In this subchapter below, I discuss the domestic laws of France and Israel as examples of the criminal prohibition against sexual harassment, but, of course, the criminal laws of other countries also provide that it is an offense. See, e.g., Russia, Criminal Code, Russian Federation art. 118, http://shsf.invisionzone.com/index.php?s=a1f5e83af0f492d74310d4d1a073 b792&showtopic=279, (last accessed 3 October 2010); India, Indian Penal Code, 1860, art. 376, http://www.netlawman.co.in/acts/indian-penal-code-1860.php (last accessed 14 April 2011); and others.

158 See Abigail Saguy, supra note 156, p. 1096.

159 Ibid., p. 1107.

of a sexual nature, by a person abusing the authority that functions confer upon him…"[160] Therefore, an employer, a colleague or a non-employee, such as a client, will be held personally and criminally liable for the act of harassment.

It is also significant to note that, according to French penal law, sexual harassment does not necessarily involve physical contact. It is sufficient for a perpetrator to use his or her official authority or the target's economic dependence to pressure a person into consenting to sexual relations for the law to interpret the action as sexual harassment. One might "consent" to sexual relations, for example, out of fear of losing one's job, without the sexual contact being "welcome",[161] at which point one is considered as having been sexually harassed but not raped or sexually assaulted. If, however, a male boss, for example, not only tells his employee that she will have to have sex with him if she wants to keep her job, but he also grabs her breast, then he would be guilty not only of sexual harassment but also of sexual assault. If he goes further and physically forces his employee into having sexual intercourse, then he would be guilty of rape, in addition to sexual assault and sexual harassment.[162]

It is apparent that the offense of sexual harassment is characterized by its victims being in situations of subordination and financial dependence.[163] This is the same subordination which is at the foundation of this study. It is this subordination which creates a situation of coercion, which makes the issue of consent irrelevant, and which ultimately establishes criminal liability.

In Israel, it was recognized that this serious social problem needs to be addressed by legal means with enactment of the Prevention of Sexual

---

160   In the original: "Le fait de harceler autrui en usant d'ordres, de menaces ou de contraintes, dans le but d'obtenir des faveurs de nature sexuelle, par une personne abusant de l'autorite que lui conferent ses fonctions…"

161   Note that sexual harassment was recognized as an offense that was distinguished from rape and sexual assault. Arguably, this distinction means that, in effect, sexual harassment is a lesser offense, and possibly punished less severely as well. Recognition of this offense also enabled reform of the laws of rape to be avoided. In my opinion, however, the recognition that circumstances involving subordination are circumstances in which there is no consent serves to strengthen one of the central claims of this book. In contrast with sexual harassment, which is recognized as an exception under domestic law because of the circumstances of subordination and coercion, in the international criminal law this kind of inherent inequality in a relationship is the norm. In other words, the presumption of nonconsent should always apply.

162   Abigail Saguy, supra note 156, p. 1098.

163   Caroline Goette, "Sexual Harassment in the Workplace in France and in the United States", *Nat'l L. Ass'n Rev.* (Spring 1997).

Harassment Law, 5758–1988. This law establishes a presumption that if the harasser is in a position of authority over the person who has been harassed, then she does not have to prove that she objected or otherwise expressed resistance to the harasser's behavior.[164] The inherent inequality between the subordinate and the employer attests to her inability to refuse.

The relationship of authority and inequality between the harasser and the harassed is prominent when one is in a position of power and the other is in a position of weakness and, typically, dependent upon the person with authority. In other words, it is presumed that under circumstances of subordination and authority, the person who has been harassed did not give full and willing consent to the harassing behavior. Hence, there is no requirement for any external expression of a lack of consent when the sexual act is committed with an employee subject to the harasser's authority.[165]

> Workplace relationships, including a relationship of authority, can be fertile ground for sexual exploitation of the person in a subordinate position, and there is actually quite a high rate of sexual harassment in the workplace. In those incidents, the economic and professional dependency of the employer on the person with authority – the harasser – can deter him from indicating to the supervisor that he is not interested in those acts which constitute sexual harassment.
>
> Therefore, even if there allegedly was consent to the harassment, a preliminary presumption should be made that this consent is not consent, in the context of a relationship of authority.[166]

To summarize, the foregoing discussion demonstrates that the offense of sexual harassment, as it has taken shape over the last thirty years in certain countries, shares two significant characteristics with sex crimes under international law. *First,* the circumstances of the offense involve an atmosphere of coercion and relationships of subordination and domination between the perpetrator and the victim. *Second,* the atmosphere of coercion creates a moral ambiguity which obscures the boundary between the permitted and the prohibited. The legal solution: adopt a presumption that, under certain circumstances, consent cannot be deemed to exist.

---

164   See Prevention of Sexual Harassment Law, 5758–1988, sec. 3(a)(6).

165   CSA (Civil Service Appeal) 1599/03 Tapiro v. Commissioner of the Civil Service, 58(2) P.D. 125 (2003), in which the accused was convicted of unlawful consensual sexual relations, with exploitation of a relationship of authority. CSA 4790/04 State of Israel v. Avraham Ben Haim (2 May 2005); HCJ 1284/99 Anon. v. Chief of Staff, 53(2) P.D. 62 (1999).

166   LCA (Labor Court Appeal) 274/06 Anon. v. Anon (26 March 2008).

3.4.2 Statutory Rape

In all jurisdictions, age sets one important limit on consent to sexual relations. The statutory rape (or age of sexual consent) law criminalizes sexual intercourse with unmarried minors under a given age. The law against statutory rape is formally known by various terms, including "unlawful sexual intercourse". Any person under the jurisdiction's legal age of consent is legally incapable of consenting to certain sexual acts, making any person who performs such acts with an underage minor liable for a sexual offense.[167]

Most states in the U.S. do not designate the crime as "statutory rape", but instead they have specific criminal provisions under such headings as "sexual assault" and "sexual abuse". These statutes are based on the presumption that until a certain age established by law, a person is not capable, from a legal perspective, of consenting to engage in sexual relations.[168] In England, there are two criminal provisions regarding the offense of "statutory rape" as a discrete crime: "Unlawful sexual intercourse with a girl under 16"[169] and "Unlawful sexual intercourse with a girl under 13".[170]

Statutory rape takes place "when an adult, through economics, deceit, violence, or romance, seduces an inexperienced and immature youth into participating in sexual acts to which the youth is not capable of consenting and whose consequences the youth is not capable of understanding."[171] Also, some people above the age of consent will by virtue of mental disability be held to lack the mental capacity to consent.[172]

---

167   Samuel Pillsbury, supra note 118, p. 258. It is worth recalling the feminist critique which maintains that the offense of statutory rape deepens the inequality between men and women and violates women's autonomy and free will. The argument is that in most cases the law is directed against women as the minors, and so the law prohibiting sexual relations with them violates their free will. See Wendy Williams, "The Equality Crisis: Some Reflections on Culture, Courts and Feminisms", 7 *Women Rts. L. Rep.* 175 (1981–1982). As I claim above, the law must equally protect both young women and young men from sexual assault. See also supra note 8 and infra notes 300, 480.

168   Sandra Norman-Eady, Christopher Reinhart & Peter Martino, "Statutory Rape Laws by State", 2003-R-0376 (14 April 2003) available at http://www.cga.ct.gov/2003/olrdata/jud/rpt/2003-R-0376.htm. (last accessed 14 April 2011). It is interesting to note, for example, that most of the laws also specify the minimum age for the perpetrator of the offense. For example, Alabama law provides that it is first-degree rape for someone age 16 or older to have sexual intercourse with someone under age 12, and it is second-degree rape for someone age 16 or older to have sexual intercourse with someone between age 12 and 16, when the perpetrator is at least two years older.

169   Sexual Offences Act 1956, sec. 6 (Eng.).

170   Ibid., sec. 5.

171   Kay L. Levine, "The Intimacy Discount: Prosecutorial Discretion, Privacy, and Equality in the Statutory Rape Caseload", 55 *Emory L.J.* 691, 710 (2006).

172   Samuel Pillsbury, supra note 118, p. 258.

For example, Section 346 of the Israeli Penal Law, 5737–1977, provides that the question of consent between parties engaging in sexual relations is not relevant under the following situations, *inter alia*: (i) sexual relations with an unmarried girl over the age of 14 and under the age of 16, or over the age of 16 and under the age of 18, while exploiting a relationship of dependency, authority, education or supervision, (ii) a mental health therapist who has a sexual relationship with a patient over the age of 16 and under the age of 18 will be deemed to have exploited the relationship of dependency, unless the sexual relationship began before the therapy, (iii) sexual relations with a woman over the age of 18 while exploiting a position of authority in employment relations or service.[173] Section 346, which criminalizes the exploitation of a relationship of authority in the workplace as unlawful consensual sexual relations, was discussed by Justice Edmond Levy in the Supreme Court's *Joseph Noy* decision:[174]

> The explicit assumption inherent in the terms of this offense is that, under circumstances in which a person is subject to another person's authority, no significance should be attributed to his consent to sexual acts with the person in the position of authority, because this consent results from an exploitation of authority. In other words, even if consent was given for performance of the sexual acts, the law – in recognition of the victim's inherently inferior position – under appropriate circumstances will view this as "technical" consent to which no significance shall be attributed, because it is the result of an inappropriate use of power and the exploitation of the power gap.

Under this provision, the *mens rea* is reduced from awareness to recklessness. In other words, the prosecution is not required to prove that the accused was actually aware that the complainant was in one of the specified age ranges. It is sufficient to prove that he was reckless and indifferent. The Supreme Court reasoned:

> The accused cannot avoid conviction for this offense by claiming, even convincingly, that he did not know anything about the complainant's age because he was not at all interested in this issue and did not think about it. If, under the circumstances, the accused at least should have been aware of the possibility that the complainant was below the age stated in the indictment, then through his lack of interest he has assumed the risk, and his recklessness will be his downfall, if objectively it becomes apparent that the

---

173   Note that this provision was added to Israeli law in a number of stages, in 1988, 2000 and 2003.

174   CrimA 9256/04 Joseph Noy v. State of Israel (10 August 2005).

complainant was indeed in one of the age categories specially protected by law.[175]

To summarize, the preceding discussion shows how domestic law has established a presumption that consent cannot be given for sexual relations with someone under a certain age, and, similarly, under certain circumstances. This presumption regarding age, as a single factor, is not derived from a situation of moral confusion about boundaries; rather, it seems that today there is a legal and moral consensus regarding this offense. However, it is noteworthy that the presumption regarding the incapacity to consent has been expanded to cover certain situations in which there is ambiguity regarding the nature of the relationship and a presumption of coercion and subordination.

3.5 SUMMARY: THE UNIQUE NATURE OF THE CRIME OF RAPE

The complexities of the offense of rape, historically, raised many issues that have not yet been resolved completely and satisfactorily under domestic law – both with respect to the elements of the *actus reus* and the appropriate way to analyze *mens rea*. However, in my opinion, international law must focus on the exceptions to the general rules of rape: those offenses in which a presumption has been adopted that consent cannot exist. The situations addressed by international criminal law are those in which an atmosphere of coercion and subordination is the norm, rather than an exception. Moreover, in light of the controversy regarding the elements of the crime of rape in national legal systems, it becomes even more important that international law address this issue. I believe that the establishment of an international offense based on widespread agreement would serve as a guide for countries around the world.

Nevertheless, despite the nexus between domestic law and international law discussed above,[176] one could still argue that the issue of sexual offenses during conflict concerns extreme conditions that are not prevalent under domestic law. When the bullets are whizzing by and survival is dependent on another person's mercy, it is much harder to assume consent – the relationships of domination and subordination are perpetuated.[177] Therefore, the unrestrained import of the laws of rape from the national law to the international sphere would be irresponsible. For example, as discussed below, there are grounds to

---

175   CrimA 5424/91 Anon. v. State of Israel, 46(4) P.D. 497 (1992).
176   Part One, subchapter 3.1: "The Nexus between International Law and National Law".
177   I discuss the presumption of nonconsent in situations of conflict below in Part Three, subchapter 9.5.2: "The Presumption of Nonconsent".

criticize the ICTY's addition of the lack of consent to the elements of the international offense of rape in the *Kunarac Judgment*[178] – instead, the analysis of the requirement for proof regarding lack of consent should be different for incidents that occur during wartime.[179]

On this point, I note Fionnuala Ni Aolain's argument that sexual violence against women during conflict exhibits different characteristics than sexual violence in the absence of a conflict:

> Exploring the military functionalism of sexual violation in conflict situations makes evident that there is a pressing need to augment traditional legal conceptualizations and their corresponding sanctions regarding the regulation of sexual violation.[180]

Yet at the same time, it must be recalled that despite the differences, there are significant links between the two legal arenas. *First*, the critique of national law is important in order to prevent its unrestrained import into the international arena and to stimulate critique of international law. *Second*, the ongoing debate over the definition of the elements of rape under national law highlights the need for an international debate on this subject and for consolidation of a broad consensus about the definition of "rape". *Third*, the accumulated experience under national legal systems provides tools for analysis of the legal treatment of the offense of rape in the international arena.

---

178 This decision is discussed below in Part Two, subchapter 6.1.2: "New Judgments, Adaptations".

179 Adrienne Kalosieh, "Consent to Genocide?: The ICTY's Improper Use of the Consent Paradigm to Prosecute Genocidal Rape in Foca", 24 *Women's Rts. L. Rep.* 121, 136 (2003) (hereinafter *Adrienne Kalosieh*).

180 Fionnuala Ni Aolain, supra note 18, p. 309.

Part Two

SEX CRIMES AND INTERNATIONAL LAW –
PAST, PRESENT

INTRODUCTION TO PART TWO

Imagine that for hundreds of years your most formative traumas, your daily suffering and pain, the abuse you live through, the terror you live with, are unspeakable – not the basis of literature. When you try to speak of these things, you are told that it did not happen, you imagined it, you wanted it, you enjoyed it. Books say this. No books say what happened to you. Law says this. No law imagines what happened to you, the way it happened.[181]

In this Part Two, I embark on an historical journey to the cradle of international criminal law and trace the development of the crime of rape. In this journey, I distinguish between several eras. First, the *Era of Silence*. This era has strong connections with the history of the crime of rape as an offense in domestic law. Next, the *Era of Honor* began when the crime of rape was recognized in international law as a criminal offense against the victim's honor, while ignoring the other substantial harms to the victim, both mental and physical. The *Third Era* commenced when sex crimes were recognized as international crimes under some of the traditional crime categories – but this recognition remained partial, without their explicit recognition as a "grave breach of the Geneva Conventions", as "genocide", or as a distinct crime. This created the *New Status Quo*, which I wish to critique.

I present both the lessons from history and the current situation in order to lay a foundation for the discussion of potential reforms of international criminal law, which is undertaken in Part Three.

---

181   Catharine MacKinnon, Only Words, supra note 36, p. 3.

Chapter 4

THE ERA OF SILENCE

"Where there is war, there is always sexual assault."[182] For a long period of time, from the beginnings of international law until the end of WWII, international law was indifferent towards all types of sex crimes. Rape was considered common and acceptable during the heat of natural instincts and battle. In any event, perpetrators of sex crimes were treated forgivingly.

4.1 ABSENCE OF LEGAL CONDEMNATION THROUGHOUT HISTORY

Throughout history, women have suffered from mass rape during times of war. In 1204, the Crusaders raped women in Constantinople.[183] In 1937, Japanese soldiers raped women in Nanking.[184] During WWII, German soldiers raped many Jewish[185] and Russian women,[186] and toward the end of the war Russian soldiers raped German women.[187] In 1971, Pakistani soldiers raped Bangladeshi women[188] and American soldiers raped Vietnamese women.[189] We cannot identify a specific moment in history when rape during war was declared a criminal act in the international context.[190]

Biblical law also did not condemn the "taking" of women from the enemy, as indicated in the following Biblical passage:

> When you go to war against your enemies and the LORD your God delivers them into your hands and you take captives, if you notice among

---

182   Kelly Dawn Askin, War Crimes against Women, supra note 9, p. 1. As noted above, both the degree and extent of violence against women rise dramatically in periods of both national and international tension. Fionnuala Ni Aolain, supra note 18, p. 309.

183   Susan Brownmiller, supra note 11, p. 35.

184   Interestingly, this event is commonly referred to as the "Rape of Nanking", thus focusing on the city and not on the actual victims of rape – the women. Rana Lehr-Lehnardt, supra note 13. See also infra note 203.

185   Joan Ringelheim, "Women and Holocaust: A Reconsideration of Research", 10 *Signs J. Women Culture & Soc'y* 741 (1985) (hereinafter *Joan Ringelheim*); Catherine MacKinnon, "Genocide's Sexuality", supra note 1, p. 317.

186   Rana Lehr-Lehnardt, supra note 13, p. 320.

187   Pascala Bos, supra note 66.

188   Rana Lehr-Lehnardt, supra note 13, p. 320.

189   Susan Brownmiller, supra note 11, pp. 104–116.

190   Ibid., p. 35.

the captives a beautiful woman and are attracted to her, you may take her as your wife. Bring her into your home and have her shave her head, trim her nails and put aside the clothes she was wearing when captured. After she has lived in your house and mourned her father and mother for a full month, then you may go to her and be her husband and she shall be your wife. If you are not pleased with her, let her go wherever she wishes. You must not sell her or treat her as a slave, since you have dishonored her.[191]

This passage refers to a "beautiful woman" from among the enemy, who has been taken captive, and her captor desires her. According to the Bible, if the warrior was aroused by a woman taken into captivity during war, he was permitted to "take her" by force.[192]

These arrangements indicate that the phenomenon was so common that Jewish law elected not to establish an absolute prohibition. This approach enabled supervision and prevention of the kinds of problems likely to occur in the absence of formal arrangements. These rules permitted a warrior who saw a "beautiful woman" during war, whom he desired, to take her as a wife even against her will, whether or not she was married and had a family. This led to various laws: a "beautiful woman" did not actually have to be beautiful; it was prohibited to take more than one woman; and it was prohibited to pressure her during the war and to scare her into acquiescing.

The historical development of women's rights in war and their anchoring in international law took place in a non-uniform manner. For example, Totila the Ostrogoth, who conquered Rome in 546 A.D., forbade his soldiers from raping the women of the city.[193] One of the oldest surviving legal codes is the Articles of War published in 1385 A.D. by Richard II of England. Among the 124 articles defining the rules of conduct for soldiers, King Richard prescribed the punishment of hanging for any soldier brazen enough to force himself upon a woman, and a similar punishment was prescribed for soldiers who dared to plunder a church.[194] Nevertheless, later during the 17th century, the Dutch

---

191 *Deuteronomy* 21:10–14 [New International Version trans.].

192 However, the Bible requires a month-long cooling-off period, enabling the woman to mourn her parents' home and adjust to the new situation. If the man tired of her, he was not permitted to make her a slave. Instead, he was required to free her, and he could not trade or sell her to someone else. Note that this law permitting marriage to a non-Israelite woman is an exception, because the Bible relates negatively to marriages with non-Israelites: "And you shall not marry them: you shall not give your daughter to his son and you shall not take his daughter for your son." (*Deuteronomy* 7:3). It seems that the temptation of battle, during which women were as a matter of course permitted to the conquering party, overrode this prohibition.

193 Susan Brownmiller, supra note 11, p. 34.

194 Ibid.

jurist Hugo Grotius wondered about the fact that certain states accepted the violation of the dignity of women in wartime as a permissible act, whereas during the same time period other states ruled otherwise.[195] In 1785, the U.S. and Prussia agreed in the Treaty of Amity and Commerce that in the event of a war between them, children and women would not be molested. In order no. 20 of the U.S. General Winfield Scott in 1847, severe punishment was provided for soldiers who committed rape. The Lieber Code of 1863, adopted by the U.S. and several European countries, provided in Article 44 that soldiers committing acts of rape against the population of an invaded country would be punished with death.[196] The Hague Conventions of 1899[197] and 1907[198] ("Hague Conventions") did not explicitly refer to rape and other sexual violence, but they provided in general language that there is an obligation toward "family honors" and "religious convictions and practice". These words were interpreted as granting protection to women against sexual violence.[199]

In light of the horrors of World War I, a commission was established in 1919 to determine the responsibilities of the war's instigators and to enforce penalties.[200] This commission placed the offenses of rape and forced prostitution near the top of thirty-two war crimes.[201]

Nearly 20 years later, the greatest horror ever documented in human history began – WWII. Again, sexual attack was an inseparable part of the inter-ethnic battle and it concomitantly continued to be a characteristic of gender subordination. During WWII, many sex crimes occurred – both as encouragement for the fighting forces and as part of the policies of the conquering forces.[202]

---

195   Ibid.

196   Ibid.

197   Hague Convention (II) Laws and Customs of War on Land, 29 July 1899, 32 Stat. 1803.

198   Hague Convention (IV) Respecting the Laws and Customs of War on Land, with Annex of Regulations, 18 October 1907, 36 Stat. 2277.

199   Yougindra Khushalanai, *Dignity and Honor of Women as Basic and Fundamental Human Rights* (M. Nijhoff, 1982) 145.

200   This commission is referred to by various titles: the "War Crime Commission", the "Peace Conference Commission", "The Commission on Responsibility of Authors of the War", and simply as the "1919 Commission". See Kelly Dawn Askin, War Crimes against Women, supra note 9, p. 42.

201   The crime of rape is listed fifth, and immediately afterwards is forced prostitution or, in the words of the commission: "kidnapping of children and women for purposes of forced prostitution". The offenses preceding these crimes were murder and slaughter, killing prisoners, torture of citizens, and intentional starvation of citizens. On this issue, see *History of the United Nations War Crimes Commission and the Development of the Laws of War* (London: H.M. Stationary, 1948).

202   Theodor Meron, "Rape as a Crime under International Humanitarian Law", 87 *Am. J. Int'l L.* 424, 425 (1993) (hereinafter *Theodor Meron*).

Both the Nazi and the Japanese regimes instituted various forms of forced prostitution and ignored the high frequency of acts of rape. For example, the Japanese regime established the institution of "comfort women", women who were kidnapped and imprisoned in order to satisfy the sexual desires of the fighting soldiers.[203] Despite the fact that the international community was aware of these sexual atrocities, not a single step was taken to prevent them. Although the Allied Forces reacted to the atrocious international crimes that were committed by establishing two international tribunals to prosecute the accused, as I discuss below, the *Era of Silence* continued.

4.2 THE NUREMBERG (IMT) AND TOKYO (IMTFE) TRIBUNALS

At the end of WWII, international tribunals were established in Nuremberg (the International Military Tribunal in Nuremberg (IMT)) and in Tokyo (the International Military Tribunal for the Far East (IMTFE)). These tribunals prosecuted the major war criminals for "crimes of war", "crimes against peace" (known today as the crime of "aggression") and "crimes against humanity". This was the first time international law imposed criminal responsibility on individuals and not states. Establishment of these tribunals commenced a trend that developed from the end of WWII, when it had become clear that the absence of legal oversight mechanisms was liable to lead to violations of the basic human rights and fundamental principles on which world order is based.[204]

The charters of the IMT and the IMTFE granted legal jurisdiction over crimes which were deemed by the Allied Forces as grave and which did not yet exist under international law: "war crimes" and "crimes against

---

203   Note that only in 1993 did the Government of Japan, in a declaration called the "Kono Statement", take responsibility for these horrendous crimes and apologize formally to the women who were kidnapped and held captive as sex slaves for the Japanese soldiers in war time. See Etsuro Totsuka, "Commentary on a Victory for 'Comfort Women': Japan's Judicial Recognition of Military Sexual Slavery", 8 *Pac. Rim L. & Pol'y J.* 47 (1999). However, years later, Prime Minister of Japan Shinzo Abe denied Japan's involvement and claimed there was no proof that the Government of Japan or its army had kidnapped women and compelled them to work in brothels for the army. This denial was severely criticized both domestically and abroad, and, due to the controversy that arose, he retracted it and said that he agreed with the 1993 apology that had confirmed involvement by the Government of Japan in operating the brothels. Reiji Yoshida, "Sex Slave History Erased from Texts; '93 Apology Next?" *Japan Times Online* (11 March 2007) in http://search.japantimes.co.jp/cgi-bin/nn20070311f1.html (last accessed 14 April 2011).

204   Amnon Reichman, "Universal Jurisdiction in State Courts – Destroying Sovereignty or Creating World Order", 17 *Mishpat v'Tzava* 49, 60–61 (2004) [Hebrew].

humanity".[205] Inclusion of "crimes against peace" in the tribunals' charters made the act of war illegal and, for the first time in international history, provided the courts with a tool for imposing responsibility on the highest governmental levels for starting a war. These trials contributed greatly to the development of international humanitarian law and international criminal law by creating an international arena that encouraged the resolution of conflicts by peaceful means.[206, 207] Moreover, many principles established by these tribunals in effect comprised the foundation for the subsequent organization of the UN.[208]

Notwithstanding this historical development, nowhere in the IMT Charter can the crime of "rape" or any other crime of a sexual nature be found. Yet there were mountains of reports explicitly documenting the incidents of rape, forced sterilization, forced abortions, pornography, sexual mutilation, and sadistic sexual attacks which took place during WWII.[209] For example, it was reported that in the last two weeks of WWII, 100,000 rapes were committed in Berlin alone.[210] All of the victims – women, men and children – were ordered

---

205   Charter of the International Military Tribunal, 8 August 1945, 82 U.N.T.S. 280 (hereinafter *IMT Charter*) and Charter of the International Military Tribunal for the Far East, 19 January 1946 (hereinafter *IMTFE Charter*).

206   Note that there is a counter-critique claiming that the IMT and IMTFE violated the "principle of legality" by retroactively inventing new international crimes, and that the justice which they laude is merely the justice of the victors. However, in my opinion, those making this claim are burying their heads in the sand. The "Nuremberg Principles" are principles of *jus cogens* which have always been part of the customary law of nations. This is because they are crimes that harm the foundations of the international community and its security, crimes that violate the universal moral values and humanitarian principles, which are:

> embedded in the systems of criminal law that cultured nations have instituted. The principle of international law regarding these crimes is that the individual who perpetrated these acts, and who is presumed to have been fully aware of their heinous character at the time of their commission, must be held accountable for his conduct.

CrimA 336/61 Adolf Eichmann v. Attorney General, 16 P.D. 2052 (1962) (Isr.) (hereinafter *Eichmann Judgment*). Consequently, due to the shocking nature of the crimes that were committed, these are crimes that were always prohibited under the customary law of the human community, and, therefore, establishment of the Nuremberg and Tokyo tribunals were not acts contradicting the principle of *nulla poena* or that violate its applicability. Ibid., p. 2059. (On the term *jus cogens*, see discussion supra note 83.)

207   However, it is important to note that "war" was not made illegal.

208   Jocelyn Campanaro, "Women, War and International Law: The Historical Treatment of Gender Based War Crimes", 89 *Geo. L.J.* 2557, 2559 (2001) (hereinafter *Jocelyn Campanaro*).

209   Astrid Aafjes, *Gender Violence: The Hidden War Crime* (Women, Law & Development Intl., 1998) 8.

210   See Kelly Dawn Askin, War Crimes against Women, supra note 9, p. 52.

to remove their clothing during the march to their death, but it was the women who were selected for an additional humiliation – sexual violence.[211]

Not only was the IMT Charter silent. Even those prosecutions brought pursuant to the IMT Charger, with their detailed charges describing offenses of murder and torture, were completely silent regarding rape and other sexual offenses.[212] In effect, the transgressions of rape and other sexual atrocities that occurred during WWII were not condemned, nor were their perpetrators punished. Moreover, the crime of rape was added at the bottom of the list of offenses, and was never accorded the status given to the other war crimes.

As I discuss below in this chapter, the wording in both the IMT and the IMTFE Charters was sufficiently flexible to have permitted an interpretation that would have, for the first time, enabled the recognition and prosecution of rape and other sex crimes during WWII. However, nothing of the kind took place.

In this *Era of Silence* when the Nuremberg trials took place, sexual crimes, along with pillage, were viewed as inevitable aspects of war, and therefore unpunishable. In addition to this equating of rape with pillage, a further obstacle presented itself: the prosecutors shied away from the subject as if it were simply too distasteful. When the French prosecutor at the Nuremberg trials was asked about the rape of French women, he responded: "The tribunal will forgive me if I avoid citing the atrocious details."[213] Rather than directly confronting rape and treating it like other crimes, it was regarded as something too atrocious to prosecute, and so impossible to prevent that it was unworthy of prosecution.[214]

The IMT Charter defined "crimes against humanity" to include murder, ethnic cleansing, slavery, expulsion and other inhumane acts perpetrated against a civilian population before or during the war, and political, racist or religious persecution.[215] While sex crimes were not explicitly mentioned in the IMT Charter, a broad interpretation could have included these crimes within the

---

211   Ibid., p. 56.

212   Ibid., pp. 97–98.

213   As reported in Susan Brownmiller, supra note 11, p. 56:

   I quote, "The Maquis had evacuated the town several days earlier … 54 women or young girls from 13 to 50 years of age were raped by the maddened soldiers."
   The Tribunal will forgive me if I avoid citing the atrocious details which follow … A medical certificate from Doctor Nicolaides, who examined the women who were raped in this region - I will pass on.

214   Sita Balthazar, "Gender Crimes and the International Criminal Tribunals", 10 *Gonz. J. Int'l L.* 43, 44 (2006).

215   IMT Charter, supra note 205, art. 6(b).

definitions that it did include. For example, Article 6(b), which provided a list of the crimes included in the offense category of "war crimes", stated explicitly that it is an open list ("Such violations shall include, but not be limited to ..."). Also, Article 6(c), which provides for the offense category of "crimes against humanity", includes the phrase "other inhuman acts". Thus, the prosecution could readily have included in the indictment charges for crimes that were not specifically listed in the IMT Charter, but which were sufficiently egregious as to be considered "inhuman crimes". However, as noted, sex crimes were neither explicitly included in the IMT Charter, nor was any attempt made to include them in indictments by utilizing the expansive language of the Charter.[216]

The failure of the prosecution to bring charges against criminals for sex offenses was but a natural continuation of the historic trend of diminishing the importance of sex crimes during war, to the point of ignoring them. Thus, the harm caused to the victims was dwarfed, and, ultimately, no meaningful precedents were established which could have served as future legal precedents for criminalizing sexual offenses during war. This result violated the purpose for which the tribunal was established:

> (To) teach individual responsibility for crimes of aggressive war and crimes against humanity, so that such crimes might never again be perpetrated.[217]

The IMTFE was also granted authority to prosecute "war crimes" and other new crimes defined as "crimes against the peace" and "crimes against humanity". Just like its counterpart, the IMTFE was silent and did not define the crime of "rape" as a violation of international criminal law. However, unlike the IMT, some of the indictments tried at the IMTFE included "rape" in the charges.

The defendants were charged with having "carried out in violation of recognized customs and conventions of war ... mass murder, rape ... and other barbaric cruelties."[218] In addition, the IMTFE found senior Japanese guilty of rape for having failed in their obligation to ensure that their subordinates would behave in accordance with international law.[219] Thus, although the crime of "rape" was one crime within the long list of sexual offenses, its inclusion in the indictments and subsequently the tribunals' judgments breached the

---

216   See Kelly Dawn Askin, War Crimes against Women, supra note 9, p. 163. In this context, it can be argued that expansion of this provision would have violated the rights of the accused. See the discussion on this point, supra note 206.

217   Jocelyn Campanaro, supra note 208, p. 2560.

218   See Kelly Dawn Askin, War Crimes against Women, supra note 9, p. 160.

219   Nicole Eva Erb, "Gender-Based Crimes under the Draft Statute for the Permanent International Criminal Court", 29 *Colum. Hum. Rts. L. Rev.* 401, 410 (1998) (hereinafter *Nicole Eva Erb*); for more on this topic, see Jocelyn Campanaro, supra note 208, p. 2561.

long-standing silence and constituted a significant precedent for future indictments.

Unfortunately, however, these precedents are not without their problems. For example, it is noteworthy that the breach of silence in Tokyo still retained certain characteristics of silence. Not one of the rape victims was called to testify at the Tokyo trials.[220] This fact reflects a lack of concern for the harm to the individual victims, in contrast with the harm to morality and society or the honor of the law of nations. Similarly, it is noteworthy that, apart from the "crime of rape", no other gender crimes were tried by this tribunal. The IMTFE did not recognize specific gender crimes as crimes that were real and distinct from the other atrocious acts worthy of prosecution.[221]

The vast amount of testimony about incidents of rape by the conquering forces (including soldiers of the Allied Forces) in Europe and Asia remained merely written testimonials. The incidents of rape, forced abortions, forced sterilization and sexual slavery – which was widespread in Asia – were dominated and overshadowed by the severe and "superior" crimes. The crimes highlighted under the floodlights of the court's stage were the "crimes against the peace"[222] – not "war crimes" and not "crimes against humanity" and certainly not gender crimes, which were, nearly exclusively, perpetrated against women and girls.[223]

4.3 SUMMARY: THE ERA OF SILENCE

The foregoing review demonstrates that prohibitions against sexual violence towards women during war have existed for over 200 years. However, historically, both treaty and customary international law have ignored sex crimes, have not explicitly addressed them in the laws, and have not punished the sex criminals.[224] While there have been legal statements denouncing the practice of sexual violence in war, and an undertaking to end the sexual violence that became so common during wars and armed conflicts, the measures taken were insufficient to protect women. Moreover, sex crimes in times of conflict have always been perceived as lesser crimes and perhaps even excused, as compared

---

220   Susan Brownmiller, supra note 11, p. 58.
221   Kelly Dawn Askin, War Crimes against Women, supra note 9, pp. 202–203.
222   Today these crimes are called "crime of aggression".
223   Kelly Dawn Askin, "The ICTY: An Introduction to its Origins, Rules and Jurisprudence" in Richard May, *et al.* eds., *Essays on ICTY Procedure and Evidence in Honour of Gabrielle Kirk McDonald* (Klur Law International, 2000) 2.
224   Jocelyn Campanaro, supra note 208, p. 2565.

to other crimes against "the rules of war".[225] As summarized by Theodor Meron:

> In many cases, however, rape has been given license, either as an encouragement for soldiers or as an instrument of policy. Nazi and Japanese practices of forced prostitution and rape on a large scale are among the egregious examples of such policies.[226]

Upon the conclusion of the Nuremberg and Tokyo tribunals, the Allied forces began a second series of trials with the objective of bringing lesser war criminals to justice. These trials were conducted in national military tribunals, which were authorized by Control Council Law No. 10 (CCL10).[227] The CCL10 included "rape" in the crime category of "crime against humanity" (in contrast with gender crimes and other sex crimes, which were not included in the CCL10). However, the crime of "rape" was not counted as a "war crime."[228]

As the CCL10 authorized the prosecution of any war criminal (not solely criminals from the "aggressor" countries), an opportunity was created to bring many rapists to justice. Yet the crime of rape was not included in even one indictment.[229]

---

225   Ibid.

226   Theodor Meron, supra note 202, p. 426.

227   Allied Control Council Law No. 10, Punishment of Persons Guilty of War Crimes, Crimes Against Peace and Against Humanity, 20 December 1945, 3 Official Gazette of the Control Council for Germany 49 (hereinafter *Control Council Law No. 10* or *CCL10*).

228   There is a substantive difference between the two categories of crime, which lies in the different elements provided for each crime category. This is not an insignificant point. The crime category of "crime against humanity" includes the requirement of a "wide-spread or systematic attack" as an element of the crime. This requirement is difficult enough, but especially so with respect to sex crimes. This element heightens the burden of proof required of the prosecutor in order to prove a "crime against humanity". I discuss the elements of each of the categories of crime under international law below in Part Three, subchapter 7.1: "Sex Crimes as 'Crimes against Humanity'" and subchapter 7.2: "Sex Crimes as 'War Crimes'"). See also Theodor Meron, supra note 202, p. 425.

229   The title I chose for this historical era, the *Era of Silence*, refers not only to the silence of international law regarding sex crimes, but also to the silence of society and even language itself. Fionnuala Ni Aolain describes these concepts as follows:

> We use the words rape, sexual assault, prostitution, and sexual violation with the sense of a distinct reference model within which the acts are understood and the harms take place. This reference model was not in place either during or immediately following the Second World War. This is not the vocabulary of women describing the violence done to them or to others.

Fionnuala Ni Aolain, supra note 18, pp. 313–314.

Chapter 5

THE ERA OF HONOR

Toward the conclusion of the *Era of Silence*, at the end of WWII, the atrocious sex crimes which had been committed by soldiers on both sides of the conflict, on the basis of race and gender, had finally begun "to be seen". This is certainly true of the crimes committed by the defeated side, which were no longer completely transparent in the eyes of the victors. However, they were still not given appropriate weight, and they were given legal recognition only by analogy. The age of silence only finally ended when the Geneva Conventions explicitly recognized the crime of rape. This opened a new era – the *Era of Honor*. No longer silence and transparency. The crime of rape was given content. The attacking army was obliged to protect women's honor. The harm to rape victims as persecuted ethnic victims was recognized not as a physical or a mental injury, but as an injury to their honor.

5.1 GENEVA CONVENTIONS

The beginning of the *Era of Honor* is marked by the signing of the Geneva Conventions.[230] These conventions provide that grave breaches of the humanitarian norms in the context of an international armed conflict lead to individual criminal responsibility and universal jurisdiction. Article 3 is common to all four Geneva Conventions and it provides that some of these acts are also prohibited in conflicts that are not international. However, it does not contain any references to sex crimes.[231]

---

230   The Geneva Conventions were supported by almost every country in the world – 192 countries ratified them. Orna Ben-Naftali & Yuval Shany, supra note 81, p. 131. The Geneva Conventions are as follows: First Geneva Convention "For the Amelioration of the Condition of the Wounded and Sick in Armed Forces in the Field", 27 July 1949, 118 L.N.T.S. 303; Second Geneva Convention "For the Amelioration of the Condition of Wounded, Sick and Shipwrecked Members of Armed Forces at Sea", 12 August 1949, 75 U.N.T.S. 85; Third Geneva Convention "Relative to the Treatment of Prisoners of War", 12 August 1949, 75 U.N.T.S. 135; Fourth Geneva Convention "Relative to the Protection of Civilian Persons in Time of War", 12 August 1949, 75 U.N.T.S. 287 (hereinafter *Geneva Conventions*).

231   A peremptory norm is considered part of the customary international law and thus obligates every country in the world, even if it is not a signatory to the Geneva Conventions. Originally rape was not considered part of the customary law, but due to the atrocious acts committed during armed conflicts in recent decades, which I discuss below, international

The international community related explicitly for the first time to "rape" in the Geneva Conventions of 1949 in the context of the protection of civilians during war. Article 27 of the Convention provides:

> Women shall be especially protected against any *attack on their honor*, in particular against rape, enforced prostitution, or any form of indecent assault.[232]

[Emphasis added by the author]

Although this provision obligates the conquering army to protect women from rape, the wording of the Convention does not explicitly provide that acts of rape or sexual violence are crimes or prohibited acts. However, the criminality of these deeds could be deduced by interpretation of Article 3(c), which prohibits "outrages upon personal dignity".

The language of these provisions clearly distinguishes between rape as it relates to an attack on honor[233] and other non-gendered crimes related to an injury to dignity.[234] On this basis, from the perspective of the Geneva Conventions, rape is an injury to the woman's "honor" in its social meaning, rather than "dignity" in the sense of her inherent dignity as a human being. This treatment not only diminishes the value of the harm, but it also obscures and fails to acknowledge the cruelty of the physical injury. It diverts the discussion toward the social aspect of the injury and diminishes the aspect that is personal to her. This treatment also reduces motivation to bring the attacker to justice for the crime of "rape" and leads the system to punish criminals for crimes that seem to be more serious. As Charlesworth explains:

---

law has changed its view of these crimes to some extent. Discussions of the International Committee of the Red Cross (ICRC) reflect this change. Theodor Meron, supra note 202, p. 426.

232   Fourth Geneva Convention, supra note 230.

233   The term "honor" was conceptualized by Orit Kamir. "Honor societies" are those in which "honor," on the one hand, and "shame," on the other hand, serve as two sides of the same value by means of which social structure and hierarchical status are constructed. Dishonorable behavior is perceived as casting a stain of disgrace on a person's good name and brings shame and humiliation. This stain of shame adheres to the individual's honor, and also casts its shadow on the honor of everyone who is defined as related to or allied with the person. Thus in many societies the rape of women is considered an injury to the entire community's honor and as a defect and a "mark of Cain" on the victim, which can never be erased. See Orit Kamir, Israeli Honor and Dignity, supra note 13, pp. 19–25.

234   In contrast with "honor", the concept "dignity" was conceptualized by Orit Kamir as a universal concept and a uniform feature of all human beings. In order to acquire honor, one must act in accordance with a specific social code. In contrast, "dignity" is an inherent characteristic with which each human being is born. See Orit Kamir, Israeli Honor and Dignity, supra note 13, pp. 27–34.

The provision assumes that women should be protected from sexual crimes because they implicate a woman's honor, reinforcing the notion of women as man's property, rather than because they constitute violence.[235]

According to this view, rape during conflict is an act against another ethnic group in its entirety, a crime that is characterized by the struggle of one group against another group. This viewpoint ignores the victim and erases the gender aspect of the act. In other words, this perspective ignores those acts of rape that stem from female subordination and male empowerment.[236]

However, even an expansive interpretation that would ignore this historical overlay and treat dignity and honor as equivalent, in reliance on Article 3(c), would nevertheless still be ineffective. This is because the very emphasis on honor does not allow for the treatment of rape as a sexual, violent and grave offense.[237] As Valerie Oosterveld argues:

> Listing sexual violence crimes as "outrages on personal dignity" would represent a step backward, and send the outdated and potentially harmful message that these violent, physical crimes were to be evaluated based on the harm done to the victim's honour, modesty or chastity.[238]

Moreover, shifting the discussion to the harm to honor both hides the victim's physical and mental harm and requires that the assessment of the victim's harm be based on the injury to honor. This shift also distances the perpetrator from the crime and places the victim at the center of the investigation.

> The focus on the victim's protection, dignity and honour serves to distance the crime from the perpetrator. This distance is potentially harmful. It could lead prosecutors and judges considering charges of sexual slavery (or enforced prostitution) to focus on an evaluation of harm on honour or dignity and overlook consideration of sexual autonomy.[239]

---

235 Hilary Charlesworth, Feminist Methods in International Law, supra note 60, p. 386.

236 I refer to those gender crimes arising from the "male urge", which is considered legitimate during battle. Acting upon this urge raises the soldiers' morale and gives them relief for their desires with their commanders' approval. This is an archaic outlook, whose origin lies in the domestic laws of a patriarchal age, a time when the crime of rape was conceived of as a civil wrong against the victim's patron or family. See Part One, subchapter 3.2: "Rape as a Gender Crime – Attacker, Victim and Society".

237 Adrienne Kalosieh, supra note 179, p. 122.

238 Valerie Oosterveld, "Sexual Slavery and the International Criminal Court: Advancing International Law", 25 *Mich. J. Int'l L.* 605, 613 (2004) (hereinafter *Valerie Oosterveld, Sexual Slavery and the International Criminal Court*).

239 Ibid., pp. 650–651.

This requirement of the abstract injury to "honor" converts the crime of rape into a theoretical offense. In order for the crime of rape to become concrete, the drafters of the Conventions would need to have adapted its elements to those of the crimes "wilful killing, torture, or inhuman treatment" and "wilfully causing great suffering or serious injury to body or health". However, since the drafters of the Conventions did not do so, they effectively made it unlikely that charges would be brought for the crime of rape.[240, 241]

This discussion about the *Era of Honor* would be incomplete without referring to Janet Halley, who supports the position taken by the Geneva Conventions. In her opinion, the Geneva Conventions protect both women and men as part of their universal protection of human beings. She believes that the declaration that protects the honor of women adds to the usual protection of women and men.

> There is no trace of the patriarchal conception of honor in the pattern or in the words that construct it, I would hazard to say. Rather, we have universal rights of man, and the claim that they require specification because of the special harms that befall women ...[242]

This position is unconvincing, in my opinion. It seems to me that this treatment of women distinguishes them from the general rule governing the protection of men. The interpretation of the Geneva Conventions in retrospect, from today's feminist standpoint, overlooks the historical background of the words that were written in the *Era of Silence*. The choice of the word "honor" and not "dignity" is by no means accidental; it points to the roots of the offense as an injury to the masculine honor.

Halley also ignores the comparison drawn between women and children, the locating of these acts within the "moral" field, and the use of language of honor and family.[243] If we were to ignore the moderate language of the

---

240   Rhonda Copelon, "Gendered War Crimes: Reconceptualizing Rape in Time of War", in Julie Peters & Andrea Wolper, eds., *Women's Rights, Human Rights* (Routledge, 1995) 197.

241   In the 1940s when the Geneva Conventions were drafted, rape was not considered "torture". Torture was considered a means to extract information. However, international law has since expanded the boundaries of the definition of the crime of "torture" to include all physical and mental harm that is intended "(to) punish, intimidate, discriminate, obliterate the victim's personality, or diminish her personal capacities." For further discussion regarding the absence of the recognition of "rape as torture", see Hilary Charlesworth & Christine Chinkin, The Gender of Jus Cogens, supra note 46, pp. 72–73; see also Adrienne Kalosieh, supra note 179, p. 124. I discuss the possibility of recognizing rape as torture under international law above in Part One, subchapter 1.1: "Private v. Public in International Humanitarian Law".

242   Janet Halley, Rape at Rome, supra note 3, p. 61.

243   This entails recognition that we are dealing with special treatment stemming not from the woman's dignity as a human being, but rather from the power to protect the honor of her

provisions, we could claim that the prohibition against rape in wartime in the Geneva Conventions indicates that many countries consider rape in wartime to be illegal. On this basis, one could claim that the prohibition of rape in wartime provided in the Geneva Conventions reflects customary international law.[244]

Arguably, however, because the anchoring of the crime of rape in international law is handled in such a patchwork manner, whereby it is either given low importance or none whatsoever, the conclusion must be drawn that it is not part of the existing legal norms of international humanitarian law. Consequently, it also can be claimed that rape cannot be considered part of the peremptory norms, or *jus cogens*, which no states are permitted to violate. For example, Patricia Sellers claims that the only way to resolve this conflict, to prohibit rape, and to prosecute sex crime offenders as part of international criminal law is through the explicit recognition of these crimes:

> It is questionable whether a general norm of the prohibition of rape, in and of itself [exists] in human rights law. It is likewise uncertain that the crime rape under humanitarian law has been considered, in and of itself, as imposing a non-derogatory obligation on the community of states other than protection against its infliction. And quite frankly, rape has never been cited, heretofore, as a peremptory norm. … [C]ould one fathom two states entering into an agreement to rape persons in a third state, without the condemnation of the international community of States? If so, why has rape, whether a commonly committed national or international crime or perhaps an emerging human rights violations that is never justifiable, not crossed the peremptory norm threshold? Is the prohibition of rape's inability to meet international law's formalistic peremptory norm requirement the gendered legacy of a patriarchal legal culture?[245]

The conclusion drawn from this discussion is thus both dual and ambivalent: on the one hand, we can conclude that the prohibitions in various conventions in general, and in the Geneva Conventions in particular, against an act

---

community and her family's rights, all because of patriarchy. The woman as a victim is perceived under the categories of family law in the framework of the paternalistic protection of a "minor". Moreover, this protection is located entirely within the moral field, not the legal field. Once again, sex crimes are an exception to general legal principles.

244 Customary international law arose from the general practices that were customary over an extended period of time, when acts of states were based on the belief that they were bound to act in accordance with the practices. Barry E. Carter & Philip R. Trimble, *International Law* (Little, Brown & Company, 2d ed., 1995) 141–144.

245 Patricia Viseur Sellers, "Sexual Violence and Peremptory Norms: The Legal Value of Rape", 34 *Case Western Reserve J. Int'l L.* 287, 303 (2002).

injuring a person's honor, and the obligation to protect women against rape, are part of international customary law. On the other hand, one can argue that "rape" and "sexual violence" are not enumerated among the crimes that constitute "grave breaches" of the Geneva Conventions, nor are they included in Article 3 common to all Geneva Conventions, which ensures minimal protection during both international and domestic armed conflicts. And, indeed, as I discuss below,[246] when the drafters of the Rome Statute subsequently established the categories of international crimes, they chose to continue this chain of legal thinking and exclude the crime of rape from the list of crimes constituting "grave violations of the Geneva Conventions".

5.2 *INTERNATIONAL TREATY LAW, POST-GENEVA CONVENTIONS*

During the fifty years after the Geneva Conventions, many treaties were signed which, to some extent, compensated for the vacuum created after the trials at Nuremberg, Tokyo and the CCL10. These treaties aroused hope that international law would deal appropriately with the issues affecting women.[247] Although they certainly were no wonder drug which could cure years of neglect of the treatment of women's rights in international law, nevertheless, these treaties played an important role in developing international humanitarian law, which was customary, for the most part. These treaties were also a significant factor in raising awareness about the need for effective deterrents against gender crimes, as well as punishments for sex criminals.

The first document relevant to this process was written in 1950 at the direction of the UN General Assembly and was called the "Nuremberg Principles". These principles recognized individual responsibility for "war crimes", "crimes against peace" and "crimes against humanity."[248] But they, too, did not contain any references to sex crimes.

---

246   Part Two, subchapter 6.3: "The ICC – A New Status Quo".

247   Jocelyn Campanaro, supra note 208, p. 2562.

248   The UN General Assembly recognized a total of seven principles as principles of international law. Principles of International Law Recognized in the Charter of the Nürenberg Tribunal and in the Judgment of the Tribunal, 29 July 1950, UN Doc. A/CN.4/SER.A/1950/Add.1. The Nüremberg Principles include, *inter alia*, recognition of individual responsibility for committing international crimes; recognition of "crimes against peace", "war crimes" and "crimes against humanity" as international crimes; and recognition of the right to a fair trial. Lucinda Saunders, "Rich and Rare Are the Gems They War: Holding De Beers Accountable for Trading Conflict Diamonds" 24 *Fordham Int'l L.J.* 1402, 1450 (2001).

The two additional Protocols to the Geneva Conventions which were adopted in 1977 can be seen as progress.[249] Article 76 of Protocol I primarily covers the protection of women and children in international armed conflicts. Protocol II, which protects victims in non-international armed conflicts, in Article 4(2)(e) prohibits rape and regards it as an outrage upon the victim's dignity. In effect, these two Protocols treat sexual violence in a fairly comprehensive manner, and they emphasize that acts of rape are prohibited in both non-international and international armed conflicts.[250] Moreover, the duration of the period of time during which they grant protection was extended under certain circumstances, such as when territory remains under foreign occupation.[251]

The Geneva Conventions and the Additional Protocols enjoyed support from an impressive number of countries. However, while the Geneva Conventions enjoy universal adherence today, this is not yet the case for other major treaties, including the Additional Protocols.[252] Although nearly every state has ratified the four Geneva Conventions, the Additional Protocols have not yet gained universal adherence[253] and are applicable only between the

---

249   Protocol Additional I to the Geneva Conventions of 12 August 1949, and Relating to the Protection of Victims of International Armed Conflicts, 8 June 1977, 1125 U.N.T.S. 3 (hereinafter *Protocol I*); Protocol Additional II to the Geneva Conventions of 12 August 1949, and Relating to the Protection of Victims of Non-International Armed Conflicts, 8 June 1977, 1125 U.N.T.S. 609 (hereinafter *Protocol II*, and together with *Protocol I*, the *Additional Protocols*).

250   Kelly Dawn Askin, War Crimes against Women, supra note 9, p. 246. For example, regarding non-international armed conflicts, Article 4(2)(e) of Protocol II prohibits "outrages upon personal dignity, in particular humiliating and degrading treatment, rape, enforced prostitution and any form of indecent assault".

251   See Article 3(b) of Protocol I, supra note 249, which provides:

Art 3. Beginning and end of application
Without prejudice to the provisions which are applicable at all times: ...
(b) the application of the Conventions and of this Protocol shall cease, in the territory of Parties to the conflict, on the general close of military operations and, *in the case of occupied territories, on the termination of the occupation*, except, in either circumstance, for those persons whose final release, repatriation or re-establishment takes place thereafter. These persons shall continue to benefit from the relevant provisions of the Conventions and of this Protocol until their final release, repatriation or re-establishment.

[Emphasis added by the author]

252   Dr. Jakob Kellenberger, Foreword to Jean-Marie Henckaerts & Louise Doswald-Beck, *Customary International Humanitarian Law*, Vol. I, Rules (Cambridge University Press, 2009) xvi (hereinafter *Customary International Humanitarian Law*).

253   Almost every country in the world – 192 in number – ratified the Geneva Conventions. Protocol I was ratified by 165 countries and Protocol II was ratified by 160. ICRC database, "International Humanitarian Law – Treaties & Documents" available at http://www.icrc.org/ihl. nsf/CONVPRES?OpenView (last accessed 14 April 2011).

parties to a conflict that have ratified them, so their efficacy is limited because some states that have been involved in international armed conflicts are not a party to them.[254] Certain prominent countries have refused to join them (the U.S., India, Israel, Turkey and others), and other countries have joined subject to broad reservations on controversial provisions (for example, Britain and Germany).[255] In this regard, it is noteworthy that the vast majority of the Geneva Convention's provisions, including common Article 3, are considered to be customary law. Moreover, because the Geneva Conventions have been ratified by 192 states, they are binding on nearly all states as a matter of treaty law.[256]

The Additional Protocols can be seen as an indication of a transition to a new era, which I discuss below in chapter six. In any event, however, this transition is limited to international treaty law. Consequently, we cannot establish a clear position regarding the impact of this treaty law on the legal situation of sex crimes under international law in general.

Another document directly related to the problems associated with women and war is the "Declaration on the Protection of Women and Children in Emergency and Armed Conflict".[257] This declaration recognizes that women fall victim, all too often, to inhuman acts during armed conflicts and therefore need special protection. However, it is only a declaration – without binding legal force. Moreover, this declaration fails to refer at all to rape or other gender crimes during war.

Throughout the twentieth century, many documents related to human rights have been signed. In addition to the Geneva Conventions, the following were drafted: the Universal Declaration of Human Rights from 1948,[258] the International Covenant on Civil and Political Rights from 1966,[259] the Convention on the Elimination of All Forms of Discrimination against

---

254   Customary International Humanitarian Law, supra note 252, p. xxxvi.

255   Orna Ben-Naftali & Yuval Shany, supra note 81, p. 133.

256   Customary International Humanitarian Law, supra note 252, p. xxxvi.

257   Declaration on the Protection of Women and Children in Emergency and Armed Conflict, 14 December 1974, UN Doc. A/9631.

258   Universal Declaration of Human Rights, 10 December 1948, UN Doc. A/810, which provides, *inter alia*, in Article 5 that "No one shall be subjected to torture or to cruel, inhuman or degrading treatment or punishment".

259   International Covenant on Civil and Political Rights, 16 December 1966, UN Doc. A/6316, 999 U.N.T.S. 171. Articles 2 and 26 expressly prohibit discrimination on the basis of sex, Article 9 protects every person's right to liberty, and Article 7 provides that "No one shall be subjected to torture or to cruel, inhuman or degrading treatment or punishment."

Women (CEDAW) from 1979,[260] and the Convention against Torture and Other Cruel, Inhuman or Degrading Treatment or Punishment from 1984.[261] However, these documents, which do not deal specifically with conflicts or wars, also do not directly relate to the issue of sexual violence.

Changing this situation requires, *first*, the explicit recognition of sex crimes as an international crime, which emphasizes the physical and the mental harm to the woman, and, *second*, the implementation and enforcement of the international prohibition, by prosecuting the sex criminals who until now have been completely immune.

5.3 SUMMARY: THE ERA OF HONOR

The signing of the Geneva Conventions broke the silence. Sex crimes were no longer transparent; international law recognized that sex criminals must be pursued. However, in exchange, these obligations included the problematic wording regarding "honor" by which the Geneva Conventions analyze sexual offenses and distinguish them from other crimes that are covered by the Geneva Conventions. Furthermore, the "honor" paradigm perpetuates the historic patriarchal baggage that sex offenses carry as inferior crimes, as crimes of property, torts and plunder, and as crimes against society's honor, rather than crimes against the body and dignity of the woman who has been attacked.

Unfortunately, the treaties and conventions signed after the Geneva Conventions also failed to provide effective and operative tools for condemning and eradicating sex crimes in the international arena. Only when the new era commences three decades later – with the establishment of the ICTY and the ICTR – does genuine change begin to take place.

---

260 Convention on the Elimination of All Forms of Discrimination against Women, 18 December 1979, UN Doc. A/RES/34/180. Article 1 of this Convention provides:

> For the purposes of the present Convention, the term "discrimination against women" shall mean any distinction, exclusion or restriction made on the basis of sex which has the effect or purpose of impairing or nullifying the recognition, enjoyment or exercise by women, irrespective of their marital status, on a basis of equality of men and women, of human rights and fundamental freedoms in the political, economic, social, cultural, civil or any other field.

261 Convention against Torture, supra note 58.

Chapter 6

A NEW DIRECTION – TOWARDS A NEW ERA?

Fifty years have passed since the time of the Nuremberg and Tokyo trials, a time when international law was silent and ignored the horrendous sex crimes perpetrated during WWII. During this period, the transparency of sex crimes began to be painted in with the colors of honor, and international law's treatment of this subject reflected the gender subordination of women. Also, during this same period, women's political power began to be consolidated. As I discuss in this chapter, women's organizations and many scholars made significant contributions towards breaking down the stereotypes and misconceptions about all types of sex crimes. This development had a significant impact. Yet at the same time as these developments, shocking gender crimes were central features of both the war in Yugoslavia and the war in Rwanda. They could no longer be ignored: rape and sexual slavery were used as tools of conquest and were part of the national struggle and ethnic cleansing that accompanied these battles. In both of these wars, atrocious sex crimes were perpetrated as part of the official policies of the war.

In 1993, as a result of these horrendous crimes, feminist women became involved in international humanitarian law in order to fight against these atrocious crimes. They also sought to use them as a platform for feminist change of the international criminal law.[262]

These wars lead to the establishment of two international criminal tribunals – one for the former Yugoslavia (the ICTY) and one for Rwanda (the ICTR), which both prosecuted sex crimes against women. As demonstrated below in this chapter, these tribunals made great progress with respect to the treatment of sex crimes during war in international law. Sex crimes were no longer related to as offenses that were subordinate to other serious crimes, but were treated instead as independent international crimes which stood on their own two feet. However, ultimately, neither the ICTY nor the ICTR provided meaningful legal tools which could enable further progress.[263] In this chapter, I show how these tribunals did not interpret the traditional crime categories in a manner that was broad enough when they applied them to sex crimes. They selectively

---

262   See Janet Halley, Rape at Rome, supra note 3, p. 5.
263   See Kelly Dawn Askin, "A Decade of the Development of Gender Crimes in International Courts and Tribunals: 1993 to 2003", 11 *Hum. Rts. Br.* 16, 17 (2004) (hereinafter *Kelly Dawn Askin, A Decade in Human Rights Law*).

applied only some of the existing crime categories, and in ways that were insufficient to deal appropriately with sexual offenses.

6.1 THE FORMER YUGOSLAVIA (ICTY)

According to the report of the United Nations Special Rapporteur on Human Rights, over 20,000 women in the former Yugoslavia were victims of abuse between 1992 and 1994.[264] Most of the incidents of rape were committed by Serbian forces.

In an operation intended as "ethnic cleansing", hundreds of thousands of Serbs raped thousands of Muslim and Croatian girls and women for the purpose of "forced impregnation". These horrific acts occurred in approximately twenty rape and death camps.[265] Perhaps even more than the incomprehensible number, the circumstances of these horrific acts are shocking. Women were imprisoned in houses, in hotels or in one of the tens of detention camps, where they were repeatedly raped by Serbian soldiers over many months, and the acts of rape were accompanied by violence and cruelty.[266] The women were used as a means to humiliate, to abuse, and ultimately, to try and destroy the entire population.

The choice of this tool was not incidental and can be explained as follows: *First*, the Serbs sought to expand the Serbian population at the expense of the Muslim population. The women were held in camps where they were repeatedly raped with the hope that they would become pregnant and give birth to Serbian children. According to Islam, the child's religion is determined by the father's religion. Thus the criminals hoped that the Serbian population would grow enough to wipe out the Muslim population. *Second*, rape was used as a means of humiliation and injury to the victim's personal and social honor[267]

---

264   Economic and Social Council, Report of the Special Rapporteur on Violence Against Women, its Causes and Consequences, Ms. Radhika Coomaraswamy, in accordance with Commission on Human Rights Resolution, 21 January 1999, 1997/44 Distr. GENERAL E/CN.4/1999/68/Add.4.

265   Note that even some of the UN soldiers sent to protect the local population compelled refugees to submit sexually in order to receive assistance. See Catharine A. MacKinnon, "Rape, Genocide and Women's Human Rights" in Alexandra Stiglmayer, ed., *Mass Rape: The War against Women in Bosnia-Herzegovina* (University of Nebraska Press, 1994) 183 (hereinafter *Catharine MacKinnon, Rape, Genocide and Women's Human Rights*). I discuss sex crimes committed by peace-keeping forces below in Part Three, chapter 8: "Part of Existing Crime Categories or a Discrete Crime?"

266   Christin Coan, "Rethinking the Spoils of War: Prosecuting Rape as a War Crime in the International Criminal Tribunal for the Former Yugoslavia", 26 *N.C. J. Int'l L. & Com. Reg.* 183, 185–186 (2000) (hereinafter *Christin Coan*).

267   For an analysis of the different kinds of honor, see Orit Kamir, Israeli Honor and Dignity, supra notes 13, 233, 234.

and to reduce the morale of the victims and their families. As discussed above, according to the Muslim tradition, a rape victim's honor is considered to be permanently damaged. This leads to dissolution of the family, banishment of the victims and, in some instances, their being murdered by family or community members. Rape victims are thought to be impure, undesirable, and unfit for marriage.[268] *Third*, rape was used as a tool to glorify the attackers' honor and raise the morale of their own soldiers.[269]

However, despite these atrocities, it seemed that, yet again, the gender crimes would remain transparent – the women's voices would again be silenced and the perpetrators of these atrocious crimes would not be held criminally responsible. The war in Serbia was first defined by the international community as a "civil war" – a national problem, not an international one – so it was not clear whether there was a basis for the international community to intervene in the conflict.[270, 271]

---

268 Jocelyn Campanaro, supra note 208, p. 2565; Amy E. Ray, "The Shame of It: Gender-Based Terrorism in the Former Yugoslavia and the Failure of International Human Rights Law to Comprehend the Injuries", 46 *Am. U. L. Rev.* 793, 802 (1997) (hereinafter *Amy Ray*).

269 Note that the second and third reasons are but two sides of the same coin: honor. Honor is always taken from one party and transferred to another, because attaining honor requires humiliating someone else in exchange. There is not enough for everyone and so, to increase your own share, you have to reduce the share of someone else. Thank you to my colleague Ofra Henman for this comment.

270 Subchapter 1.1: "Private v. Public in International Humanitarian Law".

271 I note that the international attempt to avoid taking responsibility and intervening in the conflict is puzzling. This was a war against Croatia and Bosnia-Herzegovina, involving their partial occupation by Serbian forces, in cooperation with the Serbian regime in Belgrade. The implications of this occupation were unambiguous: it involved the use of prohibited force. The prohibition on the use of force is explicitly provided by international treaty law in Article 2(4) of the Charter of the United Nations, 26 June 1945, 59 Stat. 1031 (hereinafter *UN Charter*), which states:

> All Members shall refrain in their international relations from the threat or use of force against the territorial integrity or political independence of any state, or in any other manner inconsistent with the Purposes of the United Nations.

This prohibition is subject to two exceptions, which were not present in the matter at hand: (i) self-defense, under Article 51 of the UN Charter, and (ii) the authority given to the UN Security Council by Chapter VII of the UN Charter to intervene in situations of a threat to "peace and security". It is incontestable that neither of these exceptions was relevant to this matter and that the Serbs' attack was a prohibited war. Note that the prohibition on the use of force in Article 2(4) of the UN Charter is a prohibition under international treaty law. However, in the Judgment in Case Concerning Military and Para-Military Activities in and against Nicaragua (Nicaragua v. US) 1986 ICJ 14, the ICJ held that the prohibition on the use of force is not only a treaty prohibition, but also a prohibition which is part of customary international law. Also, the whitewashing in defining the conflict as a "civilian war" blurred Belgrade's role in the invasion, beginning with Croatia and afterwards into Bosnia Herzegovina. See Catharine MacKinnon, Rape, Genocide and Women's Human Rights, supra note 265, p. 189.

A group of women active in an NGO called the Women in the Law Project (WILP) sent a delegation to the area where the fighting took place, conducted interviews and an investigation, and published a report. The WILP report recommended that an international tribunal be established, that rape be included in the international crime categories, and that rape be considered a "grave breach of the Geneva Conventions" for prosecution of the war criminals.[272] Political pressure on the countries serving on the Security Council led to the establishment of a committee tasked with writing a report about the situation. The shocking findings left no room for doubt,[273] and led in 1993 to an unprecedented step in the history of the U.N.: the establishment of the International Criminal Tribunal for the Former Yugoslavia (ICTY) in The Hague. This ad hoc international criminal tribunal was given the power to prosecute individuals who committed the crimes of "genocide", "war crimes" and "crimes against humanity". The ICTY was established by authority of Chapter VII of the UN Charter, on the basis of the UN Security Council's determination that the atrocities which took place in the Balkans constituted a threat to international peace and security.[274]

The ICTY Statute granted to the ICTY the authority to prosecute persons responsible for serious violations of international humanitarian law committed in the territory of the former Yugoslavia from 1991, including "grave breaches of the Geneva Conventions", "war crimes", "genocide" and "crimes against humanity".[275] The ICTY Statute granted the Tribunal a broad mandate

---

272   Mission of the Women in the Law Project of the International Human Rights Law Group, "No Justice, No Peace: Accountability for Rape and Gender-Based Violence in the Former Yugoslavia", 5 *Hastings Women's L.J.* 89–128 (1994).

273   Interim Report of Commission of Experts Established Pursuant to Security Council by the Secretary-General, 9 February 1993 (s/25274); Final Report of the Commission of Experts Established Pursuant to Security Council Resolution 780, 27 May 1994, s/1994/674.

274   Statute of the International Criminal Tribunal for the Former Yugoslavia, 25 May 1993, UN Doc. S/RES/827 (hereinafter *ICTY Statute*).

275   ICTY Statute, arts. 1–5, respectively. Accordingly, the ICTY became the first international criminal tribunal set up to prosecute individuals accused of grave crimes, and it was established by the UN Security Council, an international body representing the entire human community. In this regard, the ICTY is distinguishable from the prior international tribunals in Nuremberg and Tokyo, which were established by the Allied forces, the victors of WWII.

The establishment of the two international criminal tribunals to prosecute those responsible for committing international crimes in the former Yugoslavia in 1993 (discussed above) and Rwanda (discussed below in subchapter 6.2: "Rwanda (ICTR)") in 1994, mark four important developments in international criminal law, in general, and the subject of this study, in particular. *First*, from a normative perspective, establishment of a criminal tribunal by the UN Security Council ties grave breaches of human rights and universal fundamental values more closely to world peace and security. *Second*, although these tribunals, like the military tribunals in Nuremberg and Tokyo, were ad hoc tribunals and their jurisdiction was

to prosecute sex criminals. It was an important milestone in the struggle for the recognition and protection of women's rights during wartime. For example, Article 5(g) of the ICTY Statute provided for the first time in the history of international criminal law that the crime of "rape" was a "crime against humanity":

Article 5. Crimes against humanity.
The International Tribunal shall have the power to prosecute persons responsible for the following crimes when committed in armed conflict, whether international or internal in character, and directed against any civilian population:
    (a) murder;
    (b) extermination;
    (c) enslavement;
    (d) deportation;
    (e) imprisonment;
    (f) torture;
    (g) rape;
    (h) persecutions on political, racial and religious grounds;
    (i) other inhumane acts.

This explicit inclusion of rape marks considerable progress in light of the charters of the previous tribunals at Nuremberg and Tokyo. The ICTY Statute applies to all crimes committed against civilians by any agent of war in order to advance the war.[276]

The crime of rape is the only sexual offense enumerated in the list of crimes over which the Tribunal has jurisdiction; no other sex crimes were listed alongside it. Also, the offense of rape is only included in the crime category of "crimes against humanity". None of the other crime categories under the ICTY's jurisdiction included the crime of rape.

---

specifically limited to certain events, they differ from their predecessors in that their composition does not represent the victorious side in a world war. This progress towards neutral jurisdiction is quite significant. *Third*, the ICTY and ICTR jurisprudence marks a highly valuable contribution to the uniform development of procedures and rules of enforcement of international law, as well as to the development of the substantive law. Orna Ben-Naftali & Yuval Shany, supra note 81, p. 256. For example, as is apparent from the discussion in this subchapter below, the ICTY jurisprudence gradually expanded the applicability of international humanitarian law to internal armed conflicts. Prosecutor v. Tadic, Case No. IT-94-1-A, App. Ch. (ICTY, 15 July 1999) (hereinafter *Tadic Case*). *Fourth*, the very fact that these tribunals were established and functioned accelerated the implementation of the idea to form a permanent international criminal court.

276   ICTY Statute, supra note 274.

Undoubtedly, including rape in the crime category "crime against human-ity" was a genuine step forward from a procedural perspective. The crime of rape is given a prominent location, listed among the most egregious interna-tional criminal offenses, alongside murder and torture.

However, from a substantive perspective, there are numerous problems with the way sex crimes were included in the ICTY Statute. *First,* in order to convict for rape under the crime category of a "crime against humanity", it must be proven that the offense was committed at the time of a widespread or system-atic attack and that it was part of an international or internal "armed conflict" directed against a civilian population. But as many feminists have argued, and continue to argue, rape, and even rape during war, is not always linked to this kind of attack. Most incidents of rape that occur during military hostilities are sporadic and not systematic.[277] *Second,* rape is noticeably absent from the other crime categories under the ICTY's jurisdiction, "genocide", "crimes against humanity" and "grave breaches of the Geneva Convention". This fact dimin-ished the Tribunal's ability to recognize and effectively deal with the immense harm caused by sex criminals to thousands of women during the war. *Third,* the absence of an explicit definition of gender crimes in the ICTY Statute reflected the view that those offenses committed predominantly against the female gender during armed conflicts are not valued by international law with the same gravity as the crimes affecting both men and women.[278]

Nonetheless, this possibility of prosecuting rape offenses opened the door for the ICTY to fill in the gaps through case law. In practice, many sex crimi-nals were prosecuted for violations of international humanitarian law on the basis of the inclusion of rape as a "crime against humanity". Furthermore, as I discuss in this chapter, the Tribunal held that rape and other types of sexual assault were indirectly a "grave breach of the Geneva Conventions" and the customary laws of war, as well as "genocide". Hence, despite the problematic aspects and the absence of an explicit definition, the ICTY established impor-tant legal and procedural precedents related to sexual offenses during war. No longer silence, no longer an attack on honor – finally, a grave crime standing on its own two feet.

---

277   Barbara Bedont & Katherine Hall Martinez, supra note 3, p 70. Note that although this requirement is not stated in Article 5 of the ICTY Statute, it was recognized by the Tribunal as part of the requirements of customary international law. See *Tadic Judgment,* infra note 302, para. 646; see also infra note 329.

278   Amy Ray, supra note 268, pp. 817–824. Regarding the possibility of recognizing rape as torture, see above Part One, subchapter 1.1: "Private v. Public in International Humanitarian Law", and in this Part Two, subchapter 5.1: "Geneva Conventions".

One of the most impressive successes of the ICTY was that, in contrast with the Nuremberg and Tokyo tribunals, the ICTY Statute encouraged female participation in the judicial process – as investigators, as researchers, as judges, as legal advisors, and as prosecutors.[279] It can be claimed, in the Gilliganian spirit,[280] that the women who undertook this critical work contributed to the success of the proceedings. On this point, Jocelyn Campanaro notes:

> Both men and women have the capacity to understand rape allegations and take them seriously, but there is a heightened gender-specific perspective that women share, regardless of ethnicity or nationality. Because women are more often the victims of sexual assault, they "easily accept themselves as potential victims".[281]

Moreover, because these crimes had never before been adequately addressed in the legal, social and international political discourse, it was undoubtedly significant that women were among the intermediaries and spokespersons.

6.1.1 New Rules, Adaptations

One of the greatest successes of the ICTY is that it established rules of procedure and evidence suited to the special nature of the evidence in sexual offenses.[282] In Part One above,[283] I discussed the complexity of the injury to sexual offense victims, and the way their immediate environment fails to provide adequate support.

Because of the humiliation, the horrendous nature of the experience, and the terrible stigmatization of sex crime victims, it is crucial that procedural law acknowledge the severe harm caused to witnesses, provide more flexible rules for witnesses to testify, and guarantee effective protection for victims. In accordance with Gilligan's approach, I contend that the feminine voice must permeate the inflexible, masculine procedural laws. And indeed, the ICTY's Rules of Procedure and Evidence (ICTY Rules) have adopted this perspective. For example, Rule 96 provides the following rules for evidence in the case of sexual assaults:

---

279   See Kelly Dawn Askin, War Crimes against Women, supra note 9, pp. 302–303.

280   See Carol Gilligan, supra note 35.

281   Jocelyn Campanaro, supra note 208, p. 2566.

282   Rules of Procedure and Evidence of the International Criminal Tribunal for the Former Yugoslavia, 11 February 1994, UN Doc. IT/32/Rev. 44 (Last rev. 10 December 2009) (hereinafter *ICTY Rules*).

283   Subchapter 3.2: "Rape as a Gender Crime – Attacker, Victim and Society".

In cases of sexual assault:
    (i) no corroboration of the victim's testimony shall be required;
   (ii) consent shall not be allowed as a defence if the victim
        (a) has been subjected to or threatened with or has had reason to fear violence, duress, detention or psychological oppression, or
        (b) reasonably believed that if the victim did not submit, another might be so subjected, threatened or put in fear; ...
   (iv) prior sexual conduct of the victim shall not be admitted in evidence.

In other words, this Rule 96 provides that there is no need to corroborate the testimony of the victim, her sexual history is not admissible as evidence, and the victim's consent will not be a defense if she believed that she was subjected to a threat of violence against herself or another person.[284]

The ICTY Rules are intended to soften the harsh effects of the legal proceedings and somewhat ease the burden on victims testifying about the atrocities. They are especially intended to protect victims, to the extent possible, from difficult interrogations and a "second rape" by defense counsel.[285]

The broad application of Rule 96 to all "sexual assaults" indicates the ICTY's sincere intent to prosecute all sexual offenders, not only rapists.[286] These rules enabled victims to tell their stories, to make their voices heard, to shatter the historic silence that had continued for an entire era. Giving a voice in law, in general, and in a judicial proceeding, in particular, as discussed above,[287] is a political act which is part of the ongoing struggle to change society's hierarchical power structures through the courtroom battle.[288]

Article 22 of the ICTY Statute expressly requires the adoption of rules to protect victims and witnesses. Rule 34(A) of the ICTY Rules provides for the establishment of a witness and victim unit to provide counseling and support to the victims of sexual attacks and witnesses. Rule 34(B) of the ICTY Rules states that "[d]ue consideration shall be given, in the appointment of staff, to the employment of qualified women." This is another example of the

---

284   I discuss the issue of consent below in Part Three, subchapter 9.5.2: "The Presumption of Nonconsent".

285   On the phenomenon of women seeking justice in the legal system and experiencing it as a second rape, see Judith Lewis Herman, supra note 98, p. 72. I discuss this issue above in Part One, subchapter 3.2.1: "Society's Attitude toward Rape".

286   Patricia Viseur Sellers & Kaoru Okuizumi, "Prosecuting International Crimes: An Inside View: Intentional Prosecution of Sexual Assaults", 7(1) *Transnational Law & Contemporary Problems* 45, 51 (1997) (hereinafter *Patricia Viseur Sellers & Kaoru Okuizumi*).

287   Part One, chapter 1: "International Law from a Feminist Perspective".

288   See Leora Bilsky, supra note 37; Katharine Bartlett, supra note 39.

significance that the ICTY attributed to the involvement of women as investigators and prosecutors in cases of rape and sexual assault.

Yet the fear that gripped the witnesses was only partially lessened. Although the witnesses were indeed offered some protection during the legal proceedings, they were not given any protection once the legal proceedings concluded. Many of these witnesses returned to their villages after they testified. In some cases, they continued to live among their attackers. Note also that, even today, international tribunals only prosecute the major offenders – those leading the troops and high-ranking officers – so that those who are prosecuted are only a select few of those who committed gender crimes.[289] In addition, many of the victims were from small villages, and rumors about the sexual assault flew through the village as soon as the victim testified in court.[290]

There were also many cases in which the Tribunal neglected to protect victims from having their names publicized as part of the proceedings, and additional information about the victims was leaked.[291] Many rape victims refused to testify because they deeply feared the rapists and the exposure of their names and testimony.[292] As a result, some of the charges were dropped against some of the accused sex criminals, and some alleged criminals were simply released. Yet the ICTY rejected requests to allow witnesses to testify over closed circuit television in a proceeding that would have maintained the victims' privacy while they testified and allowed them to avoid a face-to-face confrontation with the alleged rapists.

However, despite the foregoing, the ICTY Rules undoubtedly served as a means to advance all matters related to victims' testimony and the recognition of sexual offenses within the framework of international criminal law. And in addition to the advancements made by the ICTY Rules, there were also prosecutors who helped significantly advance international law. Drawing upon the core of international law built on the foundations of the Nuremberg Principles, the ICTY recognized rape and sexual assault as types of torture, "genocide"

---

289   See, e.g., International Criminal Tribunal for the former Yugoslavia and International Criminal Tribunal for Rwanda, S.C. Res. 1534 (2004), U.N. Doc. S/RES/1534, para. 5.

290   Christin Coan, supra note 266, p. 81.

291   Kelly Dawn Askin, "Sexual Violence in Decisions and Indictments of the Yugoslav and Rwandan Tribunals: Current Status", 93 *Am. J. Int'l L.* 97, 101 (1999). This article discusses judgments in which certain counts charging the defendants with rape had been struck from some of the indictments because the victims were too afraid to testify against the accused. See, e.g., Prosecutor v. Tadic, Sentencing Jugdment Case No. IT-94-1, T. Ch. II. (ICTY, 11 November 1999).

292   I discuss the difficulties that victims face in testifying at rape trials above in Part One, subchapter 3.2.1: "Society's Attitude toward Rape".

and "crimes against humanity". It also contributed to the integration of gender issues into international law, as I describe below.[293]

6.1.2 New Judgments, Adaptations

The first trial held in the ICTY was the prosecution of Dusko Tadic.[294] The ICTY decision in this case created important judicial precedents which influenced the integration of sex crimes into international law.

The first count in the indictment charged Tadic with a "crime against humanity" for his involvement in a "campaign of terror which included killings, torture, sexual assaults, and other physical and psychological abuse",[295] and with participation in "torture of more than 12 female detainees, including several gang rapes".[296] In another count, Tadic was charged with subjecting a female prisoner under his guard to forcible sexual intercourse. He was accused of a grave breach of the customary laws of war, i.e., a "war crime": "inhuman treatment constituting a grave breach" of the Geneva Conventions under Articles 2(b) and 7(1) of the ICTY Statute, and the "crime against humanity" of "cruel treatment constituting violations of the laws or customs of war" under Article 3 of the ICTY Statute.

Although sexual offenses were explicitly included in the ICTY Statute only as a "crime against humanity", the ICTY prosecutor decided that they could also be included under other provisions of the ICTY Statute, specifically as "grave breaches of the Geneva Conventions", as breaches of the customary laws of war, and as "genocide".[297]

Tadic was expected to be the first instance in which a criminal was tried in an international tribunal for the specific charge of rape as a war crime – and not as someone charged only with committing rape as one offense among others.[298] However, the separate counts of rape were subsequently struck from the indictment, because all of the witnesses to these atrocious acts were too fearful to testify. Nevertheless, Tadic was convicted of other violent sexual offenses and sexual mutilation.[299] This marked the most broad recognition ever given to sex crimes under international law – broad both because the accused was charged with offenses in the framework of all of the existing traditional

---

293   Jocelyn Campanaro, supra note 208, p. 2567.
294   Prosecutor v. Tadic, Second Amended Indictment, Case No. IT- 94-1-T (ICTY, 14 December 1995), paras. 4, 4.3.
295   Ibid.
296   Ibid.
297   See Prosecutor v. Tadic, Case No. IT-94-1-AR72, T. Ch. II (ICTY, 2 October 1996) paras. 88–92; Patricia Viseur Sellers & Kaoru Okuizumi, supra note 286, p. 57.
298   See Kelly Dawn Askin, War Crimes against Women, supra note 9, p. 101.
299   Ibid.

crime categories, and because the incidents included not only rape in its traditional meaning. But surprisingly – or perhaps not so surprisingly – on this first occasion that international law gave such broad recognition to sex crimes, these convictions were for atrocities committed against *men, not women.*

The sexual abuse was perpetrated primarily against prisoners, as part of the ongoing physical and mental abuse to which they were subjected. The prisoners were forced to eat live animals, including a live bird, and they were harshly beaten all over their bodies. The sexual abuse involved forced oral sex between one prisoner and another and mutilation of sex organs, among other abuses. These facts led to a recognition that sex crime victims are not only women,[300] and that sex crimes are can be characterized as torture in the framework of a general inter-ethnic war, to which both women and men are vulnerable, as I claim above.[301]

The Tribunal's decision was highly significant because it recognized sexual offenses not only as inter-ethnic crimes, but also as gender crimes. This recognition is evident in several aspects of the decision. *First,* although the accused did not commit the crimes himself, he was held responsible for perpetration of the incidents of rape because he was "aware of the policy of discrimination against non-Serbs".[302] The Tribunal held that international customary law imposes individual personal responsibility for criminal behavior on a person who knew and influenced the perpetration of the illegal act, even if the person did not actively participate in its performance.[303] Thus, Tadic was convicted as an inactive participant in persecution which included rape and other forms of sexual violence.

Second, although the sexual offenses in the amended indictment only involved male victims, the Tribunal's opinion explicitly addressed the shocking sexual torture of female prisoners as well. Moreover, the decision acknowledged the physical and mental harm to the women that resulted from the sexual abuse.[304] This decision, by explicitly acknowledging the incidents of rape

---

300   I emphasize again that men certainly are also victims of sex crimes. However, as I discuss in this book, women are the victims in a greatly disproportionate manner. See supra notes 8, 167 and infra note 480, Moreover, we tend to view the rape of a man as a form of torture intended to break the enemy, whereas the rape of a woman is sometimes perpetrated as a form of torture and sometimes out of gender motives.

301   Part One, subchapter 1.1: "Private v. Public in International Humanitarian Law".

302   Prosecutor v. Tadic, Case No. IT-94-1-T, T. Ch. II (ICTY, 7 May 1997) (hereinafter *Tadic Judgment*).

303   Ibid., para. 477.

304   Patricia Viseur Sellers, "Emerging Jurisprudence on Crimes of Sexual Violence", 13 *Am. U. Int'l L Rev.* 1523, 1529 (1998).

and other sexual offenses against women, ensured the possibility of punishing sex offenders in the future.

Third, in its application of ICTY Rule 96, which establishes rules for testimony about sexual offenses, the ICTY emphasized the importance of this rule:

> [T]he testimony of a victim of sexual assault [is granted] the same presumption of reliability as the testimony of victims of other crimes, something long denied to victims of sexual assault by the common law.[305]

In this ruling, the ICTY equated the testimony of sexual offense victims with the testimony of victims of all other crimes, and rejected the prejudices which were widely held in the past about the testimony of victims of sexual offenses.[306]

The next indictment about sexual offenses submitted in the ICTY concerned several Bosnian soldiers accused of sexual exploitation and sexual torture of prisoners in the Celebici camp.[307] The soldiers were accused of "war crimes" and "grave breaches of the four Geneva Conventions". The judgment was delivered two years later, in November 1998.

The Tribunal held, among other things, that the accused, Hazim Delic, who served as a guard in the camp, was guilty of the repeated use of rape as a means of torture of two female prisoners in the camp and, on that basis, he was found guilty of violating Articles 2 and 3 of the ICTY Statute.[308] This was the first time that rape was recognized as a type of torture and as a primary offense in an indictment, rather than as a secondary offense under more severe crimes. Moreover, the judgment strengthened the law regarding "officers' responsibility" for rapes committed by their subordinates, and at their encouragement.

The *Furundzija Judgment*[309] strengthened the law that rape can be a form of torture, and even offered a broad, precise definition of the crime of "rape" for the first time.[310] The Tribunal had faced the following issue: is a coerced oral act on the male sexual organ ("oral penetration") rape or sexual assault? The Tribunal surveyed a range of viewpoints on this issue from around the world. Despite the lack of an international consensus, the Tribunal emphasized that

---

305　*Tadic Judgment*, supra note 302, para. 536.
306　I discuss these prejudices above in Part One, subchapter 3.2: "Rape as a Gender Crime – Attacker, Victim and Society".
307　Prosecutor v. Delalic, Indictment, Case No. IT-96-21-I (ICTY, 19 March 1996).
308　*Delalic Judgment*, supra note 65, paras. 943, 965.
309　Prosecutor v. Furundzija, Case No. IT-95-17/1-T, T. Ch. II, (ICTY, 10 December 1998) (hereinafter *Furundzija Judgment*).
310　Ibid., paras. 174–186.

the goal of humanitarian law is protection of human dignity, irrespective of gender, and a forced oral act is a degrading act that harms dignity. Therefore, the Tribunal reasoned, an act of coerced oral penetration must be considered a trauma to the victim just like vaginal or oral penetration. The Tribunal concluded that any other determination would undermine the fundamental principles underlying the crime of rape – protection of human dignity. Hence, the Tribunal held that an act which includes "oral penetration" must be classified as rape.

The ICTY found that international law lacked a specific definition of the elements of the crime of rape, and formulated it as follows:

> (i) the sexual penetration however slight:
>   (a) of the vagina or anus of the victim by the penis of the perpetrator or any other object used by the perpetrator; or
>   (b) of the mouth of the victim by the penis of the perpetrator;
> (ii) by coercion or force or threat of force against the victim or a third person.[311, 312]

Furthermore, the Tribunal clearly stated that Article 5 of the ICTY Statute grants explicit jurisdiction to prosecute war criminals for the offense of rape, and permits an indictment to be submitted for other grave sexual assaults as "crimes against humanity".[313]

In addition to the broad interpretation and the expansion of the Tribunal's jurisdiction to prosecute other sexual offenses, the *Furundzija Judgment* dealt with procedural rules governing witnesses who testify about rape. This judgment was based to a great extent on the testimony of a sexual abuse victim who suffered from posttraumatic stress disorder (PTSD). This occurred in spite of the claim raised by the defense, in reliance on historic legal roots, that a posttraumatic stress victim's memory of the events is likely to be impaired and unreliable because of the great suffering she endured during the war.[314] The Tribunal held:

> Even when a person is suffering from PTSD, this does not mean that he or she is necessarily inaccurate in the evidence given. There is no reason why a person with PTSD cannot be a perfectly reliable witness.[315]

---

311   Ibid., para. 185.
312   Note that in formulating this definition of the offense of rape, the court drew upon the definitions in several national court systems. See ibid., paras. 174–186.
313   Ibid., para. 175.
314   Ibid., paras. 108–109.
315   Ibid., para. 109.

By broadly interpreting both the definition of the crime of rape as well as the rules of evidence and procedural requirements for its proof, the Tribunal in the *Furundzija Judgment* strengthened the status of this crime as a punishable offense. Yet it can be argued that the Tribunal's broad interpretation violates the legal rights of the accused and the rule of law, in that criminal law is supposed to give warning by means of a written law prior to the illegal behavior.[316] In my opinion, however, these horrible acts were always prohibited as *jus cogens* because of their grave nature.[317] Therefore, the judicial decision in the *Furundzija Judgment* is merely a declaration about prohibited criminal behavior under international criminal law, not the establishment of a new criminal prohibition.[318]

Subsequently, in June 1996, for the first time in the history of international criminal law, the ICTY imposed criminal responsibility based only on sexual offences committed against women.[319] In this case, Serbian soldiers were charged with over sixty incidents of sexual assault of non-Serbian women. One of the Serbian officers, Dragoljub Kunarac, was charged with entering a detention camp, selecting Muslim women and girls, and taking them to a military base where they were raped and subjected to grievous sexual assault. Kunarac was found guilty of twenty-one incidents of rape and torture as "crimes against humanity" and "war crimes" in a judgment that was based nearly entirely on criminal convictions for sexual offenses.

This was the first time an international court recognized rape as a "crime against humanity" without relying on other prohibited acts. The conviction was for "enslavement" as a "crime against humanity", based on the enforced detention of Muslim women compelled to perform domestic labor and to be "sexually available" to Kunarac and the other guards. Some women were

---

316   See the discussion on this argument with respect to the establishment of the IMT and the IMTFE, supra note 206.

317   For an interesting discussion about the gender perspective of the term *jus cogens*, see Hilary Charlesworth & Christine Chinkin, The Gender of Jus Cogens, supra note 46.

318   See the discussion concerning the *Eichmann Judgment*, supra note 206. The guiding principle proposed by the ICTY for this development, which as noted is required due to the principle of legality, was the connection between "other inhumane acts" prohibited by Article 5(i) of the ICTY Statute (which was based on Article 6(c) of the London Agreement and Article II(1)(c) of the CCL10 and also was provided subsequently in Article 7(1)(g) and 7(1)(k) of the Rome Statute) and infringements of basic human rights set forth in various human rights treaties. See Prosecutor v. Kupreskic, Case No. IT-95-16, T. Ch. II (ICTY, 14 January 2000), paras. 563–566.

319   Prosecutor v. Gagovic, Case No. IT-96-23 (ICTY, 18 June 1996). In 1998, the indictment was amended and Kunarac became the only defendant in an indictment based solely on sex crimes. See Prosecutor v. Kunarac, Amended Indictment, Case No. IT-96-23-I (ICTY, 13 July 1998).

held captive in abandoned houses and subjected to repeated sexual assaults and rape, and other people were permitted to sexually abuse them in exchange for money.

In February 2001, the ICTY held that these incidents of rape were perpetrated as acts of terror, and stated in a press release that the convicted men "thrived in the dark atmosphere of the dehumanisation of those believed to be enemies".[320] Even though Kunarac was acquitted of the acts of rape committed by his subordinates, the ICTY found him guilty of using rape as a form of torture and a "crime against humanity".[321]

6.1.3 A Mixed Blessing

Although the ICTY decisions created historically significant advancements in the anchoring of sex crimes under international law, these decisions were sometimes accompanied by a heavy price. For example, although the ICTY in the *Furundzija Judgment* interpreted "rape" broadly and found credible the testimony of sexual offense victims suffering from PTSD, the Tribunal failed to provide adequate protection for the victim's privacy. Due to the defense counsel's intense opposition to the victim's testimony, the Tribunal decided to lift her immunity regarding her privacy and allowed exposure of the records about her medical and psychological treatment. The Tribunal allowed the defense to use these records and submit them as evidence in the trial.[322]

Exposure of private information that a victim has revealed as part of medical and psychological treatment for sexual abuse, without the patient's consent, undoubtedly causes real trauma (a "second rape", discussed above).[323] Once again, control over her life is taken away from the woman. Her personal heart-wrenching story is expropriated and turned into public property, without her consent. Yet the process of psychological treatment depends entirely on the trust the woman places in her therapist. This trust is based on the assumption that her experiences will remain in the therapy room, between her and the therapist.[324] A court-imposed decision, against the woman's wishes, to make her experiences public has a deep impact on the future of her psychological treatment and her willingness to confide in a professional person and seek

---

320   Press Release, ICTY, Judgment of Trial Chamber II in the Kunarac, Kovac and Vukovic Case, The Hague, 22 February 2001, JL/P.I.S./566-e.

321   Prosecutor v. Kunarac, Case No. IT-96-23-T (ICTY, 22 February 2001) paras. 630–745 (hereinafter *Kunarac Judgment*).

322   Prosecutor v. Furundzija, Decision [on Defence Motion to Strike Testimony of Witness A], Case No. IT-95-17/1-T (ICTY, 16 July 1998).

323   Part One, subchapter 3.2.1: "Society's Attitude toward Rape".

324   Judith Lewis Herman, supra note 98, p. 72.

help.[325] Note that even without this violation of her trust, a sexual abuse victim feels terrible shame and guilt when revealing her experiences.[326]

As explained above, the impact of rape is especially severe in patriarchal traditional societies, where the victim is ostracized by her family and community. This impact causes a downward spiral: a decline in the number of women seeking professional help to cope with a sexual trauma will lead to a reduction in the number of women who gather the courage to testify against their attackers. Then, without the testimony of these sexual abuse victims, the ability to prosecute the rapists and other sexual offenders will be considerably diminished.

The *Kunarac Judgment* is considered an historic decision, in that it demonstrates the seriousness of the international community about prosecuting sexual offenses against women, such as rape, sexual enslavement and gang rape. Yet despite the advances taken by this decision with respect to how international criminal law handles sex crimes during conflict, the opinion itself does not explicitly define "sexual enslavement" in the indictment. The charge of enslavement is coddled in descriptions such as the women and girls being personal property, detained, and divided among the men.[327] For some reason, the Tribunal ignored the sexual aspects of the enslavement and described the treatment of the women as objects, without stating the purpose of their objectification. In my opinion, the Tribunal missed a golden opportunity to define sexual enslavement as being of a sexual character *per se*, and to explicitly recognize it, thus exposing the gender stratum of the offense. The problematic nature of this legal development accords with Barbara Bendont's critique, in which she claims that including rape under the crime category of "torture" conceals the gendered aspects of the crime, and thus denies the distinctive harm caused to a rape victim.[328] Her conclusion is that a separate offense of "rape" should be recognized, rather than including it under the other traditional crime categories.

The foregoing analysis demonstrates that the ICTY decisions have contributed greatly to the assimilation of sex crimes into international criminal law as a "crime against humanity", torture and enslavement. However, despite these contributions, this current legal situation is filled with flaws that are likely to create obstacles in the future. For example, the ICTY Statute defines

---

325   Ibid.
326   Ibid.
327   *Kunarac Judgment*, supra note 321, para. 157.
328   Barbara Bendont, "Gender Specific Provisions in the Statute of the ICC", in F. Lattanzi & W. Schabas, eds., *Essays on the Rome Statute of the ICC* (Editoriale, 2000) 196–197.

"rape" as a "crime against humanity" but not as a "war crime", as a "grave breach of the Geneva Convention" or as "genocide". Moreover, the offense of "crime against humanity" sets a very high burden of proof, requiring proof that the specific acts attributed to the accused were part of a widespread or systematic attack against a civilian population.[329] Hence, violations of international law in the form of sexual offenses committed during conflict against an individual woman as a result of her belonging to a certain gender will not be condemned by the international community, and the perpetrators will not be prosecuted by an international tribunal.[330] Also, although criminal sentences for acts of "rape" were imposed under the other existing crime categories in the ICTY Statutes, these judgments did not directly link the incidents of rape to these other crime categories, so it is difficult to rely on these decisions as precedents.[331]

6.2 RWANDA (ICTR)

Shocking sexual offenses occurred not only in the war in Yugoslavia. In 1994, women in Rwanda were subjected to brutal sexual abuses – rape, gang rape, sexual mutilation – all as part of the violence perpetrated by the Hutu tribe against the Tutsi tribe.[332]

Major Brent Beardsley, an assistant to the general of the peace-keeping forces present in Rwanda prior to the genocide and also for a short period during it, testified before the ICTR and described the women's bodies that he saw as follows:

> [T]wo things, really. One, when they killed women it appeared that the blows that had killed them were aimed at sexual organs, either breasts or vagina; they had been deliberately swiped or slashed in those areas. And, secondly, there was a great deal of what we came to believe was rape, where

---

329   Note that although this requirement is not stated in Article 5 of the ICTY Statute, it was recognized by the Tribunal as part of the requirements of customary international law. See *Tadic Judgment*, supra note 302, para. 646.

330   I discuss the burden of proof for a "crime against humanity" below in Part Three, subchapter 7.1: "Sex Crimes as 'Crimes against Humanity'"; see also Samantha I. Ryan, "Comment, From the Furies of Nanking to the Eumenides of the International Criminal Court: The Evolution of Sexual Assaults as International Crimes", 11 *Pace Int'l L. Rev.* 447, 471 (1999).

331   See Patricia Viseur Sellers & Kaoru Okuizumi, supra note 286, p. 94. The authors note that indictments submitted in reliance on Article 5(g) of the ICTY Statute required "sophisticated recognition of how violations of international humanitarian law are prosecuted as well as some mental gymnastics."

332   Human Rights Watch, *Shattered Lives: Sexual Violence during the Rwandan Genocide and its Aftermath* (1996) 1–2 (hereinafter *Human Rights Watch*).

the women's bodies or clothes would be ripped off their bodies, they would be lying back in a back position, their legs spread, especially in the case of very young girls. I'm talking girls as young as six, seven years of age, their vaginas would be split and swollen from obviously multiple gang rape, and then they would have been killed in that position. So they were lying in a position they had been raped; that's the position they were in.[333]

Once again, sexual abuse played a significant role in a militaristic attempt to destroy a population.[334] Again an investigative committee was sent, and again it was decided that, in light of the mountains of reports and shocking testimony, an international tribunal should be established to try the individuals responsible for the crimes. The UN Security Council again exercised its authority under Chapter VII of the UN Charter and established an international criminal court in which to prosecute the people responsible for the genocide and the other grave breaches of international law in Rwanda that occurred between January and December 1994.[335]

Like the ICTY Statute, the ICTR Statute expressly provides that rape is a "crime against humanity", in Article 3(g).[336] But this Tribunal's significant contribution to international law lies in Article 4 of the ICTR Statute, which expands the Tribunal's authority and explicitly stipulates that the crime of rape may be prosecuted as a breach of common Article 3 of the Geneva Conventions and Protocol II. By using the term "breach" and not "grave breaches" as the Geneva Conventions originally used, the ICTR Statute enabled the Tribunal to avoid dealing with the distinction between breaches and grave breaches, and thereby to add rape and other crimes that can be prosecuted to the list of

---

333   Examination-in-Chief of Brent Beardsley, former aide to the force commander, General Roméo Dallaire, UN peacekeeping mission in Rwanda, Prosecutor v. Bagasora, Kabiligi, Ntabakuze, Nsengiyumva (ICTR-98-41-T), trial transcript (3 February 2004), quoted in Kelly Dawn Askin, "Gender Crimes Jurisprudence in the ICTR: Positive Developments", 3 *J. Int'l Crim. Just.* 1007, 1008 (2005) (hereinafter *Kelly Dawn Askin, Gender Crimes Jurisprudence in the ICTR*).

334   Ibid.

335   Statute of the International Criminal Tribunal for Rwanda, 8 November 1994, UN Doc. S/RES/955 (hereinafter *ICTR Statute*).

336   However, the ICTR Statute narrowed the situations that meet the definition of "armed conflict". The offense of a "crime against humanity" must be committed as part of a widespread or systematic attack against a civilian population, on national, political, ethnic, racial or religious grounds. This contrasts with the ICTY Statute, which was broader: it provided for the possibility of prosecuting the crimes listed when they are committed in an "armed conflict," whether national or international, and directed against a civilian population. But it is important to recall that the Tribunal added the requirement that the attack be widespread or systematic as case law in the *Tadic Judgment*, discussed supra note 302.

crimes. Thus the ICTR's jurisdiction, in contrast with the ICTY, explicitly covered the crime of rape through a link to the Geneva Conventions.[337]

However, since this placed the crime of rape under the wings of international humanitarian law, the essential condition that the rape must have occurred as part of an armed conflict was allowed to cast its shadow here as well.[338] As a result, from a procedural perspective, the crime of rape was upgraded by its inclusion among the leading criminal offences. From a substantive perspective, therefore, it remained linked to the approach of the Geneva Conventions, with the problematic language of "honour" embedded therein.[339]

Reports documenting the incidents of mass rape as a weapon in the inter-ethnic and inter-gender war in Rwanda began to accumulate upon establishment of the ICTR. But nothing was done to bring the criminals to justice. Judge Navanethem Pillay, a female judge and now United Nations High Commissioner for Human Rights, was the only member of the international criminal panel who ordered the prosecutors to re-examine the reports and investigate the incidents of rape, and to hire female investigators.[340]

In the end, very few of the cases heard by the ICTR concerned sex crimes during the war. Nevertheless, a significant precedent in the Jean-Paul Akayesu[341] case broke new ground and expanded the capability of the international community to prosecute wartime sex crimes.

Akayesu, a mayor in Rwanda, was the first war criminal to be tried and convicted under international law for "genocide". The twelve counts in the original indictment did not include charges of "rape" or any other sexual abuse. However, the testimony of witnesses at trial and reliable reports submitted to the Tribunal for review, along with political pressure from several human rights organizations, resulted in the opening of another investigation. This investigation ultimately led to an amended indictment which included charges of sexual violence.

The events leading to this new investigation and amended indictment began with witness testimony. During the trial, one of the witnesses testified about

---

337   Note that Article 2 of the ICTY Statute, which refers to acts constituting grave breaches, does not include the crime of rape.

338   As feminists repeatedly noted, rape, even rape during war, is rarely so clearly connected to such an attack. See Janet Halley, Rape at Rome, supra note 3, p. 68.

339   I discuss the problematic nature of the era of the Geneva Conventions above in this Part Two, chapter 5: "The Era of Honor".

340   Adrienne Kalosieh, supra note 179, p. 123.

341   Prosecutor v. Akayesu, Case No. ICTR-96-4-T, T. Ch. I (2 September 1998) (hereinafter *Akayesu Judgment*).

the gang rape perpetrated against her six-year-old daughter. The next witness testified that she herself was raped and witnessed other women being raped. Fortunately, Judge Pillay – the only female judge among the ICTR judges – had been appointed as one of the three judges sitting on this panel. Because of her extensive experience with gender violence and international criminal law, Judge Pillay ordered an investigation into the testimony of these witnesses about these particular crimes, based on an assessment that these were not isolated incidents of rape. The judges ordered the prosecution to investigate sex crimes that were committed as part of the events which had been attributed to the accused. The judges also instructed the prosecution that if it found that sexual offenses were committed and could be attributed to the accused, then it should amend the indictment against him.[342] The original indictment was amended in 1997 and Akayesu was charged with sexual abuse as an act of "genocide", a "crime against humanity" and a breach of Article 3 of the Geneva Convention (an outrage upon human dignity, primarily by means of rape and degrading treatment).[343]

Testimony about sexual abuse of indescribable magnitude continued throughout the entire trial and eliminated any doubts about the fact that sex crimes were an inseparable part of the Rwandan genocide.[344] The amended indictment charged Akayesu with awareness of the events, and with being present during sexual abuse of Tutsi tribe members on some occasions. The factual element of the sexual abuse was described in the indictment as follows:

> Forcible sexual penetration of the vagina, anus or oral cavity by a penis and/or of the vagina or anus by some other object, and sexual abuse, such as forced nudity.

The addition of the terms "forcible" and "nudity" as part of the sexual abuse charge carries great weight. It signifies the prosecution's recognition of the psychological harm caused to victims of this kind of abuse, even in the absence of physical harm.

Akayesu was found guilty of sexual abuse committed for the purpose of genocide. The Tribunal found that the acts of abuse were accompanied by an

---

342   Jean-Paul Akayesu Faces New Charges of Sexual Violence, ICTR/INFO-9-2-059; Kelly Dawn Askin, A Decade in Human Rights Law, supra note 263. See also Richard J. Goldstone, "Prosecuting Rape as a War Crime", 34 *Case W. Res. J. Int'l L.* 277, 282 (2002); Janet Halley, Rape at Rome, supra note 3, pp. 15–16.

343   "Human Rights Watch, World Report 1999", *Women's Hum. Rts.* (Human Rights Watch, 1998) 441.

344   See Kelly Dawn Askin, War Crimes against Women, supra note 9, p. 106.

intention to destroy the Tutsi group.[345] In its decision, the Tribunal explained that the acts of rape, which were committed with an intention to physically and mentally destroy the Tutsi tribe members, and which resulted in many women and girls dying from their injuries and being murdered, constituted the grave international crime of "genocide".

The Tribunal also found Akayesu guilty of committing acts of rape and forced nakedness as inhumane acts constituting a "crime against humanity". The Tribunal defined the crime of rape as a "physical invasion of a sexual nature, committed on a person under circumstances which are coercive".[346]

By recognizing that rape harms the personal dignity of the victim, the Tribunal in effect held that rape is a form of torture, and it broadened the recognition that there is no requirement for physical contact in order to prove a sexual assault. The Tribunal emphasized that, although the crime of rape is traditionally defined under state law as "non-consensual sexual intercourse," this definition is too narrow. The Tribunal found:

> Like torture, rape is used for such purposes as intimidation, degradation, humiliation, discrimination, punishment, control or destruction of a person. Like torture, rape is a violation of personal dignity, and rape in fact constitutes torture when it is inflicted by or at the instigation of or with the consent or acquiescence of a public official or other person acting in an official capacity.[347]

The *Akayesu Judgment* significantly enhanced the potential for bringing criminals to justice for sex crimes under international law – not only because this is the first time that international law recognized "rape" as a form of "genocide". It was also the first time that an international tribunal recognized the possibility of convicting an international sex criminal for the crime of rape and other sex offences that caused mental harm to the victims, and not just physical harm.[348] Also, the decision formally recognized for the first time that gender crimes were used systematically as a tool of war and terror and that these crimes had an impact that was far more extensive in its impact than the effect on the immediate victims. In its decision, the Tribunal recognized the impact of gender crimes on the victims' families, their community, all of the groups involved in the conflict, and the entire society.[349]

---

345   *Akayesu Judgment*, supra note 341, para. 734.

346   Ibid., para. 688.

347   Ibid., para. 687.

348   Jocelyn Campanaro, supra note 208, p. 2671.

349   This decision accords with Resolution 1820, which recognized sex crimes as tools of war and terror. See supra note 33.

Other major precedents were established by another ICTR case. In 1999, Pauline Nyiramasuhuko, the former Minister of Family and Women's Development for Rwanda, and her son, Arsene Ntahobali, a former militia man, were charged with two counts related to incidents of rape – one, as a "crime against humanity", and the second, as a crime constituting a "breach of the Geneva Convention", a "war crime".[350] The indictment alleged that the mother and her son set up a roadblock in order to detain, identify, abduct, rape and kill members of the Tutsi tribe.[351] Ntahobali was charged with active participation in acts of rape and abuse, and Nyiramasuhuko was charged with using her political influence in order to encourage acts of rape.[352] They were also charged with violating Article 3 of the Geneva Conventions, on the grounds that they humiliated their victims before they were transported to their deaths, and committed acts defined as "outrages to the personal dignity, in particular humiliating and degrading treatment, by forcing [Tutsi women] to publicly undress".[353]

This indictment lead to two significant precedents: Nyiramasuhuko became the first woman convicted of "genocide" under international law, *and she also has the distinction of being the first woman charged with rape* in this context. Her conviction for rape committed by her subordinate reinforced the principle that international law will not exempt violent sex criminals of any type, whether men or women, officers or civilians.[354]

Yet, despite all of the foregoing, the ICTR unfortunately did not go far enough. Thousands of testimonies and reports documenting innumerable sexual offenses notwithstanding, the number of criminals prosecuted for sex crimes was and remains miniscule. This fact is very disturbing.

Kelly Dawn Askin maintains that the problem was that the prosecutor's office did not engage in careful and sincere investigations of the sex crimes that took place during the genocide. As a result, many of the accused were acquitted of the rape charges, some charges of sex crimes were struck before trial, and there were other setbacks and missed opportunities.[355]

---

350   Prosecutor v. Nyiramasuhuko, Indictment, Case No. ICTR-97-21-I, T. Ch. I (26 May 1997).

351   Ibid., para 6.27.

352   For an explanation of the indictment submitted against the minister, see Hirondelle News Agency, "Congolese Lawyer Dismissed From Ex-Minister's Case", *ICTR On-line*, 29 September 1999, available at http://www.hirondelle.org/hirondelle.nsf/caefd9edd48f5826c-12564cf004f793d/a5b92a5b19fc040cc125682d0080772c?opendocument (last accessed 14 April 2011).

353   Ibid.

354   Jocelyn Campanaro, supra note 208, p. 2671.

355   Kelly Dawn Askin, Gender Crimes Jurisprudence in the ICTR, supra note 333, p. 81.

As a result, despite its valuable achievements, the ICTR was criticized for not conducting appropriate investigations and for refusing to amend indictments related to sex crimes during armed conflict – despite the vast amount of evidence before the Tribunal about thousands of Rwandan women who were subjected to degradation and many kinds of gender abuses. In order to contend with the challenges it faced, the ICTR needed to integrate sensitivity to gender and therapeutic issues into its investigations, but it did not.[356]

In other words, the Gilliganian perspective[357] which pervaded the ICTY was absent from the ICTR. Perhaps more women with professional training in the treatment of sex crime victims could have been appointed as investigators and translators for the victims' interviews. Clearly, the ICTR needed to take additional steps to ensure protection for the victims and trial witnesses. This protection is an essential condition for any legal proceeding dealing with sex crimes. Witness protection is required both pre-trial, during the trial and afterwards. If the women who were victims are not given adequate protection upon returning to their villages or moving elsewhere, then the proceedings cannot achieve their aims.

More generally, Charlesworth criticizes both the ICTY and ICTR Statutes for permitting charges of rape to be brought only when the offense was part of a systematic or widespread attack. She disagrees with the *Akayesu Judgment's* determination that the incidents of rape could only constitute a breach of international humanitarian law and "genocide" because they were related to the "destruction of the community". This decision, she argues, fails to give expression to an additional and important stratum, the gender stratum:

> [In the court's account,] [r]ape is wrong, not because it is a crime of violence against women and a manifestation of male dominance, but because it is an assault on a community defined only by its racial, religious, national or ethnic composition. In this account, the violation of a woman's body is secondary to the humiliation of the group. In this sense, international criminal law incorporates a problematic public/private distinction: it operates in the public realm of the collectivity, leaving the private sphere of the individual untouched. Because the notion of the community implicated here is one defined by the men within it, the distinction has gendered consequences.[358]

---

356 Human Rights Watch, supra note 332, pp. 94–95.
357 See Carol Gilligan, supra note 35.
358 Hilary Charlesworth, Feminist Methods in International Law, supra note 60, p. 387.

Thus, despite the progress made by international law, Charlesworth deplores the historical dichotomy I discuss above,[359] which continues to distinguish between those events in which the international community intervenes and those considered "private" or "national". As I note above, this boundary overlaps to a great extent with the gender line.

To summarize, the two international tribunals established by the authority of the UN Security Council during the 1990s, the ICTY and the ICTR, are making great progress with respect to the recognition of sex crimes in international criminal law, but this path has not been completed, nor is it free of defects. It must also not be overlooked that the authority of these criminal tribunals is limited both by time and territory.[360] The investigation and prosecution of criminals for sex crimes in the international arena should not be limited to specific time periods. The international community must send a universal message that sex crimes are violent and cruel crimes constituting a grave breach of international law, and that the international community will no longer act tolerantly toward their perpetrators. In order to promote justice, primarily for the victims but for the accused as well, and to enhance the effectiveness of international law, the international community must continue to consolidate new understandings about gender issues, convert them to new principles, and, finally, integrate them as an inseparable part of international law. And indeed, as discussed below in the next subchapter, the formulation of new understandings about international criminal law took place in 1998, with the drafting of the Rome Statute.

6.3 THE ICC – A NEW STATUS QUO

During the same time period that the ICTY and the ICTR continued to issue important legal precedents, and slowly but gradually included sex crimes in the traditional crime categories, the ICC was established by authority of the Rome Statute as the first permanent international criminal court.[361] This statute currently represents a broad consensus of 113 countries and reflects the accumulated legal experience of the ad hoc tribunals. The Rome Statute is considered the modern international criminal code, creating a new status quo. This code also deals with sex crimes in international law: no longer silence, no longer an honor injury, but an offense under some of the traditional crime

---

359   See Part One, subchapter 1.1: "Private v. Public in International Humanitarian Law".

360   Marcus R. Mumford, "Building upon a Foundation of Sand: A Commentary on the International Criminal Court Treaty Conference", 8 J. *Int'l L. & Prac.* 151, 165 (1999) (hereinafter *Marcus Mumford*).

361   See supra note 4.

categories in international law. Thus the ICC's impact on all aspects of sex crimes during conflicts needs to be examined.

In 1992, the UN General Assembly decided to advance the establishment of a permanent international court – the ICC.[362] The International Law Commission was given the authority to draft a constitution to establish a permanent criminal court, and it submitted a draft constitution for the court in 1994. In addition to other controversial matters in the proposed constitution, the lack of any treatment of gender issues and sex crimes was prominent.[363]

In order for the process, which had already been frozen for decades, not to be halted again, and as a response to ongoing pressure from several women's organizations and other NGOs, the UN General Assembly established a new ad hoc committee tasked with preparing "a widely acceptable consolidated text of a convention for an international criminal court … "[364] With the cooperation and active interest of many countries and NGOs, the new committee began its complex mission of conducting negotiations over the provisions of the ICC's constitution.

The Women's Caucus for Gender Justice in the International Criminal Court (Women's Caucus) was founded in 1997. It currently represents approximately three hundred women's organizations.[365] The Women's Caucus created a strong lobby for the protection of women's rights in the international sphere, and this lobby greatly influenced the development of the ICC's statute. Due to the influence of this group, gender principles and various definitions were expanded and strengthened in the constitution's draft, including gender representation among the prosecutors, judges and the staff in general, establishment of a witness and victims unit, and creation of the position of legal adviser for gender issues, whose role is to advise the prosecutor about gender crimes.[366]

Stormy discussions were held over gender issues throughout the entire time that the statute was being drafted.[367] While the final document gives expression to some of the successes that were achieved regarding the recognition of sex crimes in the international realm, nonetheless, it also contains a number of failures concerning the treatment of these subjects, which should be addressed in the future.

---

362   G.A. Res. 47/33, UN Doc. A/Res/47/33 (1992).

363   Report of the International Law Commission on its Forty-Sixth Session, Draft Statute for an International Criminal Court, UN Doc. A/49/10 (1994).

364   G.A. Res. 50/46, UN Doc. A/Res/50/46 (1995).

365   For additional information on the Women's Caucus, see http://www.iccwomen.org/ wigjdraft1/Archives/oldWCGJ/aboutcaucus.htm (last accessed 14 April 2011).

366   Rome Statute, supra note 4, art. 42(9).

367   Jocelyn Campanaro, supra note 208, p. 2560.

As indications of success, we can find in the Rome Statute progress regarding both the explicit stipulation of a list of sex crimes as "war crimes" and "crimes against humanity", as well as consideration of gender issues in the legal process. I consider these achievements to be, in many respects, a continuation of the *Third Era*.

Article 5 of the Rome Statute provides that the ICC has jurisdiction over the following crimes: "genocide", "crimes against humanity", "war crimes",[368] and the "crime of aggression".[369] Articles 7 and 8 of the Rome Statute establish the crime categories of "crimes against humanity" and "war crimes", respectively, and include, *inter alia*, the treatment of sex crimes. Article 7(1)(g) includes, in the definition of a "crime against humanity":

> Rape, sexual slavery, enforced prostitution, forced pregnancy, enforced sterilization, or any other form of sexual violence of comparable gravity[.]

Article 8(2)(b)(xxii) includes, in the definition of a "war crime":

> rape, sexual slavery, enforced prostitution, forced pregnancy, as defined in article 7, paragraph 2 (f), enforced sterilization, or any other form of sexual violence also constituting a grave breach of the Geneva Conventions[.]

In adopting these definitions, the Rome Statute continues the *Third Era*, the new era.

In addition, following in the footsteps of the ICTY and the ICTR, the Rome Statute includes a provision requiring the member states to take into account the need for a fair representation of both women and men as judges. Similarly, the Rome Statute recognizes the need for the judges to have expertise in certain subjects, including violence against women and children.[370] The Rome Statute explicitly provides that rape is prohibited in both international conflicts and armed conflicts not of an international nature,[371] and establishes appropriate and important rules of procedures regarding testimony of sex crime victims.

Moreover, following the ICTY and the ICTR, the Rome Statute requires the establishment of a victims and witnesses unit, intended to furnish protection, security, counseling and assistance to victims, witnesses, and others

---

368   Note that in the Rome Statute the crime category of "war crimes" includes the customary crime of "grave breaches of the Geneva Conventions", which I discuss above in this Part.

369   Note that the applicability of a "crime of aggression" has been placed on hold, temporarily, until a definition is added to the Rome Statute.

370   Rome Statute, supra note 4, arts. 36(8)(a)(iii) and 38(8)(b).

371   Rome Statute, supra note 4, art. 8(e)(6).

exposed to danger because of their testimony in court.[372] The Rome Statute also instructs the unit to employ staff members who have expertise in counseling and assisting victims of sexual and gender violence.[373, 374] The establishment of this unit, as well as the requirement for judicial expertise in violence against women and children, constitute an important step in the international treatment of sex crimes.

Similarly, the Rome Statute directs the prosecutor, in investigating and prosecuting crimes, to take into account the interests and personal circumstances of the victims and witnesses, particularly regarding crimes that involve sexual and gender violence.[375] Finally, the Rome Statute instructs the court to take appropriate measures, such as an exception from the principle of public hearings, in respect of the dignity and privacy of witnesses and victims when the crimes involve sexual and gender violence.[376]

The Rome Statute marks additional significant progress regarding the gender issue in Article 7(1)(h), which explicitly states that persecution on the basis of gender is a "crime against humanity". It provides:

> Persecution against any identifiable group or collectivity on political, racial, national, ethnic, cultural, religious, *gender* as defined in paragraph 3, or other grounds that are universally recognized as impermissible under international law ....

> [Emphasis added by the author]

The inclusion of the term "gender" in this list recognizes that a group of women or men is a group that can be persecuted, and thus a group with needs and

---

372   Article 43(6) of the Rome Statute, supra note 4, orders the establishment of this unit and provides:

> The Registrar shall set up a Victims and Witnesses Unit within the Registry. This Unit shall provide, in consultation with the Office of the Prosecutor, protective measures and security arrangements, counseling and other appropriate assistance for witnesses, victims who appear before the Court, and others who are at risk on account of testimony given by such witnesses. The Unit shall include staff with expertise in trauma, including trauma related to crimes of sexual violence.

373   Note the distinction between the two kinds of crimes: sexual crimes and gender crimes. This appears to be the first recognition under international law that sex crimes contain a concealed, additional crime which requires its own expertise. In other words, we must treat sexual crimes not only as a form of inter-ethnic violence, but also as a form of gendered violence, as I claim in this book. See also infra note 465.

374   Rome Statute, supra note 4, art. 42(9).

375   Again, note the distinction between sexual violence and gender violence.

376   Rome Statute, supra note 4, art. 68(1). Again, this provision distinguishes between the two types of crimes.

concerns that are unique to it and which must be protected under international law.[377] But this victory is also limited: the group "gender" is the only group whose definition is limited. Article 7(3) provides that "gender", for purposes of the Rome Statute, "refers to the two sexes, male and female, within the context of society".[378]

Not surprisingly, the implications of this definition can be interpreted in various ways. On the one hand, the definition of gender violence includes an attack on either a man or a woman, during a conflict, based on gender but not of a sexual character, such as, for example, an attack against fertility (forced sterilization or forced pregnancy, enslavement of women by means of marriage for performing domestic labor and providing sexual services, etc.).[379] This recognition is very important. On the other hand, the restrictive definition of the group "gender" creates a sense that the persecution of this group is different from persecution on the basis of other group belonging,[380] and perhaps even hints that its weight is inferior.[381]

It is noteworthy that the special treatment of persecution on the basis of gender did not exist in the draft of the statute submitted by the Preparatory

---

377   Ibid.

378   The argument about the limitation of this definition is actually less problematic from the female perspective, although it should be noted that this definition does not conform to the original intention to apply the definition to other situations of gender violence, such as persecution of homosexuals, carriers of the AIDS virus, or any mistreatment or discrimination against them. Janet Halley, Rape at Rome, supra note 3, p. 82. See also Valerie Oosterveld, "The Definition of 'Gender' in the Rome Statute of the International Criminal Court: A Step Forward or Back for International Criminal Justice?", 18 *Harvard Hum. Rts. J.* 55, 81 (2005) (hereinafter *Valerie Oosterveld, The Definition of Gender*"); see also Jocelyn Campanaro, supra note 208; Brook Sari Moshan, supra note 7, p. 184. Furthermore, Moshan and Campanaro are concerned about the narrow meaning given to the term "gender". In their opinion, this narrow meaning will restrict the actions of the court in prosecuting and convicting for crimes on the basis of gender. In Moshan's view, these crimes will be considered "somehow less grave" than, for example, crimes on the basis of race.

379   Janet Halley, Rape at Rome, supra note 3, pp. 83–84.

380   The definition of the term, which is defined so narrowly, leaves no room for a more expansive interpretation, such as a social or gendered construct. The statutory definition perpetuates the supposedly "natural" binary division into man/woman. According to Judith Butler, the category of sex is not natural, and will never be capable of definition. Judith Butler, *Gender Trouble: Feminism and the Subversion of Identity* (Routledge, 1990) 112. Thus, gender cannot only be understood within its social context, but must also be understood as a part of the arrangement which establishes the sex categories. The gendered arrangement that divides us into men and women is the cultural-discursive system by which sex is created, *as if* it is pre-discursive or pre-cultural; the two sexes are created by it, as if they are not constructed but rather are "natural". Ibid.

381   Brook Sari Moshan, supra note 7, p. 183.

Committee, and it is the outcome of one of the most contentious discussions in the Rome Conference. This controversy touched on two principle issues: one, the concern that gender would be interpreted as a social construct or as economic status; and second, the concern of Arab countries that the prohibition would supply ammunition against them and their domestic laws, which establish criminal prohibitions against homosexual relations.[382] This narrow approach to gender exists in other places in the Rome Statute, as discussed in Part Three.

6.4 SUMMARY: TOWARDS A NEW ERA?

Along with its great number of advantages and legal innovations, the Rome Statute chose to ignore many important judgments decided by the ICTY and the ICTR, as I discuss in Part Three below. For example, the Rome Statute does not list sex crimes among the prohibited acts which can constitute the offense of "genocide", nor is gender specified as a group that is protected under this crime category. Similarly, the international crime category of "grave breaches of the Geneva Conventions", which appears under the provision "war crimes", does not explicitly include sex crimes.[383] Moreover, the list of sexual offenses is not detailed and cannot be understood without future judicial interpretation. Many questions arise from these provisions. For example, *does forced nudity constitute sexual assault? What are the elements of the crime of rape under the Rome Statute?* These deficiencies are particularly prominent when they are compared with those terms that the Rome Statute chose to define explicitly, such as "gender", which is defined as "the two sexes, male or female, within the context of society", or the offense of "forced pregnancy", which is defined as requiring the intent of affecting the ethnic composition of a population or carrying out other grave violations of international law.[384]

To summarize, two eras have passed. No more silence. No longer only an honor injury. A new era has already begun, an era in which sex crimes are recognized as physical and psychological injuries, an era in which special care

---

382   Marcus Mumford, supra note 360, p. 206.

383   Rome Statute, supra note 4, art. 8(a). The Rome Statute chose to adopt the original language of the Geneva Conventions, and not to adopt the innovative version in the ICTR Statute, which explicitly included the offense of rape as a breach of the Geneva Convention. See the discussion on this point above in subchapter 6.2: "Rwanda (ICTR)".

384   Rome Statute, supra note 4, arts. 7(3) and 7(2)(f). As to the definition of "forced pregnancy", it once again reflects an ethno-centric, groupist, masculinist point of view, if you will. Why must the purpose of the forced impregnation be analyzed? Isn't forced pregnancy itself, because of a male desire for control and subordination, not sufficient?

for victims of sex crimes is part of international law.[385] The Rome Statute explicitly recognizes gender crimes and embeds sex crimes within some of the existing, traditional crime categories. However, *is this sufficient? Is this the change that we had hoped for when we embarked on our journey?*

Certainly not. The journey is incomplete.

---

385   Discussion of the developments in international law would be incomplete without mentioning the Hybrid/Mixed Courts. These courts are called 'hybrid' or "mixed" because domestic judges (from the same countries in which the alleged crimes were committed) sit on judicial panels alongside the international judges. These courts apply international law and the state's domestic law in parallel. Mixed courts have been established by agreements between the Security Council and national governments. Prior to each agreement, there is intensive negotiation between the state and the UN, leading to substantially different structures and jurisdictions for each of these courts. To date, five of these courts have been established, in Cambodia, Sierra Leone, East Timor, Kosovo and Lebanon. See Amichai Cohen, "The International Criminal Law" in Robbie Sabel, ed., *International Law* (Hebrew University, 2d ed., 2010) 347, 364–366 [Hebrew] (hereinafter *Amichai Cohen*); Antonio Cassese, "The Role of Internationlized Courts and Tribunals in the Fight Against International Criminality", in Cesare P.R. Romano, *et al.*, eds., *Internationalized Criminal Courts: Sierra Leone, East Timor, Kosovo, and Cambodia* (Oxford, 2004) 3, 35. For example, Articles 2 and 3 of the Statute of the Special Court for Sierra Leone, 16 January 2002, treat sex crimes as crimes against humanity and as a fundamental breach of common Article 3 of the Geneva Conventions and Protocol II, respectively, in the framework of that international court. Statute of the Special Court for Sierra Leone, 16 January 2002, UN Doc S/RES/1315.

Part Three

SEX AND GENDER CRIMES UNDER THE NEW INTERNATIONAL LAW AND A PROPOSED SOLUTION

INTRODUCTION TO PART THREE

"I want you to ask this man something," Baba said. He said it to Karim, but looked directly at the Russian officer. "Ask him where his shame is."
They spoke. "He says this is war. There is no shame in war."
"Tell him he's wrong. War doesn't negate decency. It demands it, even more than in times of peace."

Khaled Hosseini, *The Kite Runner* (p. 107)

The purpose of this Part Three is to describe the existing crime categories under international law as they stand today, and to explain how sex crimes fit into each and every category within this framework. The discussion will connect the threads of the critique collected during the historical journey undertaken above in Part Two, and examine their relevance to the current framework. This will illustrate the insufficiency of the current legal structure and lay the foundation for the proposal of a more suitable legal framework.

In this Part, I will argue that the inclusion of sexual offenses in only two of the crime categories that exist in international criminal law – "war crime" and "crime against humanity" – is insufficient. Similarly, I claim that there is no justification for not including the group of gender as a protected group in the framework of the crime of "genocide", and I query why sex crimes are absent from the list of prohibited acts of this international crime. I emphasize that this was an historical error and a missed opportunity, when the Rome Statute chose to leave sex crimes out of the explicit list of "grave breaches of the Geneva Conventions" and to adhere to the original version of this crime. This choice casts a shadow over the treatment of sex crimes as part of customary international law.[386] I then argue that the proper solution is to leave the existing crime categories unchanged, to insert sex crimes into the crime categories of "genocide" and "grave breaches of the Geneva Conventions" as well, and, in addition, because of the unique aspects of gendered sex crimes, to recognize them as a discrete international crime.

---

386 One may question how the Rome Statute can alter the written and signed Geneva Conventions. My response is that one of the purposes of the Rome Statute is the creation of a modern criminal code. Copying the grave breaches in the spirit of the era in which they were written would bring us back to the Era of Honor. In my opinion, the modern criminal code must specify the list of crimes in the spirit of the era in which *it* is written, by adopting the broad and up-to-date interpretations which have been given to these international crimes by the various international tribunals. See also Brook Sari Moshan, *supra* note 7, p. 428.

Chapter 7

SUMMARY OF ACHIEVEMENTS AND PROBLEMS

Today, rape and other sexual offenses are crimes that are punishable under international law. Moreover, sexual offenses are no longer offenses against honor, but rather "war crimes" and "crimes against humanity". The Rome Statute, the most modern criminal code, explicitly deals with sex crimes, including rape, a not insignificant achievement. But alongside these achievements, there are some striking flaws in the current situation.

Despite the *Akayesu Judgment*,[387] the Rome Statute includes the crime of "genocide" in its original formulation, as it was drafted after WWII in 1948, toward the end of the *Era of Silence*. In accordance with the era in which this crime category was written, sex crimes were not included as one of the five prohibited acts that give rise to the "crime of genocide" and gender is not a protected group under this crime category.

Article 8 of the Rome Statute, which enumerates the war crimes and also incorporates the criminal prohibition against a grave breach of the Geneva Conventions, disregards the ICTY jurisprudence, according to which rape and other forms of sexual assault constitute a "grave breach of the Geneva Conventions". It also disregards the ICTR Statute's adoption of this jurisprudence and its explicit provision that rape constitutes a "breach of the Geneva Conventions".[388] Contrary to the recommendations of the Preparatory Committee, the final version of the Rome Statute *does not include sex crimes in the framework of the list of grave breaches of the Geneva Conventions.*[389] As I describe above,[390] this omission ignores the gravity of these crimes. Moreover, it misses a golden opportunity to adopt the broad interpretation

---

387   *Akayesu Judgment*, supra note 341.

388   Article 4 of the ICTR Statute, which is entitled "Violations of Article 3 common to the Geneva Conventions and of Additional Protocol II", provides, *inter alia*, in subarticle (e) that the following acts constitute "serious violations of Article 3 common to the Geneva Conventions ... and of Additional Protocol II":

> Outrages upon personal dignity, in particular humiliating and degrading treatment, *rape, enforced prostitution* and any form of indecent assault[.]"
>
> [Emphasis added by author]

389   Brook Sari Moshan, supra note 7, p. 428.

390   Part Two, chapter 5: "The Era of Honor".

and define the explicit prohibition against sex crimes as part of customary international law.[391]

Surely, the explicit recognition in the Rome Statute of sex crimes in the framework of the crime categories of "war crimes" that are "serious violations" of the laws of war and "crimes against humanity" is essential and important. However, excluding sex crimes from the grave crime of "genocide" and from the list of offenses included in "war crimes" that are "grave breaches of the Geneva Conventions" continues to undermine the recognition of sex crimes as grave international crimes.

In the following chapters, I analyze the current situation from the perspective of the existing crime categories in the Rome Statute. First, I will analyze the way that sex crimes are included in the framework of the crime categories of "crime against humanity" and "war crimes" that are "other serious violations" of the laws of war, and I discuss their absence from the list of "war crimes" that are "grave breaches of the Geneva Conventions". I discuss the crime of "genocide" and the decision of the Rome Statute to leave sex crimes and the group of gender out of this crime category. I then demonstrate that certain aspects of sexual offenses are likely to meet the requirements of *all* of the crime categories that exist *today* in international law. Finally, beyond the call to include the sex crimes under each of the existing crime categories, I seek to demonstrate that this essential step would be insufficient, because the international gender crime would still be left without adequate treatment. In conclusion, I attempt to propose a new crime category, which would be recognized alongside the traditional crime categories.

7.1 SEX CRIMES AS "CRIMES AGAINST HUMANITY"

The crime category of "crimes against humanity" includes especially egregious illegal acts, which strike at the heart of human rights. The definition of this crime is intended to protect the entire human population.

Although the statutes governing the prior international criminal courts discussed in this book included the prohibition against "crimes against humanity",[392] each statute contained its own elements for establishing a "crime

---

391   I discuss the importance of recognizing sex crimes as part of the customary international law above in Part Two, subchapter 5.1: "Geneva Conventions".

392   The Nuremberg Statute of 1945 constitutes the first statute in which the provision regarding "crimes against humanity" was written as a normative rule whose perpetrators would bear individual criminal responsibility. Article 6(c), which was written in the *Era of Silence*, lists the following crimes: "murder, extermination, enslavement, deportation, and other inhumane acts committed against any civilian population, before or during the war" and, subsequently,

against humanity".[393] Prior to the Rome Statute, the international community had never explicitly determined the list of crimes constituting a "crime against humanity". Consequently, the explicit definition of sexual crimes in the Rome Statute and their inclusion as a "crime against humanity" constitutes a binding obligation on the entire human community.[394]

Article 7(1)(g) of the Rome Statute provides that the crime category of "crimes against humanity" includes sexual offenses. The formulation of this Article is reminiscent of Article 8, discussed below, which deals with "war crimes". Without a doubt, the inclusion of sexual offenses as "crimes against humanity" in an independent manner, not dependent on other crimes, emphasizes the importance of sex crimes under international law as a separate and independent crime. Sex crimes are no longer "sub-tenants" slipping in through the interpretation of other broader categories of crime, such as degrading treatment or torture.

Article 7(1) establishes the crime category of "crime against humanity" in the following formulation:

> For the purpose of this Statute, "crime against humanity" means any of the following acts when committed as part of a widespread or systematic attack directed against any civilian population, with knowledge of the attack ....

Based on this formulation, the offense includes three requirements: (i) the act must be part of a widespread or systematic attack; (ii) the attacked population must be a civilian population; and (iii) the perpetrator must have knowledge that his acts are part of the widespread or systematic attack. These elements are cumulative. Their significance is discussed in the document "Elements of the Crimes" (EOC), published by the ICC.[395] According to this document:

> The last two elements for each crime against humanity describe the context in which the conduct must take place. These elements clarify the requisite participation in and knowledge of a widespread or systematic attack against a civilian population. However, the last element should not be interpreted

---

CCL10 from 1945 authorized domestic courts to prosecute the Nazi criminals on the basis of the crimes defined in the Nuremberg Statute. Subsequently, this crime category was also included in the Statutes of the ICTY, the ICTR and the ICC. See Orna Ben-Naftali & Yuval Shany, supra note 81, pp. 268–269.

393   Jelena Pejic, "The International Criminal Court Statute: An Appraisal of the Rome Package", 34 *Int'l Law* 65, 73 (2000).

394   Nicole Eva Erb, supra note 219, p. 432.

395   This document was published by the ICC pursuant to Article 9 of the Rome Statute, supra note 4. With respect to each of the categories enumerated in Articles 6–8 of the Rome Statute, this document details the elements that must be proven for conviction. Finalized Draft Text of the Elements of Crime, 2 November 2000, PCNICC/2000/1/Add.2 (hereinafter *EOC*).

as requiring proof that the perpetrator had knowledge of all characteristics of the attack or the precise details of the plan or policy of the State or organization. In the case of an emerging widespread or systematic attack against a civilian population, the intent clause of the last element indicates that this mental element is satisfied if the perpetrator intended to further such an attack.[396]

Legal problems with all aspects of the prosecution of sex criminals are apparent from the elements of the offense.

The first problem arises from the element of the crime that requires a widespread or systematic attack – meaning, an intensive attack from the perspective of quantity or quality. This element is not a common characteristic of sex crimes during conflict. Most sexual attacks are perpetrated in a sporadic manner and not as part of an overall, organized plan. Therefore, it would not be possible to bring their perpetrators to justice because of this requirement.[397] Moreover, the language used in Article 7 as to "part of a widespread or systematic attack" indicates that sex crimes must rise to a certain level of severity in order for the international law to intervene and condemn them by means of criminal sanctions. This requirement creates a genuine obstacle for future prosecutions of sex crimes. Worse, this problematic language regarding the threshold for intervention could be interpreted as hinting that a certain degree of sexual violence would be tolerated and acceptable under international law.

Ben-Naftali and Shany try to minimize the results of this requirement by claiming that, with respect to the qualitative dimension, a systematic attack can be the result of a single act, so long as that attack has a political or ideological purpose. They support their position with the *Blaskic* decision, in which the Tribunal stated:

> The systematic character refers to four elements which for the purposes of this case may be expressed as follows: the existence of a political objective, a plan pursuant to which the attack is perpetrated, or an ideology, in the broad sense of the word, that is, to destroy, persecute or weaken a community; the perpetration of a criminal act on a very large scale against a group of civilians or the repeated and continuous commission of inhumane acts linked to one another; the preparation and use of significant public or private resources, whether military or other; the implication of high-level

---

396   Ibid., art. 7, introduction, para. 2.

397   See Women's Caucus for Gender Justice in the International Criminal Court Recommendations and Commentary (December 1997), Part III, Recommendation 2 (hereinafter *WCGJ Recommendations December 1997*); Janet Halley, Rape at Rome, supra note 3, p. 71.

political and/or military authorities in the definition and establishment of the methodical plan.[398]

Ben-Naftali and Shany also claim that, with respect to the quantitative dimension, the multiple acts could be committed by several different people, because of the requirement that a "crime against humanity" be perpetrated as part of the attack.[399] As a result, in their opinion, it would be possible to convict someone for a "crime against humanity" even if the perpetrator commits only one offense perpetrated against a single person.

It is noteworthy that the language of this provision in the Rome Statute finally separates the link that had existed in the past between sexual crimes and armed conflict – a requirement that became outdated both from a factual perspective and a legal perspective. From a factual perspective, many women were raped under dictatorial regimes like Chile, even though there was no conflict. From a legal perspective, the CCL10 from 1945[400] had already separated "crimes against humanity" from "war crimes" and "crimes against the peace".[401]

The absence of the requirement for a connection to conflict had become the norm in the Genocide Conventions[402] in 1948, as I discuss below in subchapter 7.3, "Genocide or Femicide". This detachment is also expressed in the relevant provisions of the ICTY Statute and the ICTR Statute. Although at first the ICTY Statute maintained this connection, in the *Tadic Case*, the ICTY found that the absence of a requirement that there be a connection between "crimes against humanity" and an international armed conflict reflects the customary international law.[403]

---

398   Orna Ben-Naftali & Yuval Shany, supra note 81, pp. 270–271, citing Prosecutor v. Blaskic, Case No. IT-95-14-T, T. Ch. I. (ICTY, 3 March 2000), para. 203.

399   Ibid., citing para. 206.

400   Upon the conclusion of the Nuremberg and Tokyo trials, the Allied forces enacted the CCL10 law to grant jurisdiction to national and military courts to prosecute Nazis for the crimes defined in the Nuremburg Statute, which I discussed above in Part Two, subchapter 4.2: "The Nuremberg (IMT) and Tokyo (IMTFE) Tribunals"; see CCL10, supra note 227.

401   I note again that the difference in the elements between the two crimes is not insignificant. This is because the burden of proof required of the prosecution is immeasurably high for proving "crimes against humanity". The requirement for proof of a widespread or systematic attack as a basis for the crimes sets a high requirement, particularly when the matter concerns sexual crimes, as I discuss in this Part Three, subchapter 7.1: "Sex Crimes as 'Crimes against Humanity'". See, e.g., Theodor Meron, supra note 202, p. 425.

402   Convention on the Prevention and Punishment of the Crime of Genocide, 9 December 1948, 78 U.N.T.S. 277 (hereinafter *Genocide Convention*).

403   *Tadic Judgment*, supra note 302, para. 627; Orna Ben-Naftali and Yuval Shany, supra note 81, pp. 268–269.

Moreover, the requirement that the injured population be a civilian population is difficult to comprehend. *Why is it not sufficient that the victims are
human beings?* When we are dealing with crimes, in general, and sex crimes,
in particular, *why should any relevance be given to their attributes as civilians,
or their ethnic belonging?* It could be viewed as simply a matter of semantics,
i.e., that the term "civilian population" is meant only to distinguish them
from the "military population". However, the wording is deeply significant.
The protection of the law must apply to every human, as such. Moreover,
assuming that the connection between the category of "crimes against humanity" and the situation of a war has indeed been separated, then this detachment is more consistent with an expansion of the identity of the potential
victims, so that it would also include military personnel. This is because in
the absence of a war, they are not granted protection under the category of
"war crimes".

To summarize, with respect to sexual offenses, there is no basis for including
the requirement of a widespread or systematic attack in the crime category of
"crime against humanity", nor is it appropriate to include any reference to a
"civilian population". The crime category must be aimed at protecting the common human denominator of any population and it should be applicable during
times of peace as well.[404]

Ironically, despite explicitly providing that committing any of the sex crimes
specified on the list are a "crime against humanity", Article 7 is likely to restrict
the ICC's capability to prosecute sexual offenses.[405] In addition, the complexity
of the criminal act points also to the complexity of the *mens rea* required for a
conviction – an element that requires knowledge that the act is part of a widespread or systematic attack. This requirement is stated in paragraph 4 of the
elements of the crime category of "crime against humanity of rape" in EOC,
Article 7(1)(g)-1, as follows:

---

404   Janet Halley, Rape at Rome, supra note 3, p. 78, quoting "The Women's Caucus for Gender
Justice in the International Criminal Court Recommendations and Commentary on Crimes
against Humanity" (March 1998) (hereinafter *WCGJ Recommendations (March 1998)*):

> Crimes against humanity should … encompass the enumerated crimes of official as well
> as non-state actors when committed on a widespread or systematic basis against any
> population *whether in war or peace* ….
>
> [Emphasis added by the author]

For additional discussion of the feminist position that the ICC should have complementary
jurisdiction if national courts do not act against violations of women's human rights during
times of peace, see ibid., pp. 67–69.

405   Brook Sari Moshan, supra note 7, p. 182.

The perpetrator knew that the conduct was part of or intended the conduct to be part of a widespread or systematic attack directed against a civilian population.

This provision of the EOC establishes the elements of the offense that are necessary for a rape conviction under international law. The crime is formulated in gender-neutral language, as follows (internal citations omitted):

Article 7 (1) (g)-1
Crime against humanity of rape
Elements
1. The perpetrator invaded the body of a person by conduct resulting in penetration, however slight, of any part of the body of the victim or of the perpetrator with a sexual organ, or of the anal or genital opening of the victim with any object or any other part of the body.
2. The invasion was committed by force, or by threat of force or coercion, such as that caused by fear of violence, duress, detention, psychological oppression or abuse of power, against such person or another person, or by taking advantage of a coercive environment, or the invasion was committed against a person incapable of giving genuine consent.
3. The conduct was committed as part of a widespread or systematic attack directed against a civilian population.
4. The perpetrator knew that the conduct was part of or intended the conduct to be part of a widespread or systematic attack directed against a civilian population.

The EOC provides that the offense is based on the following elements: (1) penetration; (2) force, threat of force or taking advantage of a coercive environment; (3) the crime is part of a widespread or systematic attack against a civilian population; and (4) the perpetrator knew the crime was part of a widespread or systematic attack against a civilian population, or intended the conduct to be part of such an attack.

The first element, penetration, is drafted broadly and in gender-neutral language. In my opinion, however, it should prohibit every act whose purpose is sexual humiliation. For example, it appears that "enforced nudity" is not a prohibited criminal act under the definition of this crime. The second element should also be more broad. As I discuss both above and below, the extreme imbalance of power between the parties is sufficient for the presumption that during battle there is always a coercive environment. This presumption of fact should have been incorporated into the second paragraph of the elements of the crime.

The third and fourth elements, requiring the systematic or widespread nature of the attack and the perpetrator's knowledge about the attack's qualitative or quantitative extent, makes it difficult and perhaps even impossible to bring sex criminals to justice under international law. As I discuss above, these elements regarding the extent of the attack are not suited to crimes such as sexual offenses. This requirement demonstrates that the purpose of the protection is inter-ethnic protection – not inter-gender protection. As a result, if a rape is committed because of sexual desire, but not as part of a broad attack against another ethnic group, then international law would not punish the perpetrator. Similarly, the threshold *mens rea* required for the offense is too high. Even if it were proven that a reasonable person would have known that the rape was part of the widespread or systematic attack, this would be insufficient – it must be shown that the perpetrator knew or intended that the conduct would be part of the widespread or systematic attack. This requirement is unambiguous and difficult to prove, and negligence is not a basis for conviction.

The elements of the crime are not the only problems with Article 7(1)(g). This Article includes a list of additional sex crimes and does not only include rape. On the one hand, this list could enhance the possibilities for prosecuting future criminals who commit these other sexual offenses. It is also more just because the other sexual offenses are explicitly stated, making it unnecessary to engage in linguistic gymnastics to make the crime of rape cover various other sex crimes.[406] On the other hand, however, this list has the potential to function as a double-edged sword. The specific examples of sexual offenses listed in Article 7(1)(g) – rape, sexual slavery, enforced prostitution, forced pregnancy, and enforced sterilization – could be interpreted as a closed list. Such an interpretation would close the court's doors to future prosecution of sexual offenses that have not even been defined yet by international law.[407]

I examined other examples of the Rome Statute's narrow approach earlier in this section. For example, I discussed the restrictive definition of the crime of "forced pregnancy". One of the elements of "forced pregnancy" is that the intent of the forced pregnancy must be to affect the ethnic composition of the population. In other words, the issue of a conviction under this crime category will be examined from a collective, racist, militaristic point of view. Therefore, it seems that forced pregnancy stemming from male urges, from the desire for control and gender degradation, would not be covered by this offense.

The foregoing discussion illustrates that it is difficult to prove the elements of the offense "crime against humanity", particularly the high standard for the required mental state of knowledge, and that these elements are likely

---

406   Patricia Viseur Sellers & Kaoru Okuizumi, supra note 286, p. 78.
407   Jocelyn Campanaro, supra note 208, p. 2574.

to make it difficult for the international community to prosecute sex criminals. This is because sex criminals sometimes lack the high *mens rea* standard of "knowledge" or "intention". Sometimes, they use sexual force as part of a battle celebration, or even due to a genuine belief that the inferior gender wants to have sex with the victorious ethnic group, the powerful conqueror.

7.2 SEX CRIMES AS "WAR CRIMES"

The crime category of "war crimes" is comprised of those acts constituting violations of the laws of international humanitarian law. Not every violation of international humanitarian law carries criminal responsibility – only grave breaches.[408] Article 8 of the Rome Statute sets forth a broad list of all of the war crimes, most of which are also crimes under customary international law.

The origin of the crime category of "war crime" is the Nuremberg Statute of 1945,[409] which was formulated in the *Era of Silence*. This explains why it does not define sex crimes as "breaches of the laws of war". I mark the start of the second era, the *Era of Honor*, as beginning in 1949, upon the signing of the Geneva Conventions. These treaties provided that "grave breaches" of humanitarian norms in the framework of an international armed conflict carry individual criminal responsibility and are subject to universal legal jurisdiction. As noted above,[410] in accordance with the *Era of Honor* in which it was written, the list of grave breaches of the Geneva Conventions in the Nuremberg Statute does not include sex crimes. Article 3 common to all four Geneva Conventions, which provides that some of these acts are also prohibited in the context of a conflict that is not international, similarly does not include sex crimes in the list of prohibitions. The Additional Protocols to the Geneva Conventions expanded the list of grave breaches and added a provision converting any violation of their provisions to a "grave breach" imposing criminal liability not only on the state but also on the perpetrator.[411]

The ICTY's holding in the *Tadic Judgment* interpreted the crime category of "war crimes" expansively and determined that these crimes also include serious violations of the norms governing a non-international armed conflict. This position was adopted by the ICTR Statute[412] and, as discussed below, by the Rome Statute.[413]

---

408 Orna Ben-Naftali & Yuval Shany, supra note 81, pp. 260–261.
409 IMT Charter, supra note 205.
410 Part Two, subchapter 5.1: "Geneva Conventions".
411 Orna Ben-Naftali & Yuval Shany, supra note 81, p. 262.
412 ICTR Statute, supra note 335, art. 4.
413 Rome Statute, supra note 4, arts. 8(2)(c) – 8(2)(f).

Article 8(1) of the Rome Statute establishes the crime category of "war crimes" and provides the following conditions for this crime:

> The Court shall have jurisdiction in respect of war crimes in particular when committed as part of a plan or policy or as part of a large-scale commission of such crimes.

According to this formulation, a "war crime" must be carried out as part of a plan or policy or as part of a large-scale commission of these crimes. Again, the element of the systematic or widespread nature of the attack has been included in the definition of the crime. But, as I argue above,[414] the majority of sexual attacks take place in a sporadic manner and not as part of an overarching organized plan, which makes it difficult to bring the perpetrators to justice.[415] It is important to note, however, that as opposed to the "crime against humanity", in the offense established by Article 8 of the Rome Statute the requirement as to the attack's systematic nature has been moderated. The Article includes the phrase "in particular" with respect to "war crimes" that are perpetrated as part of a plan or policy, or part of a large-scale commission. Therefore, it is possible that this category will be extended to cover sexual violence that is not systematic and planned. In the view of Ben-Naftali and Shany, this provision should be understood as setting a threshold for the severity of the events over which the ICC will have jurisdiction (a threshold that distinguishes between which incidents are subject to the court's jurisdiction and which are not).[416]

Article 8, which discusses the prohibition against "war crimes", distinguishes between "outrages upon personal dignity" in Articles 8(2)(b)(xxi) and 8(2)(c)(ii), and the prohibition against sexual crimes in Articles 8(2)(b)(xxii) and 8(2)(e)(vi). This distinction recognizes what international law had refused to recognize in the past: sexual violence involves not only an injury to a person's honor and name, but also a potentially severe injury to the person's mind and body. This important distinction indicates that the Rome Statute can eliminate some of the historic obstacles which had made it difficult to prosecute sex crimes and had viewed them as abstract crimes against a person's honor, as

---

414   Part Three, subchapter 7.1: "Sex Crimes as 'Crimes against Humanity'".

415   WCGJ Recommendations (December 1997), supra note 397, Part III, Recommendation 2; Janet Halley, Rape at Rome, supra note 3, p. 68.

416   See Orna Ben-Naftali & Yuval Shany, supra note 81, p. 265, discussing Article 53(1)(c) of the Rome Statute, which grants discretion to the prosecutor to weigh the severity of the crime in the context of the decision whether to initiate proceedings. These two provisions will work together to restrict the number of incidents brought before the court.

I discuss above.[417] Moreover, Article 8(2)(e)(vi) provides that sexual offenses shall be recognized as "war crimes" even in conflicts not of an international character. This provision erodes part of the private/public and the national/international dichotomies that existed in the past, as I discuss above.[418]

"War crimes" can be committed by military personnel against an enemy's soldiers or its civilians, and by civilians against the enemy's soldiers or its civilians. So long as there is a connection to an armed conflict, a civilian can commit a war crime against a civilian.[419]

Article 8 distinguishes the Rome Statute from the statutes of the international criminal tribunals established in the past, and it includes the most current and comprehensive codification to date of the offense of "war crimes". In the past, it was customary to discuss "grave breaches of the Geneva Conventions" and other "war crimes" as separate crime categories. Article 8 sets forth both of these offenses in one crime category. Article 8 effectively categorizes war crimes into four groups: the *first group* of crimes in Article 8(2)(a) are acts committed in the framework of an international armed conflict. This provision contains the eight war crimes that constitute "grave breaches" of the Geneva Conventions, literally copying the latter. Of course, sexual crimes do not appear in this group, given the spirit of the *Era of Honor* in which the Geneva Conventions were written. The *second group* contains the offenses in Article 8(2)(b), which are also relevant to international armed conflicts and which include 26 "war crimes" that are violations of other laws. Sex crimes are in the "respectable" place of 22nd on the list. The *third group* contains the crimes in Article 8(2)(c). This provision defines "war crimes" as acts perpetrated in the framework of an armed conflict that is not international, but distinguishes them from sporadic acts of violence within a state.[420] This third group is defined in a general manner, and includes killing, torture, outrages upon dignity and degradation, taking hostages and carrying out executions without a fair trial. This group is also silent about sexual offenses, in accordance with the emphasis on honor in the Geneva Conventions; it does not explicitly specify sex crimes. The *fourth group* contains the crimes in Article 8(2)(e), which also deals with non-international armed conflicts, and distinguishes between sporadic acts of violence, riots and internal disturbances (to which it does not apply)

---

417 Part Two, chapter 5: "The Era of Honor".

418 Part One, subchapter 1.1: "Private v. Public in International Humanitarian Law".

419 However, crimes by one state's soldiers against its own soldiers are not covered by the crime category of "war crimes" under international law. Orna Ben-Naftali & Yuval Shany, supra note 81, p. 261.

420 Rome Statute, supra note 4, art. 8(2)(d).

and protracted conflict between the government and organized armed groups or between such groups (to which it does apply).[421] According to Ben-Naftali and Shany, this provision contains 12 crimes that are ranked less severely.[422] Sex crimes are in sixth place on the list.

Hence, sex crimes are mentioned in two of the four groups. True, no longer silence, no longer only a crime against honor. However, there is no doubt that the inferiority of these crimes is still prominent, as compared to the "truly grave" crimes. This attitude about their inferiority prevails to this day, in an era in which these crimes have become specific and independent crimes. The final version of the Rome Statute does not adopt the broad interpretation of the ICTY and ICTR, and does not explicitly list sex crimes as grave breaches, or even breaches, of the Geneva Conventions.[423] This omission ignores the gravity of these crimes, and, even more significantly, it potentially misses a golden opportunity to include an explicit prohibition against sex crimes as part of customary international law. This version was adopted despite the fact that the ICTY had interpreted "war crimes" as including sex crimes, and Article 4 of the ICTR Statute had explicitly included sex crimes as "war crimes".[424]

Rana Lehr-Lehnardt suggests another reason why it is especially important to allow the prosecution of sex crimes as "grave breaches of the Geneva Conventions". Although the offense of a "crime against humanity" presents rape as a crime that injures humanity in general, an indictment for rape as a "grave breach of the Geneva Conventions" highlights the nature of the crime, distinguishes it from other crimes, and exposes the gender stratum of the crime – by emphasizing the harm to the individual as an individual, rather than to society as society:

> [L]isting rape as a war crime in addition to a crime against humanity was an advancement for women, because it reinforced the notion that the injury was suffered by the individual instead of by the society, or even more generally, by humanity, which is inferred by listing rape as a crime against humanity.[425]

It is also noteworthy that Article 8(2)(e), which enumerates crimes related to national conflicts, distinguishes between the specific sex crimes listed in

---

421   Rome Statute, supra note 4, arts. 8(2)(e), 8(2)(f).
422   Orna Ben-Naftali and Yuval Shany, supra note 81, p. 264.
423   Jocelyn Campanaro, supra note 208, p. 2571; Nicole Eva Erb, supra note 219, p. 428.
424   I discuss the importance of recognizing sex crimes as part of the customary law above in Part Two, subchapter 5.1: "Geneva Conventions".
425   Rana Lehr-Lehnardt, supra note 13, p. 341.

the first part of Article 8(2)(e)(vi) from the other forms of sexual violence that constitute a "serious violation" of the Article 3 common to the Geneva Conventions, which are specified in the latter part of this provision, as follows:

> (e) Other serious violations of the laws and customs applicable in armed conflicts not of an international character, within the established framework of international law, namely, any of the following acts: ....
>
> (vi) Committing rape, sexual slavery, enforced prostitution, forced pregnancy, as defined in article 7, paragraph 2 (f), enforced sterilization, and any other form of sexual violence also constituting a serious violation of article 3 common to the four Geneva Conventions; ....

From this perspective, the Rome Statute reflects a retreat from the progressive development of international criminal law. Moreover, this strange division between how the criminal prohibitions apply in international conflicts and in non-international conflicts is not consistent with the *Tadic Judgment*. In that case, as noted, the ICTY held that the same logic should apply to the two types of conflict situations and that the same prohibitions are applicable to both.[426]

Despite this failure to clearly determine that sex crimes are a "grave breach of the Geneva Conventions", it is important to note that the category of "war crimes" covered by Article 8(2)(b) includes the following general provision: "Other serious violations of the law and customs applicable in international armed conflict". Article 8(2)(b)(xxii) then lists the following sex crimes: rape, sexual slavery, enforced prostitution, forced pregnancy, enforced sterilization, "or any other form of sexual violence also constituting a grave breach of the Geneva Conventions". Arguably, the fact that Article 8(2)(b)(xxii) uses the phrase "any other form of sexual violence also constituting a grave breach" indicates that sex crimes and sexual violence constitute a grave breach of the customary law. However, this interpretation is not self-evident; the ICC will need to rule on this issue. If this interpretation were to be adopted, it could be claimed that sex crimes are part of the customary law.[427] An advantage of this interpretation is that it would be consistent with the decisions of the ICTY and ICTR.

---

426   *Tadic Case*, supra note 275, paras. 119–124; Orna Ben-Naftali & Yuval Shany, supra note 81, p. 265, fn. 86.
427   Nicole Eva Erb, supra note 219, p. 430; Valerie Oosterveld, The Definition of Gender, supra note 378, pp. 81–82.

Articles 8(2)(b)(xxii) and 8(2)(e)(vi)-1 of the EOC clarify the elements of the crime required for conviction of the crime of rape as a "war crime" under international law. The offense is worded in gender neutral language, as follows:

Article 8 (2) (b) (xxii)-1
War crime of rape
Elements
1. The perpetrator invaded the body of a person by conduct resulting in penetration, however slight, of any part of the body of the victim or of the perpetrator with a sexual organ, or of the anal or genital opening of the victim with any object or any other part of the body.

2. The invasion was committed by force, or by threat of force or coercion, such as that caused by fear of violence, duress, detention, psychological oppression or abuse of power, against such person or another person, or by taking advantage of a coercive environment, or the invasion was committed against a person incapable of giving genuine consent.

3. The conduct took place in the context of and was associated with an international armed conflict.

4. The perpetrator was aware of factual circumstances that established the existence of an armed conflict.

Hence, the crime is based on the following elements: (1) penetration; (2) force, the threat of force, or taking advantage of a coercive environment; (3) the crime took place in the context of an international armed conflict; and (4) the perpetrator was aware of the circumstances establishing the existence of the armed conflict.

In effect, if we compare the elements of the crime of rape as a "war crime" under international law to the elements of the crime of rape as a "crime against humanity", we see that they are identical, apart from the requirement for the systematic or widespread nature of the attack, which has been replaced with the requirement for the existence of an armed conflict.

The *mens rea*, element, just like the *mens rea* for rape in the context of a "crime against humanity", requires a high standard of "awareness" about the occurrence of the conflict between tribes/nations/ethnic/racial groups. Once again, the prosecution must meet a very high burden of proof – and anyone who is negligent, deliberately ignores the circumstances, or is simply indifferent to them, will be immune from prosecution. Therefore, once again, an opportunity has been squandered to prosecute those rapists whose motives derive not from the external conflict, but rather from the inter-gender conflict intensified by the war, where national norms become irrelevant and the international norms make an exception and exclude this crime.

In contrast with the two crime categories discussed above, "crime against humanity" and "war crime", the crime category of "genocide" which is discussed in the next subsection, is silent about sex crimes. The offense of "genocide" does not include sex crimes as prohibited acts in any manner, nor does it establish gender as a protected group – even though the Rome Statute could easily have done so by adopting the precedents established in the ICTY and ICTR.

7.3 "GENOCIDE" OR "FEMICIDE"

Sex crimes are completely absent from the crime category of "genocide". Because of the gravity of this crime and the fact that it continues to occur,[428] in this subchapter I elaborate on this crime category, its origins, and its importance with respect to the possibility of it including sex crimes.

The term "genocide" is based on the Greek word "*genos*", which means "race, nationality or tribe", combined with the Latin word "*caedere*" meaning "to kill".[429] Article 2 of the Convention on the Prevention and Punishment of the Crime of Genocide[430] defines "genocide" as follows:

[A]ny of the following acts committed with intent to destroy, in whole or in part, a national, ethnical, racial or religious group, as such:

  (a) Killing members of the group;
  (b) Causing serious bodily or mental harm to members of the group;
  (c) Deliberately inflicting on the group conditions of life calculated to bring about its physical destruction in whole or in part;
  (d) Imposing measures intended to prevent births within the group;
  (e) Forcibly transferring children of the group to another group.

The Article emphasizes that in order for acts to be recognized as "genocide" from a legal perspective, the defined crimes ("prohibited acts") must be perpetrated with an intent to destroy ("special intent") a racial, ethnic, religious or

---

428 For example, genocide by means of sexual assault, sterilization and forced pregnancy was prominent in Croatia and Bosnia-Herzegovina between 1991–1994. Along with mass murder, the Serbs, whose aim was to expel and exterminate non-Serb people, sexually attacked women and sometimes men, in a mass manner. See Catharine MacKinnon, Genocide's Sexuality, supra note 1.

429 The Jewish Polish jurisprudent Raphael Lemkin first coined the term "genocide" in 1944.

430 Genocide Convention, supra note 402.

national group as such ("protected group"). Today "genocide" is considered the most egregious international crime,[431] the "crime of crimes" in the words of the ICTR.[432]

The UN General Assembly was the first institution to treat "genocide" as an autonomous crime in adopting the decision in December 1948 that led to the Genocide Convention.[433] The Genocide Convention emphasized the differences between this crime and other international crimes: "genocide" does not have to be part of a systematic or widespread attack, and it may be perpetrated during either war or peace. The definition of "genocide" was copied verbatim into Article 4 of the ICTY Statute, Article 2 of the ICTR Statute, and Article 6 of the Rome Statute.

The Genocide Convention was drafted soon after the atrocities of the Holocaust in Europe, and, in the spirit of the silence of that era, its drafters never address sexual atrocities in an explicit manner. Also, in defining the *mens rea* that is required for genocide, which as noted is a "special intent" (*dolus specialis*)[434] to destroy all or part of a group as such, the group "gender" is not mentioned as a protected group.

This narrow definition raises two important questions. *First*, do the crimes defined in the Genocide Convention also include sexual acts as a prohibited act? *Second*, if one of the five prohibited acts is committed with the intention to destroy a group based on the gender of the victims, then are the elements of the crime established, i.e., is a group based on gender a protected group?[435]

7.3.1 Sex Crimes as Crimes of Genocide

Between the months of April and July, 1994, as part of the organized slaughter of a half million to a million people which took place in Rwanda in less than four months, the Hutus raped and sexually abused Tutsi women on a massive

---

431   Orna Ben-Naftali and Yuval Shany, supra note 81, p. 272.

432   Prosecutor v. Akayesu, Case No. ICTR-96-4-T, T. Ch. I. (2 October 1998).

433   The Genocide Convention, supra note 402, has been signed by 133 countries and it is considered to reflect the norms of customary law. It was given this recognition by the International Court of Justice in The Hague (*ICJ*) in its advisory opinion regarding reservations to the Genocide Convention. See Reservations to the Convention on the Prevention and Punishment of the Crime of Genocide, 1951 ICJ 15, p. 24.

434   The "special intent" (*dolus specialis*) is in addition, of course, to the criminal intention that accompanies the physical act.

435   Of course, these acts are likely to be "crimes against humanity" if they meet the definition of this crime category – for example, if these crimes were committed in the framework of a systematic or widespread attack, as I discuss above in this Part Three, subchapter 7.1: "Sex Crimes as 'Crimes against Humanity'".

scale, as part of their attempt to eradicate and genetically destroy the Tutsi ethnic group. *Should these acts be considered "genocide"?*[436] In other words, *do acts of rape which were as a matter of fact committed as part of a genocide also constitute "genocide" as a matter of law?*

As discussed above,[437] in the precedent-setting *Akayesu Judgment* the ICTR found that genocide can be committed by means of rape.[438] Similarly, the view has developed in international law that "genocide" can be perpetrated by means of "forced pregnancy", primarily in societies in which the infant's group belonging is based on the father (hence the forced pregnancies are intended to destroy the mother's group, because if the children belong to the father's group, then the former will be diminished until it completely disappears).

Article 2 of the Genocide Convention, as discussed above, provides that the forcible transfer of children from the group sought to be destroyed to another group is a crime defined as "genocide". Unlike the four other prohibited acts which involve a physical injury to the group sought to be destroyed, this crime theoretically does not involve a physical injury. Transferring children is not an act that necessarily causes a bodily injury to the members of the group intended to be destroyed. In contrast, rape and forced pregnancy are crimes that both involve a physical harm yet they are not on the list of prohibited acts.

This distinction is also interesting in light of the fact that "cultural extinction" does not constitute "genocide", despite the attempt that was made to include it in the Genocide Convention.[439] In other words, the attempt to destroy a specific culture through a prohibition on use of its language, customs or certain institutions which characterize that culture is not included in the definition of "genocide", which focuses on the physical destruction of the group. Yet the crime of transferring children without a physical injury is enumerated among the defined crimes. This lack of coherence points to potential directions for this crime's development.[440]

One of the possibilities for the development of this crime that is relevant for our purposes is the addition of sex crimes to the list of the prohibited acts.

---

436   See similar questions raised by Catharine MacKinnon in Catharine A. MacKinnon, Genocide's Sexuality, *supra* note 1, pp. 313–315.

437   Part Two, subchapter 6.2: "Rwanda (ICTR)".

438   *Akayesu Judgment*, *supra* note 341.

439   Thomas W. Simon, "Defining Genocide", 15 *Wis. Int'l L.J.* 243, 252 (1996) (hereinafter *Thomas Simon*).

440   Orna Ben-Naftali and Yuval Shany, *supra* note 81, p. 276.

7.3.2 GENDER AS A PROTECTED GROUP

The basis for group belonging in the Genocide Convention is narrowly defined. The draft of the Genocide Convention explicitly rejected including groups based on language, politics and economics. The challenge, as Thomas Simon explains, is to find groups with a basis of belonging that fits the Genocide Convention's language.[441]

International tribunals have applied the purposive theory of statutory interpretation when ruling on charges of "genocide". For example, the ICTR held that the provision was intended to recognize acts of genocide not only to the groups explicitly listed in the Genocide Convention, so long as the injured group comprises a "stable" group, meaning a group to which belonging is determined from birth.[442] This test is an "objective" test of belonging from birth. According to this interpretation, destroying women because they belong to the group women should constitute genocide, in addition to the limited number of examples presented by the Genocide Convention.

A broader interpretation was adopted by the ICTY, which determined on the basis of the explanatory notes to the Genocide Convention that the drafters' intention was to protect "stable" groups, defined objectively and as to which belonging is not dependent upon its members' individual will, but it found that it is more appropriate to view the definition of a group from the point of view of those who are trying to separate it from the community.[443] Thus, the test applied by the Tribunal is broader than the "objective" test (although it is only from the perpetrators' point of view and not from the "target" group's perspective).[444] This interpretation would also allow the argument to be made that gender is a basis of belonging intended by the Genocide Convention, in addition to the limited number of examples it presents.

---

441   Thomas Simon, supra note 439, p. 245.

442   *Akayesu Judgment*, supra note 341, para. 516.

443   Prosecutor v. Krstic, Case No. IT-98-3-T, T. Ch. I (ICTY, 2 August 2001) paras. 559–560; Prosecutor v. Jelisic, ICTY Case No. IT-95-10-T, T. Ch. I (14 December 1999) paras. 70–71.

444   Thomas W. Simon, *The Laws of Genocide: Prescriptions for a Just World* (Praeger Security International, 2007) 101 (hereinafter *Thomas Simon, The Laws of Genocide*). I note that Ben-Naftali and Shany raise an important argument: the exclusion of a certain group by someone who is not from among its rank, on the basis of belonging from birth, is not necessarily more severe than exclusion of a certain group whose basis of belonging is cultural. Orna Ben-Naftali & Yuval Shany, supra note 81, p. 275. In other words, even if this interpretation were to expand the basis for group belonging beyond the groups listed in the provision defining the crime, it is hard to contest the internal logic. In any event, gender would be a protected group based on either of these interpretations.

In the *Rutaganda Judgment*[445] the ICTR held that objective criteria do not always exist for defining a certain group as a national, ethnical, racial or religious group, and that in any event a subjective test must be applied, as noted. This subjective test requires an examination of whether a certain group was identified by society as a unique group. Of course, the injury to the group must stem from the specific intent to destroy it in order to constitute "genocide".[446] Simon proposes a similar test: the "negative group" test. This test looks at the negative definition of a group as seen from the perspective of the perpetrators of the crime.[447] This necessitates finding evidence about the identity and collective negative treatment of the specific group by the perpetrator. Application of this test would surely lead to a conclusion that the attempt to destroy a group on the basis of gender is "genocide".[448]

Furthermore, the Rome Statute recognizes the group of gender in Article 7(1)(h), which expressly provides that persecution on the basis of gender is a "crime against humanity":

> Persecution against any identifiable group or collectivity on political, racial, national, ethnic, cultural, religious, *gender* as defined in paragraph 3, or other grounds that are universally recognized as impermissible under international law.
>
> [Emphasis added by the author]

Inclusion of the term "gender" in this provision acknowledges that a group of women is a group that can be persecuted. This is a group with its own special needs and concerns, deserving of recognition and special treatment under international law.[449]

7.3.3 "Genocide" – From Silence to a New Era

The Genocide Convention adopted at the end of WWII includes the specific, horrific acts that the Nazis used in their attempt to annihilate the Jewish people. However, it did so without sufficient attention to the crimes committed against women at the time. The sex victims who survived this time

---

445   Prosecutor v. Rutaganda, Case No. ICTR-96-3, T. Ch. I (6 December 1999) para. 56.

446   *Dolus specialis,* see *Akayesu Judgment*, supra note 341, para. 517.

447   In his later book, Simon elaborates on this test. See Thomas Simon, The Laws of Genocide, supra note 444, p. 102.

448   Prosecutor v. Kayishema and Ruzindana, Case No. ICTR-95-1-T, T. Ch. II (21 May 1999) para. 98 (hereinafter *Kayishema Judgment*).

449   Ibid.

period were compelled to remain silent – while the rest of the world preferred to forget and to ignore, as if any discussions about sexuality would desecrate the memory of the dead, the living, or even the Holocaust itself.[450] WWII broke out during the period of silencing – the *Era of Silence*. Clearly, the Genocide Convention's silence about sex crimes is not because sexual atrocities did not occur.

However, the historical context sheds light only on the first version of the crime of "genocide". Since 1948, many more women have been raped, international decisions have been handed down, and treaties have been signed. The *Era of Silence* was replaced with the *Era of Honor* and, over time, this era also came to an end and the *Third Era* has begun. These developments should have been reflected in the Rome Statute.

During the genocide in Bosnia, the Serbs raped their Muslim neighbors in the name of "Greater Serbia". Serbian forces raped women of Muslim and Croatian ethnic origin in order to "produce" Serb babies, and they used sex as a means of reproduction on an ethnic basis primarily in order to create a dominant ethnic group, as an inherent part of the "ethnic cleansing" policy of the Serbs.[451] *Is this not genocide?*

As noted above, the ICTY and the ICTR determined that under certain circumstances rape is one of the defined crimes for the offense of "genocide".[452] However, this development was left out of the Rome Statute.

Some feminists argue that including the crimes of rape and other sexual offenses in the crime category of "genocide" would subordinate feminism to nationalism, by obscuring the fact that rape takes place on both sides of the battle lines.[453] In my opinion, including rape in the existing crime categories under international criminal law in general, and in the crime category of "genocide" in particular, would mean treating this crime with the seriousness that it deserves. Naming and defining this crime does not legitimize some

---

450   MacKinnon draws attention to the analysis of Joan Ringelheim, who interviewed Jewish women survivors of the Holocaust:

> Although there are many stories about sexual abuse, they are not easy to come by. Some think it inappropriate to talk about these matters; discussions about sexuality desecrate the memories of the dead, or the living, or the Holocaust itself. For others, it is simply too difficult and painful. Still others think it may be a trivial issue.

Joan Ringelheim, supra note 185, p. 745. See Catharine MacKinnon, "Genocide's Sexuality", supra note 1, p. 317.

451   Catharine MacKinnon, Genocide's Sexuality, supra note 1, pp. 314–315.

452   See Part Two, subchapters 6.1: "The Former Yugoslavia (ICTY)" and 6.2: "Rwanda (ICTR)".

453   Karen Engle, supra note 70, pp. 785–794, 798–803.

other illegal act. Excluding the offense of rape from the crime category of "genocide" actually diminishes this crime's stature, making it an inferior crime as compared to other international crimes.

7.4 THE MENTAL STATE - MENS REA

In international criminal law, as in domestic criminal law, there is a requirement that the *actus reus* of the crime be accompanied by the *mens rea*. However, a uniform rule of customary law defining the requisite *mens rea* for the commission of an international crime has not yet crystallized.[454]

The first instance in which international treaty law addresses *mens rea* is Article 2 of the Genocide Conventions, which requires a special intent to destroy all or part of one of the protected groups, as I discuss above.[455] Article 1 of the Convention against Torture and Articles 85(3) and (4) of Protocol I to the Geneva Conventions also require this highest level of *mens rea* – "intentionally" and "willfully", respectively.

Article 30 of the Rome Statute provides the first definition for the *mens rea* required for conviction of an international crime enumerated in the Statute. This provision states that, in general, "intent" and "knowledge" are the required *mens rea*. Article 30 states that, unless otherwise provided by the Rome Statute, the requisite *mens rea* is the intention to engage in the conduct, and, if there are consequences, then the intent to cause that consequence is required, or at least an awareness that the ordinary course of events will lead to this consequence, as follows (footnote added):

1. Unless otherwise provided, a person shall be criminally responsible and liable for punishment for a crime within the jurisdiction of the Court only if the material elements are committed with intent and knowledge.

2. For the purposes of this article, a person has intent where:
   (a) In relation to conduct, that person means to engage in the conduct;
   (b) In relation to a consequence, that person means to cause that consequence or is aware that it will occur in the ordinary course of events.

---

454   Antonio Cassese, supra note 59, p. 159.

455   Part Three, subchapter 7.3: "'Genocide' or 'Femicide'".

456   The interpretation given to the term "knowingly" by the ICTY is related to the mental state of "intention" or "criminal recklessness". By contrast, the jurisprudence of the ICTR is more strict and requires premeditation. See *Kayishema Judgment*, supra note 448, paras. 138–139.

3. For the purposes of this article, "knowledge" means awareness that a circumstance exists or a consequence will occur in the ordinary course of events. "Know" and "knowingly"[456] shall be construed accordingly.

The foregoing provides that this is a residual requirement. In other words, so long as the elements of the crime itself do not establish a different requirement regarding *mens rea*, then the requisite *mens rea* is the high standard of "intent" and "knowledge".[457] This high level for the *mens rea* element is intended to avoid the possibility that, by default, international criminal law would allow convictions on the basis of the *mens rea* of negligence.[458]

The provisions of the Rome Statute concerning sex crimes as a "war crime" and as a "crime against humanity" are silent regarding *mens rea*. Consequently, the *mens rea* that they require is determined under Article 30 – "intent" and "knowledge". Thus, the Rome Statute establishes a stringent and high level for the *mens rea* required to convict for sex crimes, as compared to that required by the domestic laws of nation-states, or even customary international law.[459]

This high level for *mens rea*, which makes it difficult for the international prosecutor to prove *mens rea*, is problematic in both conservative and modern societies. Moreover, as I discuss above,[460] even when there is an awareness that the woman is not interested in the sexual act, there is a tendency to assume that she does not know what is best for her and that she is not capable of making wise decisions. This argument is amplified during war, particularly from the perspective of the soldier who sees himself as representing the superior race/religion/tribe/nationality. Therefore, if the soldier willfully ignores the victim's subordination and her inability to object, then the prosecution will not be able to meet its burden of proof.

Another aspect of this problem is the deeply rooted gender construct, which I discuss above, of an active, conquering masculinity and a passive, conquered femininity. The problematic nature of this construct is intensified on the battlefield, where the soldier hero represents the stronger group. In other words, the blurring of the senses and the moral ambiguity of conflict

---

457   This can also be understood from paragraph 2 of the general introduction to the EOC, supra note 395. As stated in Article 30 of the Rome Statute, unless otherwise provided, a person shall be criminally responsible and liable for punishment for a crime within the jurisdiction of the ICC only if the material elements are committed with intent and knowledge. See also Antonio Cassese, supra note 59, p. 176.

458   Amichai Cohen, supra note 385, p. 399.

459   Antonio Cassese, supra note 59, p. 176.

460   Part Two, subchapter 3.3.2: "The Guilty Mind – *Mens Rea*".

sharpen the gender gaps that still exist, remnants of patriarchal culture. These gender gaps lead to a dominating and conscious sexual activeness and a presumption that the victims' will to survive is the same as consent to the act of rape.[461]

Therefore, because the crime categories of "war crime" and "crime against humanity" require "knowledge" that a circumstance exists or conduct will occur, then it requires "awareness" about the conflict or the inter-ethnic attack taking place – and the prosecution has to meet a very high burden of proof. This high burden of proof will lead to acquittals of those who are negligent or willfully ignorant by objective standards. The result will be an inability to prosecute rapists whose motives are unrelated to the external inter-ethnic conflict, but are related to the inter-gender conflict which is intensified during battle – a conflict in which the national norms are typically irrelevant and the international norms make an exception and exclude these sex and gender atrocities from coverage of the law.

---

461 This issue is at the heart of Janet Halley's article, "Rape in Berlin: Reconsidering the Criminalization of Rape in the International Law of Armed Conflict", 9(1) *Melb. J.I.L.* 78 (2008) (hereinafter *Janet Halley, Rape in Berlin*). *Are sexual relations between the enemy's soldiers and a conquered population rape?* Or *are they within the women's decision-making capacity in the context of war?* I discuss this issue, focusing on the question of consent, below in Part Three, subchapter 9.5.2: "The Presumption of Nonconsent".

Chapter 8

PART OF EXISTING CRIME CATEGORIES OR A DISCRETE CRIME?

The ICC Statute has partly lifted the traditional immunity historically granted by international law to sex criminals. However, much remains to be done. The problems under the Rome Statute stem from the artificial means by which international law has tried to adapt all sex crimes to the existing crime categories.

As Charlesworth and Chinkin describe this problem:

> They do not move beyond the "add women and stir" approach ... and would not lead to a restructuring of the international legal system that would address the continued subordination of women.[462]

The struggle for inclusion of sexual offenses in the framework of the traditional crime categories that have existed for so long in international law conceals the unique characteristics of sex crimes. This struggle describes sexual offenses solely as crimes of violence, or to be more precise, as crimes of violence which in the past had been excluded from coverage of the general norms, as expressed by Agamben,[463] and which have now come to be recognized as one example among many violent crimes. The problem is that the crime categories that have been developed by men, intended for the male point of view, are too narrow to address the complexities of sex offenses.

The drafters of the Rome Statute were aware of some of these complexities, as I discuss above,[464] but only marginally. As noted, the Rome Statute requires that the prosecution appoint advisers who have expertise in sexual

---

462   Hilary Charlesworth & Christine Chinkin, The Boundaries of International Law, supra note 44, p. 335.

463   Giorgio Agamben, supra note 6. Agamben discusses the abandoned person, the one who is excluded from the norm, such that in effect a violation of the excluded person is immune. My claim is that excluding sexual offenses from the criminal law – taking them outside of the general norms – leaves the victim's body permissible. The exclusion of sexual offenses in the past, and the current inadequate legal arrangement, places the victims of sexual offenses outside the shelter of the law.

464   Part Three, subchapter 6.3: "The ICC – A New Status Quo".

and gender violence.[465, 466] In other words, the Rome Statute recognized that sexual offenses are composed of two strata – general and gendered. The Rome Statute further instructs the prosecutor to consider at the time of investigating witnesses the interests and personal circumstances of the victims of sexual violence and gender violence – another recognition of the two strata of the offense.

In a nutshell, my claim is as follows: rape is both a violent crime and a sexual crime.[467] Violent, in the physical sense; and sexual in the sense that it is a part of the social subordination of women that already exists. During conflict, national law has never been relevant, and international law did not address sexual offenses. As it developed, international law regarded sexual offenses as crimes against honor, while ignoring the two components of its physical aspect and its sexual aspect. Finally, in its current stage of development, the *New Status Quo* of the *Third Era*, international law has placed sex crimes within the framework of the existing categories for violent crimes – and it thereby ignores the second stratum, the sexual/gender stratum. Thus, the recognition of sex crimes in the Rome Statute solely in the framework of the existing violent crime categories does not furnish a comprehensive solution to this problem, because it continues to ignore the gender stratum of these crimes.

Using the existing crime categories to cover sexual crimes of violence equates rape with other international crimes. Yes, rape is a violent international crime, but it also contains within it an additional stratum – by being a tool for feminine subordination, sexual satisfaction, masculine empowerment, and perpetuation of male domination over the female gender.

As discussed above,[468] reform as to how sexual offenses are handled at the national level is well underway. These reforms have taken place in both the legislative and enforcement arenas, and they have begun to have an impact.

Nevertheless, during conflict, when the lights are out, the seeds of gender violence sprout and grow into that old patriarchal monster. During times of conflict, rape is again in many cases excluded from the general norms. The battlefield becomes the battle site for subordination on the basis of

---

465   I discuss this distinction between the two types of offenses above in Part Two, subchapter 6.3: "The ICC - A New Status Quo". As noted, this provision can be understood as recognition that sexual offenses embody an additional offense that requires expertise and treatment – that they are not only sexual offenses as part of inter-ethnic violence but also offenses that are part of the inter-gender violence. See also supra note 373.

466   Rome Statute, supra note 4, art. 42(8)(b).

467   See Janet Halley, Rape at Rome, supra note 3, p. 58–59.

468   Part One, chapter 3: "Rape as a Unique Crime under Domestic Law".

hate towards the other and the desire for revenge. Women become a double prey. Although some women now serve in combat positions,[469] they are also still used to glorify the fighters, injure the enemy, and raise morale – and through their own subordination and weakness, they perpetuate the weakness of the enemy and enable his destruction.

Halley critiques the feministic discourse regarding sex crimes during war, claiming that men are also tortured and murdered in war, not only women.[470] And I maintain: not exactly. Women are tortured and murdered, and they are *also* raped. They are murdered and tortured as the enemy, and they are tortured and raped as women. The dualism continues.

My conclusion is unambiguous: both crimes must be punished – both the murder and torture, as well as the rape. Men are not tortured because of their gender; they are tortured because of their ethnicity, nationality, or politics. Yet women are tortured not only because of their ethnicity, nationality, or politics – they are also tortured and raped because they are women. On both sides of the battle lines.

Furthermore, when international third parties arrive to liberate those who have been conquered or to help maintain peace, they too rape and forcibly conquer the female gender. Prior to October 2003, this phenomenon of "peace forces" committing sexual crimes was passed over in silence, or by a shrugging of the shoulders, or perhaps a hidden smile that slipped out, saying: "boys will be boys". For example, Dianne Otto cites an incident from the early 1990s in which a high-ranking UN officer in Cambodia, Under-Secretary General Yashusui Akashi, casually dismissed harsh allegations that the Bulgarian peacekeeping forces were sexually exploiting girls in Cambodia "by saying that he was not a puritan and that '18-year-old, hot-blooded soldiers' have a right to chase 'young beautiful beings of the opposite sex'".[471]

MacKinnon discusses a woman who wrote to her about some of the UN soldiers who participated in the rape of Muslim and Croatian women taken from the rape/death camps under Serbian control.[472] She comments on the perverse contradiction inherent in the image of UN soldiers raping those

---

469   In the interest of full disclosure, I note that the author of this book has served as an officer and trained soldiers.

470   Janet Halley, Rape at Rome, supra note 3, p. 86.

471   Dianne Otto, "Making Sense of Zero Tolerance Policies in Peacekeeping Sexual Economies", in Vanessa Munro & Carl F. Stychin, eds., *Sexuality and the Law: Feminist Engagements* (Oxon/Routledge-Cavendish, 2007) 265 (hereinafter *Dianne Otto, Making Sense of Zero Tolerance*).

472   Catharine MacKinnon, Rape, Genocide and Women's Human Rights, supra note 265, pp. 192–193.

whom they have come to rescue and protect.[473] She presents this as an example of the fearless male bonding that crosses official borders.[474]

In October 2003, UN General Secretary Kofi Annan instituted the "zero-tolerance" policy, which forbade representatives of the UN peace-keeping forces from engaging in a range of activities related to sexual exploitation of the local population in locations in which UN forces are stationed. For example, "peacekeeping forces" are not permitted (i) to engage in sex for money; (ii) to engage in sex with anyone under the age of 18, even if the local law permits it; or (iii) to engage in sexual relations with anyone being given assistance by the UN representatives. Annan explained the policy as follows: "Based on inherently unequal power dynamics ... these relations undermine the credibility and integrity of UN efforts."[475]

As I discuss above,[476] Halley supports the narrative of the Geneva Conventions.[477] In her opinion, the Geneva Conventions protect women as human beings, and add an additional protection rooted in a sincere concern for their wellbeing. If so, and on the basis of this logic, then she should support the double protection offered here. The purpose of this double protection is not to abolish the protection granted to men, but to grant appropriate and suitable legal coverage to those victims who have been excluded until now.

Regarding rape as only a crime of violence but not as a gender crime ignores the social reality in which rape is perpetrated primarily by men against women. Of course, it is a violent phenomenon, but violence of a very specific type.[478]

Gender crimes against women take place both during conflicts and in their absence. In recent decades, the patriarchal grip on society has somewhat

---

473   Ibid., p. 192.

474   Ibid., pp. 192–193. MacKinnon describes reports about one of the former officers of the United Nations Protection Forces (UNPROFOR) who complied with a Serbian commander's request to supply him with Muslim girls for sex.

475   Secretary-General, "Special Measures for Protection from Sexual Exploitation and Abuse", Secretary-General's Bulletin, 9 October 2003, U.N. Doc. ST/SGD/2003/13. For more about this policy, discussion and critique, see Dianne Otto, Making Sense of Zero Tolerance, supra note 471. Otto critiques the "zero tolerance" approach, claiming that sometimes "survival sex" or "sex in exchange for payment" is all that the local population has left in order to survive. This claim is similar to Halley's questions: *under these circumstances, is it rape? Or perhaps it is within the decision-making capacity of women in the framework of war?* Janet Halley, Rape in Berlin, supra note 461. In my view, the response to these queries is unambiguous: consent in a coercive environment is not consent. I discuss this issue further below in Part Three, subchapter 9.5.2: "The Presumption of Nonconsent".

476   Part Two, subchapter 5.1: "Geneva Conventions".

477   See Janet Halley, Rape at Rome, supra note 3, p. 61.

478   See Orit Kamir, Israel's Dignity-based Feminism, supra note 94, p. 161.

declined in Western liberal countries. Unfortunately, it has not completely dis-
appeared. It has diminished; it has begun to be buried. However, the seeds of
patriarchy sprout during conflicts. In other words, the subordination becomes
intensified under conditions of battle – a woman who is both a member of the
enemy's ethnic group and also female is doubly exposed to harm, both as the
enemy and as the vulnerable gender. Her vulnerability to day-to-day rape is
intensified by conflict, when it becomes a tool of war which, in the past, was
considered legitimate both during war and peace. Her submission is twofold –
it is both a gender submission and an ethnic submission. Recognizing rape and
sexual offenses as discrete international crimes will draw a clear red line of
prohibition, during both war and peace.

In the darkness of battle, women were excluded from the protection of the
law and abandoned. Their bodies were permitted to any taker, under the protection of the law. The attempt to include women in the general norms according to their masculine characteristics has left gaps in those places where there
are differences. The attempt to construct rape and address it as ordinary violence, rather than as a phenomenon with characteristically typical gender
attributes, inevitably overlooks significant aspects of this issue, and thus can
never be effective.

Including sexual crimes of violence under the existing crime categories
equates rape with other international crimes, which is an important step – but
it is not sufficient. Only by breaking the masculine dichotomy can the second
stratum be exposed – the gender stratum. This goal can only be accomplished
by recognizing a new international crime category, one which can address the
unique features of these crimes and succeed in protecting and enforcing all of
its violent, sexual *and* gendered aspects.[479]

---

479 This argument would also be the correct response to those feminist scholars who claim
that including rape and other sexual offenses in the crime category of "genocide" would subordinate feminism to nationalism by concealing the fact that rape takes place on both sides of the
battle lines. See above in this Part, subchapter 7.3.3: "'Genocide' – From Silence to a New Era".
Moreover, this argument is also the response to those who are concerned about the rights of the
accused. A precisely defined offense will counter the arguments about violations of rule of law
and the prohibition against retroactivity which I discuss above, supra notes 206, 318.

Chapter 9

SEX AND GENDER CRIMES AS A DISCRETE CRIME – A PRELIMINARY DRAFT

A new international crime category prohibiting sexual offenses must address all the disadvantages of the current law. In this chapter, I aim to present the priorities that international legislators should consider when drafting and adopting the new crime category of "sex and gender crimes".

9.1 DEFINING THE VICTIMS

The new crime category must be blind to race, religion, sexual orientation, political or citizenship belonging and, especially, the victim's gender. In other words, the crime category must be directed towards the broadest common human denominator, so as to cover each person in every population. This point is significant because, although women are the victims of the vast majority of sex crimes, sometimes men are also the victims of sexual offenses.[480] Moreover, treating only women as potential victims of sex crimes would be a double-edged sword, labeling them as perpetual victims. Every victim of sexual offenses needs to be protected by international law.[481] In this regard, the new crime category will be distinguished from the offense of "crimes against humanity".

9.2 DEFINING THE SITUATION

This crime must be applicable not only to international and non-international armed conflicts, but, like "genocide" and "crimes against humanity", it should also apply in peacetime.[482] When a national government fails to provide a

---

480   See supra notes 8, 167, 300.

481   This conflicts with Orit Kamir's view that, although the definition of the crime should explicitly address both genders, it should be drafted in feminine language. She argues, rightfully so, that this is the gender harmed far more frequently. Orit Kamir, Israel's Dignity-based Feminism, supra note 94, p. 171. Although I think the point is valid, in my opinion, the crime should be drafted in gender-neutral language in order to peel the label of victim off the female gender, and to emphasize that the harm to the male gender is no less severe.

482   Janet Halley, Rape at Rome, supra note 3, p. 68; WCGJ Recommendations (March 1998), supra note 404.

solution to sexual offenses, then international law must intervene. When the government or the current political climate excludes sex crimes from the general norms of the rule of law, then international law must make decisions on behalf of that dark government, tearing down those walls between private and public which used to stand everywhere. In this regard, the new crime category will be distinguished from the offense of "war crimes".

9.3 THE COERCED SEXUAL ACT

The definition of the prohibited sexual act must be as broad as possible. In this context, I adopt the ICTY's decision in *Furundzija*,[483] which strengthened the law according to which rape can be considered torture, and, for the first time, proposed a broad and concise definition of the crime of rape.[484] The ICTY ruled that the objective of humanitarian law is the protection of a person's dignity, without regard to gender. Finding that a forced oral act is a degrading act that harms a person's dignity, the ICTY ruled that forced oral penetration is as traumatic to the victim as genital or anal penetration. The ICTY found that any other conclusion would rest on a shaky foundation, and would undermine the central principle underlying the crime of rape – protection of a person's dignity.

The ICTY found that the definition of the crime of rape was not sufficiently specific, and proposed the following precise definition:

(i) the sexual penetration however slight:
  (a) of the vagina or anus of the victim by the penis of the perpetrator or any other object used by the perpetrator; or
  (b) of the mouth of the victim by the penis of the perpetrator;
(ii) by coercion or force or threat of force against the victim or a third person.[485, 486]

Moreover, terms such as "forced nudity" need to be added in the context of sexual abuse.[487] These kinds of additions would recognize the psychological harm caused to victims of sexual abuse even in the absence of bodily harm.

---

483   *Furundzija Judgment*, supra note 309.
484   Ibid., paras. 174–186.
485   Ibid., para. 185.
486   Note that in drafting this definition, the ICTY drew on the definitions of the crime of rape in several national court systems, see ibid., paras. 174–186.
487   On this point, see *Akayesu Judgment*, supra note 341.

Askin listed the following prohibited offenses, which were left out of the Rome Statute's definitions:

> impregnation, forced maternity, forced abortion, forced sterilization, forced marriage, forced nudity, sexual molestation, sexual mutilation, sexual humiliation and sex trafficking.[488]

These gaps in the law must be filled in. At the same time, the new crime category must separate any connection between sex crimes and an injury to the victim's honor.

9.4 ELIMINATING THE ELEMENT OF THE SYSTEMATIC NATURE OF THE ATTACK

As I discussed at length above,[489] the requirement for the systematic or widespread nature of the attack, which is found in the crime categories of "war crime" and "crime against humanity", is not appropriate for sex crimes. In many instances, sexual offenses are committed sporadically, not as part of a systematic or widespread attack. Moreover, the harm to each specific victim of discrete acts of rape is no different than if they were part of a systematic or widespread attack. The offense of rape, therefore, must be recognized without any requirement for it to be part of a systematic or widespread attack, in order to protect each individual woman from the gender and sexual violence directed against her.[490]

Furthermore, the pervasive patriarchal model that discriminates against and subjugates all women on the basis of gender is reinforced by sexual offenses. Hence the rape of an individual woman under the cover of battle is not only an injury to the individual woman, her dignity and her right to equality, but it also reinforces the inferiority of all women. Sex crimes that are perpetrated out of masculine urges, even if they are unrelated to the inter-ethnic battle taking place, compel each woman as such to conceive of herself as "female" in the patriarchal sense of a second-class citizen and sexual object for men.[491]

---

488   Kelly Dawn Askin, "Prosecuting Wartime Rape and Other Gender-Related Crimes under International Law: Extraordinary Advances, Enduring Obstacles", 21 *Berkeley J. Int'l L.* 288, 305 (2003).

489   Part Three, subchapter 7.1: "Sex Crimes as 'Crimes against Humanity'" and subchapter 7.2: "Sex Crimes as 'War Crimes'".

490   See also Rana Lehr-Lehnardt, supra note 13, p. 347.

491   See Orit Kamir, Israel's Dignity-based Feminism, supra note 94, p. 295; Catharine MacKinnon, Afterword, supra note 151, pp. 672–673, 680–682.

9.5 DEFINING THE MENTAL STATE

Due to the special character of sexual offenses, the requirement for the *mens rea* for the new crime category should be minimal. As I discuss above,[492] historically the crime of rape was one of the exceptions to the customary requirements for proof of the mental state. The court had to focus on the factual elements and ignore the mental state of the accused.[493] The reason for this was simple and logical: it is nearly impossible to prove beyond a reasonable doubt that the accused himself heard, saw, listened, internalized and understood the woman's position with respect to the sexual contact – meaning, that he was aware. It may be possible to prove objectively that he possessed the reasonable tools to be aware, but it is nearly impossible to prove that he had indeed formulated a state of awareness.

9.5.1 ELIMINATING THE REQUIREMENT FOR "KNOWLEDGE"

For the *mens rea* requirement, it is inappropriate to require "intent", as required for the crime category of "genocide", or "knowledge", as required for the crime category of "war crimes" or "crimes against humanity". The lesser mental state of "negligence" – an objective standard for *mens rea* – should be sufficient. In other words, in order to meet the requisite *mens rea*, it should be sufficient to find that the reasonable man or woman in the defendant's shoes would not have believed that the victim had consented.

9.5.2 THE PRESUMPTION OF NONCONSENT

Adrienne Kalosieh attempts to demonstrate the absurdity of the search for consent in the context of war. She explains that the real question hidden beneath the search for consent is, in effect, the following:

> Whether the victim enjoyed the sexual violence perpetrated by her enemy for the purposes of ethnically cleansing, demoralizing, and invading her ethnic group, and whether she did anything to prevent it.[494]

In contrast with some of the domestic laws I surveyed above,[495] international law elected not to include the element of the victim's "lack of consent" as one of the elements of the crime category of sexual violence. Yet "consent" can be a

---

492   Part One, subchapter 3.3.2: "The Guilty Mind – *Mens Rea*.
493   The court had only to focus on the *actus reus* and to ignore the *mens rea* of the accused regarding the physical acts other than, of course, penetration.
494   Adrienne Kalosieh, supra note 179, p. 122.
495   Part One, subchapter 3.3: "The Elements of the Crime of Rape under Domestic Law".

defence,[496] as the ICTY and ICTR prosecutors believed.[497] Today, as discussed above, rape is subject to the ICC's jurisdiction only when it is part of an armed conflict or a widespread or systematic attack against a civilian population. Under these circumstances, genuine consent is impossible.[498] Moreover, rape should be treated in the same way that international law deals with crimes like torture or slavery, in which the prosecution does not need to prove a lack of consent.

According to Rule 96(ii) of the Rules of Procedure and Evidence of the ICTR, consent may be raised as a defense under limited circumstances:

In cases of sexual assault:
    (i) Notwithstanding Rule 90 (C), no corroboration of the victim's testimony shall be required;
  (ii) Consent shall not be allowed as a defence if the victim:
       (a) Has been subjected to or threatened with or has had reason to fear violence, duress, detention or psychological oppression; or
       (b) Reasonably believed that if the victim did not submit, another might be so subjected, threatened or put in fear;
 (iii) Before evidence of the victim's consent is admitted, the accused shall satisfy the Trial Chamber *in camera* that the evidence is relevant and credible;
 (iv) Prior sexual conduct of the victim shall not be admitted in evidence or as defence.[499]

Allowing consent only as a defense transfers the burden of proof regarding the existence of consent to the accused.[500] The question of consent in sexual offenses will always be problematic, the classic "his word against hers" issue. The answer to this question will not always succeed in distinguishing between consensual sexual relations and penetration without consent – and even more so when the issue concerns sex crimes that are part of a "genocide", "crimes against humanity" or "war crimes".[501]

---

496   Adrienne Kalosieh, supra note 179, pp. 121–122.

497   See, e.g., Prosecutor v. Gacumbitsi, Case No. ICTR-2001-64-A, App. Ch. (7 July 2006) paras. 147–157 (hereinafter *Gacumbitsi Judgment*); Prosecutor v. Kunarac, Case No. IT-96-23-I, App. Ch. (ICTY, 12 June 2002) para. 130.

498   *Gacumbitsi Judgment*, supra note 497, para. 157.

499   Rule 96 of the ICTR Rules of Procedure and Evidence, 29 June 2005, UN Doc. IT/32 (Last rev. 1 October 2009), is the same in principle as Rule 96 of the ICTY Rules, supra note 282.

500   Wolfgang Schomburg & Ines Peterson, "Notes and Comments: Genuine Consent to Sexual Violence under International Criminal Law", 101 *Am. J. Int'l L.* 121, 124 (2007).

501   Ibid.

A presumption regarding the absence of consent can be found in the Rules of Procedure and Evidence of the Rome Statute.[502] The Rome Statute itself is silent regarding the elements of the crime of rape and other sex crimes. However, Rule 70 of the Rules of Procedure and Evidence provides that the ICC's decision with respect to sex crimes will be guided by the following:

a. Consent cannot be inferred by reason of any words or conduct of a victim where force, threat of force, coercion or taking advantage of a coercive environment undermined the victim's ability to give voluntary and genuine consent;
b. Consent cannot be inferred by reason of any words or conduct of a victim where the victim is incapable of giving genuine consent;
c. Consent cannot be inferred by reason of the silence of, or lack of resistance by, a victim to the alleged sexual violence.

Therefore, due to the special characteristics of sex crimes in the intensity of conflict, the element of consent should be eliminated, as it is for the crimes of torture and enslavement. At the same time, under certain unusual circumstances, the possibility that consent could be a defense should be considered.

Wolfgang Schomburg and Ines Peterson, who critique radical feminism, argue that a careful line should be drawn between a solitary act of rape and an act of rape covered under the categories of "genocide", "crime against humanity" or "war crime". They argue that when sexual violence is used as a tool of war, it is different from sexual violence tried in state courts. Victims of armed conflict undergo a severe and continuous harm that can even cause death. In their view, this atrocity cannot be compared to an act based "only" on sexual relations without consent. This is sexual violence which, in addition to the injury to the sexual autonomy of the victim, has more of a harmful impact on the victim's physical and mental state. Those factors that in domestic law are considered "aggravating circumstances" could be the conditions that would provide a basis for criminal responsibility in the international arena.

In this context, it is important to contend with the various critiques that have been proposed regarding the presumption of nonconsent. These other critiques include, for example, Otto, who argues against the "zero tolerance" approach which the UN has adopted toward the conduct of sexual relations between peacekeeping forces and the local population. She claims that sometimes "survival sex" or "sex in exchange for payment" may be all that the local population has left for survival.[503] Recall Halley's queries as well: *are sexual*

---

502   Rules of Procedure and Evidence of the International Criminal Court, 3–10 September 2000, Doc ICC-ASP/1/3.
503   Dianne Otto, Making Sense of Zero Tolerance, supra note 471.

*relations between an enemy soldier and the civilian population in exchange
for items of sustenance, for example, always rape? Or perhaps it is possible
that this is a decision made by women in the context of war?*[504]

My response to these critiques is that the background of subordination
and domination cannot be ignored. These are dependent relations, if you will.
As I described in Part One above, relationships of dependency are exceptions
under domestic law, which adopts a presumption that the issue of consent
is inapplicable in the context of such relationships.[505] These are hierarchical
systems in which there will always be an inherent power gap. This is the
approach taken with regard to sexual relations with minors and relationships
between an employee and employer. These types of relationships are acknowledged as an exception in domestic law, but they are the general rule in the
international arena.

Furthermore, all sexual relations involving coercion can be seen as contain-
ing some aspect of "survival sex" – to be or to cease to exist. In focusing on
what is exchanged, our vision is too narrow. If we allow sex under coercion in
exchange for sustenance and survival, then we are ignoring the "bigger picture". *Does the headline really matter?* Rape is rape; a decision made in an environment of duress is not a decision. There is no meeting of the minds or true
will in the relationship. Just as entering into an international agreement under
coercion is void,[506] and just as entering a private contract under coercion is
voidable,[507] a choice made under conditions of coercion does not indicate
consent.

Hence, the question of consent in the international realm is far less relevant.
We need a new perspective which will accurately reflect the nature of the relationships, especially under international law. The concept of "sexual coercion",
which characterizes all sex and gender crimes, more accurately clarifies the
essence of those crimes.[508]

---

504 Janet Halley, Rape in Berlin, supra note 461.

505 Subchapter 3.4: "The Presumption of Nonconsent in Domestic Law".

506 See Vienna Convention on the Law of Treaties, 23 May 1969, 1155 U.N.T.S. 331,
art. 52.

507 Coercion or duress was the only kind of improper pressure which the common law recognized as affecting the validity of a contract. See, e.g., Black's Law Dictionary, 6th ed., p. 504, Law
of Contracts (General Part) – 1977, art. 17 (Isr.); Restatement (Second) of Contracts, sec. 175(2)
(1979).

508 For additional discussion about basing sex crimes on the new perception of "sexual coer-
cion", see Orit Kamir, "A Different Kind of Sex: Conceptualizing Rape in Terms of Human
Dignity, and a Model of Suggested Legislation", 7 *Misphat Umimshal* 669, 765–766 (2005)
[Hebrew]; Orit Kamir, Israel's Dignity-based Feminism, supra note 94, pp. 170–173.

The legal discussion about the issue of consent would be incomplete without addressing the ICC's coverage of the new sex crime adopted by the Rome Statute, the crime of sexual slavery. As I discuss above,[509] the crime of sexual slavery is covered in the Rome Statute both as a "war crime" and a "crime against humanity". As I discuss below in the concluding chapter, the ICC prosecutor preferred to prosecute the crime of rape and other sex crimes as "sexual slavery". The preference for this crime is important, because the term "slavery" embeds in it the presumption of the lack of consent. As expressed by Valerie Oosterveld:

> By definition, [an] exercise of … [the powers attaching to the right of ownership] involves a negation of consent, which is why the Special Rapporteur on systematic rape, sexual slavery and slavery-like practices in armed conflict stated: "As a *jus cogens* crime, neither a State nor its agents, including government or military officials, can consent to the enslavement of any person under any circumstances. Likewise, a person cannot, under any circumstances, consent to be enslaved or subjected to slavery. Thus, it follows that a person accused of slavery cannot raise consent of the victim as a defense." If a judge finds that the actions of the perpetrator fall within the first element of the crime of slavery, an evaluation of whether a defense of consent can apply to the sexual acts of the second element is not necessary. … The fact that consent cannot serve as a defense to the crime of sexual slavery is another advance in international law.[510]

Therefore, as with the crimes of torture and enslavement, the presumption for this crime would be the absence of consent. As noted, the possibility of allowing the accused to prove otherwise as a defense would be considered under certain unusual circumstances.

9.6 DEFINING THE PERPETRATOR

The perpetrator is anyone who committed, ordered someone else to commit, or was found responsible for the prohibited act. Also, a person in a position of

---

509   Part Three, subchapter 7.1: "Sex Crimes as 'Crimes against Humanity'" and subchapter 7.2: "Sex Crimes as 'War Crimes'".

510   Valerie Oosterveld, Sexual Slavery and the International Criminal Court, supra note 238, p. 640, quoting UN Commissioner on Human Rights Sub-Commission on the Promotion and Protection of Human Rights, Contemporary Forms of Slavery, Systematic Rape, Sexual Slavery and Slavery-like Practices During Armed Conflict: Update on the Final Report Submitted by Ms. Gay J. McDougall, UN Doc, E/CN.4/Sub.2/2002/21 (6 June 2000) 51.

power or level of command who could have prevented or stopped the attack can be convicted along with those who actually committed the crime.

9.7 SUMMARY: ELEMENTS OF THE NEW CRIME CATEGORY

The new crime category I propose will eliminate both the requirement for a systematic or widespread attack, which currently exists for a "crime against humanity", and the requirement for the circumstances of armed conflict, which currently exists for a "war crime". The new offense must protect every victim against any sexual act committed with indifference to his will, because it is presumed that during an armed conflict, a person's choice to survive is not "consent". With respect to *mens rea,* it is sufficient for the accused to have been indifferent to the circumstances of the coerced sexual act.

One could claim that eliminating the elements of the systematic nature of the attack, the armed conflict and special intent will create a crime category that is too broad in its coverage. My response is that the legal vacuum in the protection of sex crime victims and enforcement of the laws against sexual offenses *mandates* the intervention of international law. Universal jurisdiction developed where domestic jurisdiction was short-handed, in the areas in which terrible wrongs occurred, and where, in the absence of this jurisdiction, there is neither justice nor law.

I am certain that there is no reason to be apprehensive about the extent of the new crime's applicability. The new crime category not only will assist in creating a uniform legal norm, which will condemn sex and gender crimes resulting from relationships of subordination and domination, but it will also create a genuine incentive for domestic courts to implement the law and to capture and punish perpetrators of these crimes.

In order to further clarify my view, I wish to respond to some broader potential critiques of it. The primary critiques of my view are expressed by the following questions: *Can there be an international crime category which lacks international features? Is a single grave crime enough in order to be prosecuted in the framework of the international criminal law?* I will respond to these two questions in order.

First, Article 5(1) of the Rome Statute, which establishes the extent of the ICC's jurisdiction, provides: "The jurisdiction of the Court shall be limited to the most serious crimes of concern to the international community as a whole…" This wording does not limit the ICC only to prosecuting crimes of an international character, but rather it grants jurisdiction to try cases that concern the entire international community. As I have discussed at length in this book, sex and gender crimes are crimes that contain within them a long history of inter-gender subordination and control, and in my view, because of their nature they constitute *jus cogens*.[511] It is this nature which justifies the ICC's jurisdiction to prosecute these crimes. An example of similar commentary can be found regarding the crime of "torture" as a discrete crime, as described by Antonio Cassese.[512] The *Pinochet Judgment* held:

> The jus cogens nature of the international crime of torture justifies states in taking universal jurisdiction over torture wherever committed. International law provides that offences jus cogens may be punished by any state because the offenders are "common enemies of all mankind and all nations have an equal interest in their apprehension and prosecution". Demjanjuk v. Petrovsky (1985) 603 F. Supp. 1468; 776 F. 2d. 571.[513]

Furthermore, if we analyze each and every one of the three categories in the international criminal law, we will discover, excluding a few exceptions, that the crime categories do not require international characteristics! The crime category of "genocide" requires that, in order for the actions to be recognized as "genocide" from a legal perspective, one or more of the prohibited acts must be committed with an intention to destroy a protected group – racial, ethnical, religious or national, as such, in all or in part.[514] This definition does not include international characteristics. The crime category of "crime against humanity" has three requirements: the act must be part of a widespread or systematic attack; the attacked population must be a civilian population; and the perpetrator must be aware that his acts are part of that widespread attack. Again, there is no requirement for different nationalities.[515] And similarly, even the crime category of "war crime" includes an entire subarticle 8(2)(c) which deals with a "war crime" that takes place during an armed conflict that is not of an international character.[516]

Second, the nature of sex crimes as *jus cogens* should be a sufficient basis for them to be subject to international jurisdiction, whether they are perpetrated as a single act or a systematic attack. For example, as stated by Judge Lord

---

511   See supra notes 83, 206.

512   Antonio Cassese, supra note 59, p. 150.

513   Regina v. Bartle and the Commissioner of Police for the Metropolis and Others ex parte Pinochet, House of Lords, 2 I.L.M. 827 [1999] (hereinafter *Pinochet Judgment*).

514   I discuss the crime category of "genocide" above in this Part Three, subchapter 7.3: "'Genocide' or 'Femicide'".

515   I discuss the crime category of "crimes against humanity" above in this Part Three, subchapter 7.1: "Sex Crimes as 'Crimes against Humanity'".

516   I discuss the crime category of "war crimes" above in this Part Three, subchapter 7.2: "Sex Crimes as 'War Crimes'".

Hutton of the House of Lords, who joined the majority opinion in the *Pinochet Judgment*, regarding the crime of torture:

> Therefore I consider that a single act of torture carried out or instigated by a public official or other person acting in an official capacity constitutes a crime against international law, and that torture does not become an international crime only when it is committed or instigated on a large scale. Accordingly I am of opinion that Senator Pinochet cannot claim that a single act of torture or a small number of acts of torture carried out by him did not constitute international crimes and did not constitute acts committed outside the ambit of his functions as head of state.[517]

Therefore, the possibility that the new crime category will be devoid of international characteristics or, alternatively, that it will protect against an isolated crime does not constitute an exception or precedent under international law.

I wish to clarify: the new crime category that I propose is not intended to apply primarily to the isolated sex crime committed out of relationships of subordination and domination in the framework of the state. Under those circumstances, it is appropriate for the domestic law of the nation-state to act in the first instance. However, if the domestic law chooses to remain silent, or, alternatively, the judicial and enforcement systems under the domestic law ignore sex and gender crimes, as they will be defined in the new crime category I propose in chapter ten below, then the resulting international criminal jurisdiction is appropriate, in my opinion. In other words, in a place where sex and gender crimes are perpetrated under the passive shelter of domestic law, the international community must shatter the anachronistic dichotomy of private/public and national/international – and act.[518] Gender crimes are the result of a history of exclusion, the perpetuation of subordination, and the strengthening of male domination, and therefore international law must act to eradicate them. For this purpose, all of humanity must take action together.

It is important to recall that in contrast with prior international criminal tribunals, the ICC only has complementary jurisdiction. In the race for jurisdiction, domestic courts enjoy priority.[519] This rule is upheld except under very special circumstances – according to Article 17(1)(d) of the Rome Statute,

---

517   *Pinochet Judgment*, supra note 513.

518   I discuss the problematic nature of the existing dichotomy between the international and national law above in Part One, subchapter 1.1: "Private v. Public under International Humanitarian Law".

519   The complementary jurisdiction of the ICC can be learned from Article 1 of the Rome Statute, and also from Articles 10, 15, 17, 18 and 19, supra note 4. See Antonio Cassese, supra note 59, pp. 342–346.

the ICC is authorized to exercise jurisdiction, even if the matter is before a state court, when the state in which the crime was perpetrated is unwilling or genuinely unable to investigate or prosecute the case, or when the decision not to prosecute the suspect results from an unwillingness or genuine inability to prosecute him, and the act is of sufficient gravity to justify action by the ICC.

As stated, gender subordination is intensified and prominent under conditions of conflict, during which rape becomes a tool of war. The international community unanimously and officially recognized this in Resolution 1820 of the UN Security Council.[520] This tool of war primarily threatens the female gender. This is the same tool of war which, in the past, was considered legitimate and immune from condemnation, during times of peace as well as war. The recognition of the new international crime category, as proposed in chapter ten below, will make sex crimes into discrete international crimes, address all of the ethnic and gender aspects of the offense, and establish an explicit prohibition against these crimes during times of peace and conflict.

As I have described at length here, the difficulty in prosecuting sex criminals under the existing crime categories is a genuine problem. The role of the entire human community is to condemn these crimes and supply the international court with the legal tools that will enable it to prosecute the sex criminals who are enjoying the absence of the law. Even today, in many cases, under the darkness of battle, the victims of sex crimes are excluded from the protection of international law, and their bodies are still permitted to every indifferent taker, immune from the law. The new crime category I have proposed seeks to address all of the unique aspects of sex and gender crimes and their circumstances, in order to ensure that international criminal law will succeed in protecting all sex victims and provide a response to all of the violent aspects of life in the sex and gender realm.

---

520   See Resolution 1820, supra note 33.

Chapter 10

PRELIMINARY DRAFT OF A NEW CRIME CATEGORY

My bringing together of the historical evidence with the various critiques leads me to propose a new crime category to cover "sex and gender crimes". This offense will require the *mens rea* of negligence. Set out below is my proposed wording for the crime category, drafted so as to integrate it into the original language of the Rome Statute:

Article 9
Sex and Gender Crimes

For the purpose of this statute, 'Sex and Gender Crimes' means any use of a person's body for the sexual satisfaction of the perpetrator or that of a third person, or for the sexual humiliation of a person, by committing one or more of the following acts with indifference to the violation of the victim's will or to the coercive nature such as described in Paragraph (2) below:

(a) any penetration however slight (i) of the vagina or anus of the victim by the penis of the perpetrator or by any other body part or any other object used by the perpetrator; or (ii) of the mouth of the victim by the penis of the perpetrator;

(b) other forms of sexual violence including but not limited to (i) sexual slavery, (ii) forced impregnation, (iii) forced maternity, (iv) forced abortion, (v) forced sterilization, (vi) forced marriage, (vii) forced nudity, (viii) sexual molestation, (ix) sexual mutilation, (x) sexual humiliation, and (xi) sex trafficking.

For the purpose of Paragraph 1, coercive nature *includes, but is not limited to*, circumstances in which a crime is committed through coercion, force, or the threat of force directed at the victim or at a third person, such as that caused by taking advantage of a coercive environment, by taking advantage of a person incapable of giving genuine consent, by abuse of power, or by exercising or threatening to exercise violence, duress, detention, or psychological oppression against the victim or a third person.

SUMMARY AND CONCLUSIONS

In this book, I have sought to document the use of rape as a weapon throughout history: rape for the purpose of "genocide", the systematic rape of a civilian population, rape as part of wartime activity, and rape simply for the sake of rape, while exploiting relationships of subordination during armed conflicts or other domestic political tension. The woman's body has been nationalized, expropriated, and turned into a battleground, an instrument for sprouting the victor's seed, for the soldiers' consolation and their physical relief.

I have surveyed how international law has related to sex crimes, from its origin through today. This historic journey allowed me to identify three main areas in the treatment of rape under international law.

The *Era of Silence*. An era when rape was permitted, in the absence of law. Occasionally, rape was morally condemned, but the law itself remained silent. Rape was perceived both as a legitimate tool for defeating the enemy and for raising the troops' morale. An era when society, morality, language and law were all mute. An era when the silence continued through two world wars, casting a hush over the statutes of the first two international tribunals, in Nuremberg and Tokyo. Despite the mountains of testimony, documents and evidence about all types of sex crimes – forced abortions, sexual slavery, forced prostitution, sexual mutilation – the silence continued, and these offenses were excluded from the trials of the war criminals.

The *Era of Honor*. An era when rape was finally recognized as a crime under international law, beginning with the signing of the Geneva Conventions in 1949. But the harm protected by law recognized rape as an attack on the victim's honor – not her dignity as a person, not a bodily harm, not a mental harm. Rape was perceived as an inferior crime, not worthy of addition to the list of crimes constituting a "grave breach of the Geneva Conventions".

The next era commenced with establishment of the ICTY and the ICTR following the horrific wars in Yugoslavia and Rwanda. These international tribunals included sex crimes within the framework of *all* of the existing crime categories under international law. Yet just a few years later, when the Rome Statute was signed in 1998, this treaty halted the progress partway, instead of continuing down the full length of the important path paved by the ICTY and ICTR precedents.

My argument is that this *New Status Quo* – marked by only partial recognition of sex crimes in today's modern criminal code, the Rome Statute – is inadequate. I demonstrated that sex crimes can be included within each of the Rome Statute's existing crime categories, by interpreting "genocide" and "grave breaches of the Geneva Conventions" more broadly. Rape and forced pregnancy should be enumerated among the acts that can constitute "genocide", as the ICTR ruled in the *Akayesu Judgment*,[521] and sex crimes should constitute "grave breaches of the Geneva Conventions", as the ICTR Statute provides.[522] This silence about sex crimes under the serious crime categories of "genocide" and "grave breaches of the Geneva Conventions" in the Rome Statute vividly demonstrates that international law still views sexual offenses as less serious than other international crimes.

Again and again throughout history, women have been tortured, murdered *and* raped. They have been murdered and tortured as an enemy, and they have been tortured and raped as women. *All aspects must be punished – the murder and torture, as well as the rape.* Women are tortured not only because of their color, their race, their ethnic group, or their politics. They are tortured and raped because they are women – on both sides of the battle lines. Parallel actions are called for: including sex crimes under the traditional crime categories in international law, and creating a new crime category suited to the characteristics of sexual offenses.

I wish to emphasize that I am not arguing that crimes against women are more serious than other crimes – only that each offense possesses its own unique traits. My argument is not that sex crimes should be elevated to the top of the crime list, but rather that sex and gender crimes should be addressed by a crime category suited to their unique features, and this crime category must stand alongside the other existing serious offenses.

In particular, the covert stratum of these crimes must be exposed – the gender stratum. To do so, a new international crime category must be adopted, which will enable protection against all of the violent aspects of this phenomenon as well as proper enforcement. The new crime category I propose will bring sex crimes within the bounds of the general norms, by enabling comprehensive protection against sex crimes under international law. Moreover, it will enable international harmonization of the elements of the offense of rape. This harmonization will also assist states with the reform of their domestic laws, and will provide them with incentives for enforcement. In other words, broad international agreement about the new category of sex crimes will serve as a guideline that can influence the domestic law of all states that are parties to the Rome Statute.[523]

---

521 *Akayesu Judgment*, supra note 341.

522 ICTR Statute, supra note 335, art. 4(e).

523 Regarding international law's impact on domestic law, see, e.g., Gerald L. Neuman, "International Law as a Resource in Constitutional Interpretation", 30 *Harvard J. L. & Pub. Pol.* 177 (2006); Gerald L. Neuman, "The Uses of International Law in Constitutional Interpretation,"

International law was created and formulated by men to protect men, and so, historically, it ignored violence against women. The incontestable historical masculinity of the battle field, the lack of involvement of women in decisions to instigate armed conflicts, the miniscule number of women in the international legal field, and the predominance of men as legislators and judges of international law, are all factors that have contributed to the failure of international law to deal effectively with matters related to women. These factors also perpetuate women's inferiority and prevent assistance regarding the issues affecting women.

Now is the time for the international legal community to unite and condemn forced pregnancy, rape and sexual abuse, just as the international community has united and condemned other intolerable crimes: enslavement, torture, hijacking, and terror. Integration of women as judges and gender experts enriches the international discourse and enables the silence to be broken. Adopting new legal terms and a new crime category will arm international law with better tools to fight sex and gender crimes. After thousands of years of silence, international criminal law must mercilessly pursue sex criminals and uproot the gender-biased subordination of women that is exposed during times of conflict as well as peace. International law must do so, not only because these are atrocious and grave offenses, but also because the only effective way to fight sex crimes is a comprehensive effort by society to devote resources towards destroying the distorted societal perspectives that foster gender subordination.

The proposed new crime category is tailored to the unique features of sex and gender crimes, and it would protect every person who is a victim as such. It recognizes that the issue of consent must be analyzed differently in the context of relationships of subordination and control in which the choice to survive cannot be considered consent. This crime category would apply to times of peace as well as war, and it would eliminate the requirement regarding a systematic or widespread attack which is embedded in the crime category of "crime against humanity".

So long as this comprehensive proposed reform is not adopted, the question remains as to *whether the ICC will interpret the crime categories in the Rome Statute as including sex crimes in those provisions which do not explicitly recognize them?* The future will tell.

---

98 *Am. J. Int'l L.* 82 (2004); Percy E. Corbett, "Quincy Wright's Contribution to International Law", 14(4) *J. Conflict Resolution* 465, 466 (December 1970); Robert O. Keohane, Stephen Macedo & Andrew Moravcsik, "Democracy-Enhancing Multilateralism", *IILJ Working Paper* (Princeton University, 2007/4).

At the time of writing this book, the ICC prosecutor has begun prosecuting alleged criminals under the categories of crime that include sex crimes. One of the first matters adjudicated in the ICC concerned Germain Katanga, who was charged with "war crimes" and "crimes against humanity" he allegedly committed in the eastern Democratic Republic of the Congo in 2003. He was charged with the commission of violent sexual crimes in the indictment under the new crimes of "sexual slavery" and "rape".[524] In a pre-trial hearing on 29 September 2008, the court unanimously found the evidence sufficient to warrant prosecution in the ICC on charges of "sexual slavery" and "rape" as a "crime against humanity", and a majority found sufficient evidence for charges of "sexual slavery" and "rape" as a "war crime". The trial against Congolese warlords Germain Katanga and Matthieu Ngudjolo Chui (whose case was joined by the pre-trial chamber), which commenced on 24 November 2009, is the ICC's second trial. Katanga and Ngudjolo are accused of "war crimes" and "crimes against humanity", which they allegedly committed in the village of Bogoro in the Ituri district of the Democratic Republic of the Congo from January to March 2003.[525]

Will the ICC continue along the course set by its predecessors, the ICTY and the ICTR, and adopt broad interpretations in matters related to sex crimes? For example, will it rule that forced impregnation can constitute "genocide"? Will it pave the way for integrating sex crimes into customary law? Will it rule that rape constitutes a "grave breach of the Geneva Conventions"? Will the gender stratum of sex crimes finally be exposed in international law? This book demonstrates that it is appropriate for the ICC to do so, and that it already has all the necessary legal tools to do so.

---

524   Regarding sexual slavery as a "crime against humanity", see Rome Statute, supra note 4, art. 7(1)(g); regarding sexual slavery as a "war crime", see Rome Statute, supra note 4, art. 8(2)(b)(xxii).

525   See Prosecutor v. Germain Katanga and Mathieu Ngudjolo Chui, ICC-01/04-01/0. Details regarding all of the offenses and charges in the indictment of which Germain Katanga and Matthieu Ngudjolo Chui were accused are located at http://www.icc-cpi.int/menus/icc/situations%20and%20cases/situations/situation%20icc%200104/related%20cases/icc%200104%200107/democratic%20republic%20of%20the%20congo?lan=en-GB (last accessed 14 April 2011).

BIBLIOGRAPHY

INTERNATIONAL TREATIES (IN CHRONOLOGICAL ORDER):

Hague Convention (II) Laws and Customs of War on Land, 29 July 1899, 32 Stat. 1803.

Hague Convention (IV) Respecting the Laws and Customs of War on Land, with Annex of Regulations, 18 October 1907, 36 Stat. 2277.

Allied Control Council Law No. 10, Punishment of Persons Guilty of War Crimes, Crimes Against Peace and Against Humanity, 20 December 1945, 3 Official Gazette of the Control Council for Germany.

Charter of the International Military Tribunal, 8 August 1945, 82 U.N.T.S. 280.

Statute of the International Court of Justice, 26 June 1945, 59 Stat. 1055.

Charter of the United Nations, 26 June 1945, 59 Stat. 1031.

Charter of the International Military Tribunal for the Far East, 19 January 1946.

Convention on the Prevention and Punishment of the Crime of Genocide, 9 December 1948, 78 U.N.T.S. 277.

First Geneva Convention "For the Amelioration of the Condition of the Wounded and Sick in Armed Forces in the Field", 27 July 1949, 118 L.N.T.S. 303.

Second Geneva Convention "For the Amelioration of the Condition of Wounded, Sick and Shipwrecked Members of Armed Forces at Sea", 12 August 1949, 75 U.N.T.S. 85.

Third Geneva Convention "Relative to the Treatment of Prisoners of War", 12 August 1949, 75 U.N.T.S. 135.

Fourth Geneva Convention "Relative to the Protection of Civilian Persons in Time of War", 12 August 1949, 75 U.N.T.S. 287.

International Covenant on Civil and Political Rights, 16 December 1966, UN Doc. A/6316, 999 U.N.T.S. 171.

Vienna Convention on the Law of Treaties, 23 May 1969, 1155 U.N.T.S. 331.

Protocol Additional I to the Geneva Conventions of 12 August 1949, and Relating to the Protection of Victims of International Armed Conflicts, 8 June 1977, 1125 U.N.T.S. 3.

Protocol Additional II to the Geneva Conventions of 12 August 1949, and Relating to the Protection of Victims of Non-International Armed Conflicts, 8 June 1977, 1125 U.N.T.S. 609.

Convention on the Elimination of All Forms of Discrimination against Women, 18 December 1979, UN Doc. A/RES/34/180.

Convention against Torture and Other Cruel, Inhuman or Degrading Treatment or Punishment, 10 December 1984, UN Doc. A/39/46.

Rules of Procedure and Evidence of the International Criminal Tribunal for the Former Yugoslavia, 11 February 1994, UN Doc. IT/32/Rev. 44 (Last rev. 10 December 2009).

Rome Statute of the International Criminal Court, 17 July 1998, UN Doc. A/CONF. 183/9, 2187 U.N.T.S. 3.

Rules of Procedure and Evidence of the International Criminal Court, 3–10 September 2000, Doc ICC-ASP/1/3.

ICTR Rules of Procedure and Evidence, 29 June 2005, UN Doc. IT/32 (Last rev. 1 October 2009).

INTERNATIONAL JURISPRUDENCE:

ICJ

Reservations to the Convention on the Prevention and Punishment of the Crime of Genocide, 1951 ICJ 15.

Judgment in Case Concerning Military and Para-Military Activities in and against Nicaragua (Nicaragua v. US) 1986 ICJ 14.

ICTY

Prosecutor v. Blaskic, Case No. IT-95-14-T, T. Ch. I. (ICTY, 3 March 2000).

Prosecutor v. Delalic, Indictment, Case No. IT-96-21-I (ICTY, 19 March 1996).

Prosecutor v. Delalic, Case No. IT-96-21-T, T. Ch. II (ICTY, 16 November 1998).

Prosecutor v. Furundzija, Decision [on Defence Motion to Strike Testimony of Witness A], Case No. IT-95-17/1-T (ICTY, 16 July 1998).

Prosecutor v. Furundzija, Case No. IT-95-17/1-T, T. Ch. II, (ICTY, 10 December 1998).

Prosecutor v. Gagovic, Case No. IT-96-23 ICTY, (ICTY, 18 June 1996).

Prosecutor v. Jelisic, ICTY Case No. IT-95-10-T, T. Ch. I (ICTY, 14 December 1999).

Prosecutor v. Krstic, Case No. IT-98-3-T, T. Ch. I (ICTY, 2 August 2001).

Prosecutor v. Kunarac, Amended Indictment, Case No. IT-96-23-I (ICTY, 13 July 1998.)

Prosecutor v. Kunarac, Case No. IT-96-23-T (ICTY, 22 February 2001).

Prosecutor v. Kunarac, Case No. IT-96-23-I, App. Ch. (ICTY, 12 June 2002).

Prosecutor v. Kupreskic, Transcript, Case No. IT-95-16-T (ICTY, 14 January 2000).

Prosecutor v. Kupreskic, Case No. IT-95-16, T. Ch. II (ICTY, 14 January 2000).

Prosecutor v. Tadic, Second Amended Indictment, Case No. IT- 94-1-T (ICTY, 14 December 1995).

Prosecutor v. Tadic, Case No. IT-94-1-AR72, T. Ch. II (ICTY, 2 October 1996).

Prosecutor v. Tadic, Case No. IT-94-1-T, T. Ch. II (ICTY, 7 May 1997).

Prosecutor v. Tadic, Case No. IT-94-1-A, App. Ch. (ICTY, 15 July 1999).

Prosecutor v. Tadic, Sentencing Judgment, Case No. IT-94-1, T. Ch. II. (ICTY, 11 November 1999).

ICTR

Prosecutor v. Akayesu, Case No. ICTR-96-4-T, T. Ch. I (2 September 1998).

Prosecutor v. Akayesu, Case No. ICTR-96-4-T, T. Ch. I (2 October 1998).

Prosecutor v. Gacumbitsi, Case No. ICTR-2001-64-A, App. Ch. (7 July 2006).

Prosecutor v. Kayishema and Ruzindana, Case No. ICTR-95-1-T, T. Ch. II (21 May 1999).

Prosecutor v. Nyiramasuhuko, Indictment, Case No. ICTR-97-21-I, T. Ch. I (26 May 1997).

Prosecutor v. Rutaganda, Case No. ICTR-96-3, T. Ch. I (6 December 1999).

ICC

Prosecutor v. Germain Katanga and Mathieu Ngudjolo Chui, ICC-01/04-01/07.

SECURITY COUNCIL RESOLUTIONS
(IN CHRONOLOGICAL ORDER):

S.C. Res. 780 (1992), Establishing a Commission of Experts to Examine and Analyze Information Submitted Pursuant to Resolution 771, U.N. Doc. S/RES/780.

S.C. Res. 827 (1993), Statute of the International Criminal Tribunal for the Former Yugoslavia, U.N. Doc. S/RES/827.

S.C. Res. 955 (1994), Statute of the International Criminal Tribunal for Rwanda, U.N. Doc. S/RES/955.

S.C. Res. 1315 (2002), Statute of the Special Court for Sierra Leone, U.N. Doc. S/RES/1315.

S.C. Res. 1534 (2004), International Criminal Tribunal for the former Yugoslavia and International Criminal Tribunal for Rwanda, U.N. Doc. S/RES/1534.

S.C. Res. 1820 (2008), U.N. Doc. S/RES/1820, on widespread sexual violence in conflict.

GENERAL ASSEMBLY RESOLUTIONS
(IN CHRONOLOGICAL ORDER):

G.A. Res. 217A (1948), Universal Declaration of Human Rights, U.N. Doc A/810.

G.A. Res. 2200A (1966), International Covenant on Civil and Political Rights, U.N. Doc. A/6316.

G.A. Res. 3318 (1974), Declaration on the Protection of Women and Children in Emergency and Armed Conflict, U.N. Doc. A/9631.

G.A. Res. 34/180 (1979), Convention on the Elimination of All Forms of Discrimination against Women, U.N. Doc. A/RES/34/180.

G.A. Res. 39/46 (1984), Convention against Torture and Other Cruel, Inhuman or Degrading Treatment or Punishment, U.N. Doc. A/RES/39/46.

G.A. Res. 47/33 (1992), Report of the International Law Commission on the work of its 44th session, U.N. Doc. A/RES/47/33.

G.A. Res. 48/104 (1993), Declaration on Elimination of Violence against Women, U.N. Doc. A/Res/48/104.

G.A. Res. 50/46 (1995), Establishment of an International Criminal Court, U.N. Doc. A/Res/50/46.

G. A. Res. 58/144 (2003), Improvement of the Status of Women in the United Nations System, U.N. Doc. A/Res/58/144.

OTHER INTERNATIONAL DOCUMENTS AND RESOLUTIONS:

DECLARATIONS (IN CHRONOLOGICAL ORDER):

Declaration on the Protection of Women and Children in Emergency and Armed Conflict, 14 December 1974, U.N. Doc. A/9631.

Universal Declaration of Human Rights, 10 December 1974, U.N. Doc. A/810.

Vienna Declaration and Programme of Action, World Conference on Human Rights, 25 June 1993, U.N. Doc. A/Conf.157/23.

REPORTS (IN CHRONOLOGICAL ORDER):

Interim Report of Commission of Experts Established Pursuant to Security Council by the Secretary-General, (1993) (s/25274).

Report of the International Law Commission on its Forty-Sixth Session, Draft Statute for an International Criminal Court, UN Doc. A/49/10 (1994).

Final Report of the Commission of Experts Established Pursuant to Security Council Resolution 780, 27 May 1994, s/1994/674.

Economic and Social Council, Report of the Special Rapporteur on Violence Against Women, its Causes and Consequences, Ms. Radhika Coomaraswamy, in accordance with Commission on Human Rights Resolution, 21 January 1999, 1997/44 Distr. GENERAL E/CN.4/1999/68/Add.4.

UN Commissioner on Human Rights Sub-Commission on the Promotion and Protection of Human Rights, Contemporary Forms of Slavery, Systematic Rape, Sexual Slavery and Slavery-like Practices During Armed Conflict: Update on the Final Report Submitted by Ms. Gay J. McDougall, UN Doc E/CN.4/Sub.2/2002/21 (6 June 2000).

Improvement of the Status of Women in the United Nation System, Report of Secretary General, UN Doc. A/59/357 (20 September 2004).

OTHER INTERNATIONAL DOCUMENTS (IN CHRONOLOGICAL ORDER):

Principles of International Law Recognized in the Charter of the Nürenberg Tribunal and in the Judgment of the Tribunal, 29 July 1950, U.N. Doc. A/CN.4/SER.A/1950/Add.1.

Finalized Draft Text of the Elements of Crime, 2 November 2000, U.N. Doc. PCNICC/2000/1/Add.2.

Special Measures for Protection from Sexual Exploitation and Abuse, Secretary-General's Bulletin, 9 October 2003, U.N. Doc. ST/SGD/2003/13.

NATIONAL DOCUMENTS:

LEGISLATION:

Canada

Criminal Code of Canada.

England

Sexual Offences Act 1956, sec. 6 (Eng.).

India

Penal Code, 1860 (Ind.).

Israel

Law of Contracts (General Part) – 5733-1973, art. 17 (Isr.).

Prevention of Sexual Harassment Law, 5758-1988, sec. 3(a)(6) (Isr.).

Sexual Offenses Act, 2003 (Isr.).

Russian Federation

Criminal Code (Rus.).

JURISPRUDENCE:

Israel

CrimA 5424/91 Anon. v. State of Israel, 46(4) P.D. 497 (1992) (Isr.).

HCJ 1284/99 Anon. v. Chief of Staff, 53(2) P.D. 62 (1999) (Isr.).

LCA (Labor Court Appeal) 274/06 Anon. v. Anon (26 March 2008) (Isr.).

CSA 4790/04 State of Israel v. Avraham Ben Haim (2 May 2005) (Isr.).

CrimA 336/61 Adolf Eichmann v. Attorney General, 16 P.D. 2052 (1962) (Isr.).

CrimA 9256/04 Joseph Noy v. State of Israel (10 August 2005) (Isr.).

CSA 1599/03 Tapiro v. Commissioner of the Civil Service, 58(2) P.D. 125 (2003) (Isr.).

England

Regina v. Bartle and the Commissioner of Police for the Metropolis and Others ex parte Pinochet, House of Lords, 2 I.L.M. 827 [1999] (Eng.).

PUBLICATIONS:

BOOKS:

Deuteronomy 21:10–14 [New International Version trans.].

History of the United Nations War Crimes Commission and the Development of the Laws of War (London: H.M. Stationary, 1948).

Astrid Aafijes, *Gender Violence: The Hidden War Crime* (Women, Law & Development Intl., 1998).

Giorgio Agamben, *Homo Sacer, Sovereign Power and Bare Life* (Daniel Heller-Roazen, trans., Stanford University Press, 1998).

Anonyma, *Eine Frau in Berlin: Tagebuch-aufzeichnungen vom 20, April bis 22. Juni 1945* (2005) [German].

Kelly Dawn Askin, *War Crimes against Women: Prosecution in International War Crimes Tribunals* (M. Nijhoff, 1997).

M. Cherif Bassiouni, *Introduction to International Criminal Law* (Transnational Publishers, 2003).

Orna Ben-Naftali & Yuval Shany, *International Law Between War and Peace* (Ramot, Tel Aviv University, 2006) [Hebrew].

Black's Law Dictionary, (6th ed.).

Susan Brownmiller, *Against Our Will: Men, Women and Rape* (Simon & Schuster, 1975).

Judith Butler, *Gender Trouble:* Feminism and the Subversion of Identity (Routledge, 1990).

Barry E. Carter & Philip R. Trimble, *International Law* (Little, Brown & Company, 2d ed., 1995).

Antonio Cassese, *International Criminal Law* (Oxford, 2008).

Hilary Charlesworth & Christine Chinkin, *The Boundaries of International Law: A Feminist Analysis* (Manchester University Press, 2000).

Simone de Beauvoir, *The Second Sex* (H.M. Parshley, trans., Vintage Classics, 1997).

Yoram Dinstein, *The Internal Powers of the State* (Schocken, Tel Aviv University Press, 1972) [Hebrew].

Susan Estrich, *Real Rape* (Harvard University Press, 1987).

S.Z. Feller, *Foundations of Criminal Law*, Vol. A (1984) [Hebrew].

Nancy Fraser, *Unruly Practices: Power, Discourse and Gender in Contemporary Social Theory* (University of Minnesota Press/Polity Press, 1989).

Judith G. Gardam & Michelle J. Jarvis, *Women, Armed Conflict and International Law* (Kluwer International Law, 2001).

Carol Gilligan, *In a Different Voice: Psychological Theory and Women's Development* (Harvard University Press, 1982).

Jonathan Gottschall, *The Rape of Troy: Evolution, Violence, and the World of Homer* (Cambridge University Press, 2008).

Human Rights Watch, *Shattered Lives: Sexual Violence during the Rwandan Genocide and its Aftermath* (1996).

Orit Kamir, *Israeli Honor and Dignity: Social Norms, Gender Politics and the Law* (Carmel, 2004) [Hebrew].

Orit Kamir, *Israel's Dignity-based Feminism in Law and Society* (Carmel, 2007) [Hebrew].

Dr. Jakob Kellenberger, Foreword to Jean-Marie Henckaerts & Louise Doswald-Beck, *Customary International Humanitarian Law* (Cambridge University Press, 2009).

Yougindra Khushalanai, *Dignity and Honor of Women as Basic and Fundamental Human Rights* (M. Nijhoff, 1982).

Yuval Levy & Eliezer Lederman, *Principles of Criminal Responsibility* (1981) [Hebrew].

Judith Lewis Herman, *Trauma and Recovery: The Aftermath of Violence – From Domestic Abuse to Political Terror* (BasicBooks, Harper Collins, 1992).

Catharine A. MacKinnon, *Feminism Unmodified: Discourses on Life and Law* (Harvard University Press, 1987).

Catharine A. MacKinnon, *Only Words* (Harvard University Press, 1993)

Catharine A. MacKinnon, *Toward a Feminist Theory of the State* (Harvard University Press, 1989).

Catherine A. MacKinnon & Reva B. Siegel, eds., *Directions in Sexual Harassment Law* (Yale University Press, 2003).

Gilad Noam, "A Feminist Perspective of Public International Law", in Daphne Barak-Erez, *et al.*, eds., *Studies in Feminism, Gender and Law* (Nevo, 2007) [Hebrew].

Samuel H. Pillsbury, *How Criminal Law Works* (Carolina Academic Press, 2009).

Restatement (Second) of Contracts (1979).

Liora Rofman, "Battered Women as Torture Victims? A Feminist Critique of Women's Human Rights Discourse", 2006 (unpublished master's thesis, Bar Ilan University) [Hebrew].

Stephen J. Schulhofer, *Unwanted Sex: The Culture of Intimidation and the Failure of Law* (Harvard University Press, 1998).

Ayelet Shachar, "The Sexuality of Law: The Legal Discourse About Rape", 18(1) *Tel Aviv Univ. L. Rev.* 160 (1994) [Hebrew].

Malcolm Shaw, *International Law* (Cambridge University Press, 5th ed., 2005).

Thomas W. Simon, *The Laws of Genocide: Prescriptions for a Just World* (Praeger Security International, Westport, Conn., 2007).

ARTICLES:

Michelle J. Anderson, "All-American Rape", 2 *St. John's L. Rev.* 625 (2005).

Kelly Dawn Askin, "A Decade of the Development of Gender Crimes in International Courts and Tribunals: 1993 to 2003", 11 *Hum. Rts. Br.* 16 (2004).

Kelly Dawn Askin, "Sexual Violence in Decisions and Indictments of the Yugoslav and Rwandan Tribunals: Current Status", 93 *Am. J. Int'l L.* 97 (1999).

Kelly Dawn Askin, "Gender Crimes Jurisprudence in the ICTR: Positive Developments", 3 *J. Int'l Crim. Just.* 1007 (2005).

Kelly Dawn Askin, "Prosecuting Wartime Rape and Other Gender-Related Crimes under International Law: Extraordinary Advances, Enduring Obstacles", 21 *Berkeley J. Int'l L.* 288 (2003).

Kelly Dawn Askin, "The ICTY: An Introduction to its Origins, Rules and Jurisprudence" in Richard May, *et al.* eds., *Essays on ICTY Procedure and Evidence in Honour of Gabrielle Kirk McDonald* (Klur Law International, 2000).

Sita Balthazar, "Gender Crimes and the International Criminal Tribunals", 10 *Gonz. J. Int'l L.* 43, 44 (2006).

Daphne Barak-Erez, "Introduction: The Legal Feminism of Catharine A. MacKinnon and the Move from the Margin to the Center" in Daphne Barak-Erez, ed., *Legal Feminism in Theory and Practice* (Resling, 2005) [Hebrew].

Katherine T. Bartlett, "Feminist Legal Methods", 103 *Harv. L. Rev.* 829 (1990).

Barbara Bedont & Katherine Hall Martinez, "Ending Impunity for Gender Crimes under the International Criminal Court", VI(1) *Brown J. World Aff.* 65 (1999).

Barbara Bendont, "Gender Specific Provisions in the Statute of the ICC", in F. Lattanzi & W. Schabas, eds., *Essays on the Rome Statute of the ICC* (Editoriale, 2000).

Liora Bilsky [sic], "The Violence of Silence: Legal Proceeding between Distribution and Voice", 23 *Tel Aviv Univ. L. Rev.* 421 (2000) [Hebrew].

Pascala R. Bos, "Feminists Interpreting the Politics of War Time Rape: Berlin, 1945; Yugoslavia, 1992–1993", 31(4) *Signs J. Women Culture & Soc'y* 995 (2006).

David P. Bryden, "Forum on the Law of Rape: Redefining Rape", 3 *Buff. Crim. L. Rev.* 317, 325 (2000).

Andrew Byrnes, "The Convention Against Torture", in Kelly Dawn Askin & Dorean M. Koening, eds., *Women and International Human Rights Law* (1999–2001).

Jocelyn Campanaro, "Women, War and International Law: The Historical Treatment of Gender Based War Crimes", 89 *Geo. L.J.* 2557 (2001).

Antonio Cassese, "The Role of Internationalized Courts and Tribunals in the Fight Against International Criminality", in Cesare P.R. Romano, *et al.*, eds., *Internationalized Criminal Courts: Sierra Leone, East Timor, Kosovo, and Cambodia* (Oxford, 2004) 3.

Hilary Charlesworth, Christine Chinkin & Shelley Wright, "Feminist Approaches to International Law", 85 *Am. J. Int'l L.* 613 (1991).

Hilary Charlesworth & Christine Chinkin, "The Gender of Jus Cogens", 15 *Hum. Rts. Q.* 63 (1993).

Hilary Charlesworth, "Feminist Methods in International Law", 93 *AJ.I.L. (Symposium on Method in International Law)* 379 (1999).

Christin Coan, "Rethinking the Spoils of War: Prosecuting Rape as a War Crime in the International Criminal Tribunal for the Former Yugoslavia", 26 *N.C. J. Int'l L. & Com. Reg.* 183 (2000).

Amichai Cohen, "The International Criminal Law" in Robbie Sabel, ed., *International Law* (Hebrew University, 2d ed., 2010) [Hebrew].

Rhonda Copelon, "Gendered War Crimes: Reconceptualizing Rape in Time of War", in Julie Peters & Andrea Wolper, eds., *Women's Rights, Human Rights* (Routledge, 1995).

Percy E. Corbett, "Quincy Wright's Contribution to International Law", 14(4) *J. Conflict Resolution* 465 (Dec. 1970).

Anne M. Coughlin, "Sex and Guilt", 84 *Virginia L. Rev.* 7 (1998).

Donald Dripps, "After Rape Law: Will the Turn to Consent Normalize the Prosecution of Sexual Assault?" 41 *Akron L. Rev.* 957 (2008).

Karen Engle, "Feminism and Its (Dis)Contents: Criminalizing Wartime Rape in Bosnia and Herzegovina", 99 *Am. J. Int'l L.* 778 (2005).

Nicole Eva Erb, "Gender-Based Crimes under the Draft Statute for the Permanent International Criminal Court", 29 *Colum. Hum. Rts. L. Rev.* 401 (1998).

Caroline Goette, "Sexual Harassment in the Workplace in France and in the United States", *Nat'l L. Ass'n Rev.* (Spring 1997).

Richard J. Goldstone, "Prosecuting Rape as a War Crime", 34 *Case W. Res. J. Int'l L.* 277 (2002).

Aeyal M. Gross & Amalia Ziv, "Between Theory and Politics: Gay and Lesbian Studies and Queer Theory" in Yair Kedar, Amalia Ziv & Oren Kenner, eds., *Beyond Sexuality: Selected Articles in Gay and Lesbian Studies and Queer Theory* (Hakibbutz Hemeuchad, 2001) [Hebrew].

Aeyal M. Gross, "Impersonation as Another Person: Imitation and Gender Insubordination in the Trial of Hen Alkobi" in Orna Ben-Naftali & Hannah Naveh, eds., *Trials of Love*, (Ramot, Tel-Aviv University, 2005) 365 [Hebrew].

Alona Hagay-Frey, "Sex and Gender Crimes in International Law: Silence, Honor or New International Crime?" in Klaus Hoffman-Holland, ed., *Ethics and Human Rights in a Globalized World* (Mohr Siebeck, 2009).

Janet Halley, "Rape at Rome: Feminist Interventions in the Criminalization of Sex-Related Violence in Positive International Criminal Law", 30(1) *Michigan J. Int'l Law* 75 (2008).

Janet Halley, Prabha Kotiswaran, Hila Shamir & Chantal Thomas, "From the International to the Local in Feminist Responses to Rape, Prostitution/Sex Work, and Sex Trafficking: Four Studies in Contemporary Governance Feminism", 29 *Harv. J. L. & Gender* 335 (2006).

Janet Halley, "Rape in Berlin: Reconsidering the Criminalization of Rape in the International Law of Armed Conflict", 9(1) *Melb. J.I.L.* 78 (2008).

Janet Halley, "Take a Break from Feminism?" in Karen Knop, ed., *Gender and Human Rights* (Oxford, 2004).

Kerry M. Hodak, Note, "Court Sanctioned Mediation in Cases of Acquaintance Rape: A Beneficial Alternative to Traditional Prosecution", 19 *Ohio St. J. Disp. Resol.* 1089 (2004).

Shelley Hoffman, "Violence against Women in Armed Conflicts", available at http://lib.civics.cet.ac.il/pages/item.asp?item=16937 (last accessed 14 April 2011) [Hebrew].

Michael Howard, "Temperamenta Belli: Can War Be Controlled?" in Michael Howard, ed., *Restraints on War: Studies in the Limitation of Armed Conflict* (Oxford, 1979).

"Human Rights Watch, World Report 1999", *Women's Hum. Rts.* (Human Rights Watch, 1998).

Sharon Hunter, Gail Burns-Smith & Carol Walsh, "Equal Justice? Not Yet for Victims of Sexual Assault" (Newsletter, Connecticut Sexual Assault Crisis Services, 1996).

Chris Jochnick & Roger Normand, "The Legitimization of Violence: A Critical History of the Law of War", 35 *Harv. Int'l L.J.* 49 (1994).

Adrienne Kalosieh, "Consent to Genocide?: The ICTY's Improper Use of the Consent Paradigm to Prosecute Genocidal Rape in Foca", 24 *Women's Rts. L. Rep.* 121 (2003).

Orit Kamir, "A Different Kind of Sex: Conceptualizing Rape in Terms of Human Dignity, and a Model of Suggested Legislation", 7 *Misphat Umimshal* 669 (2005) [Hebrew].

Mustafa K. Kasubhai, "Destabilizing Power in Rape: Why Consent Theory in Rape Law is Turned on its Head", 11 *Wis. Women's L.J.* 37 (Summer 1996).

Robert O. Keohane, Stephen Macedo & Andrew Moravcsik, "Democracy-Enhancing Multilateralism", *IILJ Working Paper* (Princeton University, 2007/4).

Heather L. Kleinschmidt, "Comment, Reconsidering Severe or Pervasive: Aligning the Standards in Sexual Harassment and Racial Harassment Causes of Action", 80 *Ind. L.J.* 1119 (2005).

Nicola Lacey, "Feminist Legal Theory", 9 *Oxford J. Legal Stud.* 383 (1989).

Tamara Larsen, "Comment, Sexual Violence is Unique: Why Evidence of Other Crimes Should be Admissible in Sexual Assault and Child Molestation Cases", 29 *Hamline L. Rev.* 177 (2006).

Rana Lehr-Lehnardt, "One Small Step for Women: Female-Friendly Provisions in the Rome Statute of the International Criminal Court", 16 *BYU J. P. L.* 317 (2002).

Kay L. Levine, "The Intimacy Discount: Prosecutorial Discretion, Privacy, and Equality in the Statutory Rape Caseload", 55 *Emory L.J.* 691 (2006).

Catharine A. MacKinnon, "A Sex Equality Approach to Sexual Assault", 989 *Annals of the New York Academy of Sciences* 265 (2003).

Catharine A. MacKinnon, "Feminism, Marxism, Method and the State: Toward Feminist Jurisprudence", 8 *Signs J. Women Culture & Soc'y* 515 (1983).

Catharine A. MacKinnon, "Rape, Genocide and Women's Human Rights" in Alexandra Stiglmayer, ed., *Mass Rape: The War against Women in Bosnia-Herzegovina* (University of Nebraska Press, 1994).

Catharine A. MacKinnon, "Genocide's Sexuality", in Melissa S. Williams and Stephen Macedo, eds., *Political Exclusion and Domination: NOMOS XLVI* (New York University Press, 2004).

Catharine A. MacKinnon, "Afterword", in Catharine A. MacKinnon & Reva B. Siegel, eds., *Directions in Sexual Harassment Law* (Yale University Press, 2003).

Theodor Meron, "Rape as a Crime under International Humanitarian Law", 87 *Am. J. Int'l L.* 424 (1993).

Marcus R. Mumford, "Building upon a Foundation of Sand: A Commentary on the International Criminal Court Treaty Conference", 8 *J. Int'l L. & Prac.* 151 (1999).

Gerald L. Neuman, "International Law as a Resource in Constitutional Interpretation", 30 *Harvard J. L. & Pub. Pol.* 177 (2006).

Gerald L. Neuman, "The Uses of International Law in Constitutional Interpretation," 98 *Am. J. Int'l L.* 82 (2004).

Fionnuala Ni Aolain, "Rethinking the Concept of Harm and Legal Categorizations of Sexual Violence During War", 1(2) *Theoretical Inquiries in Law* 307, 309 (2000).

Binaifer Nowrogee, "'Your Justice Is Too Slow': Will the ICTR Fail Rwanda's Rape Victims?" *UNRISD Occasional Paper Gender Policy* 10 (UNRISD, 2005).

Valerie Oosterveld, "Sexual Slavery and the International Criminal Court: Advancing International Law", 25 *Mich. J. Int'l L.* 605 (2004).

Valerie Oosterveld, "The Definition of 'Gender' in the Rome Statute of the International Criminal Court: A Step Forward or Back for International Criminal Justice?", 18 *Harvard Hum. Rts. J.* 55 (2005).

Dianne Otto, "Making Sense of Zero Tolerance Policies in Peacekeeping Sexual Economies", in Vanessa Munro & Carl F. Stychin, eds., *Sexuality and the Law: Feminist Engagements* (Oxon/Routledge-Cavendish, 2007).

Jelena Pejic, "The International Criminal Court Statute: An Appraisal of the Rome Package", 34 *Int'l Law* 65 (2000).

Sharon Rabin-Margaliot, "Who is Concerned about Sexual Harassment at Work?" in Aharon Barak & Haim Berenzon, eds., *Berenzon Yearbook* (Nevo, 1997) [Hebrew].

Amy E. Ray, "The Shame of It: Gender-Based Terrorism in the Former Yugoslavia and the Failure of International Human Rights Law to Comprehend the Injuries", 46 *Am. U. L. Rev.* 793 (1997).

Amnon Reichman, "Universal Jurisdiction in State Courts – Destroying Sovereignty or Creating World Order", 17 *Mishpat v'Tzava* 49 (2004) [Hebrew].

Joan Ringelheim, "Women and Holocaust: A Reconsideration of Research", 10 *Signs J. Women Culture & Soc'y* 741 (1985).

Darryl Robinson, "Defining 'Crimes Against Humanity' at the Rome Conference", 93(1) *Am. J. Int'l L.* 57 (1999).

Samantha I. Ryan, "Comment, From the Furies of Nanking to the Eumenides of the International Criminal Court: The Evolution of Sexual Assaults as International Crimes", 11 *Pace Int'l L. Rev.* 447 (1999).

Robbie Sabel, "Sources of International Law", in Robbie Sabel, ed., *International Law* (Hebrew University, 2d ed., 2010) [Hebrew].

Abigail C. Saguy, "Employment Discrimination or Sexual Violence? Defining Sexual Harassment in American and French Law", 34 *Law & Soc'y Rev.* 1091 (2000).

Brook Sari Moshan, "Women, War, and Words: The Gender Component in the Permanent International Criminal Court's Definition of Crimes against Humanity", 22 *Fordham Int'l L.J.* 154 (1998).

Lucinda Saunders, "Rich and Rare Are the Gems They War: Holding De Beers Accountable for Trading Conflict Diamonds" 24 *Fordham Int'l L.J.* 1402 (2001).

Wolfgang Schomburg & Ines Peterson, "Notes and Comments: Genuine Consent to Sexual Violence under International Criminal Law", 101 *Am. J. Int'l L.* 121, 124 (2007).

Leslie Sebba, "The Crime of Rape: Legal Trends and Criminality", 3 *Plilim* 46 (1993) [Hebrew].

Yaacov Shapira, "Preserving the Relationship between a Cohen and his Wife who has been Raped – Law and Cinema", 1 *Family Law* 303 (2007) [Hebrew].

Nitza Shapiro-Libai, "The Requirement for a 'Dvar Mah' in Sexual Offenses– An Unjustified Exception", 33 *Hapraklit* 422 (1979–1980) [Hebrew].

Thomas W. Simon, "Defining Genocide", 15 *Wis. Int'l L.J.* 243 (1996).

Sandesh Sivakumaran, "Sexual Violence against Men in Armed Conflict", 18 *Eur. J. Int'l L.* 253 (2007).

Kim Stevenson, "Observations on the Law Relating to Sexual Offences: The Historic Scandal of Women's Silence", *Web J. Current Legal Issues* in association with Blackstone Press Ltd. (1999).

Kwong-leung Tang, "Rape Law Reform in Canada: The Success and Limits of Legislation", 42(3) *Intl. J. Offender Therapy & Comp. Criminology* 258 (1998).

Andrew E. Taslitz, "Willfully Blinded: On Date Rape and Self-Deception", 28 *Harv. J.L. & Gender* 381 (2005).

Morrison Torrey, "When Will We Be Believed? Rape Myths and the Idea of a Fair Trial in Rape Prosecutions", 24 *U.C. Davis L. Rev.* 1013 (1991).

Etsuro Totsuka, "Commentary on a Victory for 'Comfort Women': Japan's Judicial Recognition of Military Sexual Slavery", 8 *Pac. Rim L. & Pol'y J.* 47 (1999).

Patricia Viseur Sellers, "Sexual Violence and Peremptory Norms: The Legal Value of Rape", 34 *Case Western Reserve J. Int'l L.* 287 (2002).

Patricia Viseur Sellers & Kaoru Okuizumi, "Prosecuting International Crimes: An Inside View: Intentional Prosecution of Sexual Assaults", 7(1) *Transnational Law & Contemporary Problems* 45 (1997).

Patricia Viseur Sellers, "Emerging Jurisprudence on Crimes of Sexual Violence", 13 *Am. U. Int'l L Rev.* 1523 (1998).

Nicole Westmarland, "Rape Law Reform in England and Wales", *University of Bristol, School for Policy Studies, Working Paper Series* (2004).

Wendy Williams, "The Equality Crisis: Some Reflections on Culture, Courts and Feminisms", 7 *Women Rts. L. Rep.* 175 (1981–1982).

Mission of the Women in the Law Project of the International Human Rights Law Group, "No Justice, No Peace: Accountability for Rape and Gender-Based Violence in the Former Yugoslavia", 5 *Hastings Women's L.J.* 89 (1994).

PERIODICALS:

Jean-Paul Akayesu Faces New Charges of Sexual Violence, ICTR/INFO-9-2-059, 1 July 1997.

Robert Capps, "Sex-slave Whistle-blowers Vindicated", salon.com, 6 August 2002.

Hirondelle News Agency, "Congolese Lawyer Dismissed From Ex-Minister's Case", *ICTR On-line*, 29 September 1999.

Press Release, ICTY, Judgment of Trial Chamber II in the Kunarac, Kovac and Vukovic Case, The HagueJL/P.I.S./566-e, 22 February 2001.

Sandra Norman-Eady, Christopher Reinhart & Peter Martino, "Statutory Rape Laws by State", 2003-R-0376, 14 April 2003, available at http://www.cga.ct.gov/2003/olrdata/jud/rpt./2003-r-0376.htm (last accessed 14 April 2011).

Reiji Yoshida, "Sex Slave History Erased from Texts; '93 Apology Next?" *Japan Times Online* (11 March 2007) in http://search.japantimes.co.jp/cgi-bin/nn20070311f1.html (last accessed 14 April 2011).

INDEX